FOGHORN

THE NEARLY TRUE STORY OF A SMALL PUBLISHING EMPIRE

VICKI DeARMON

Sibylline Press

AN IMPRINT OF ALL THINGS BOOK

**Sibylline
Press**

For Dave

FOGHORN

THE NEARLY TRUE STORY OF
A SMALL PUBLISHING EMPIRE

VICKI DeARMON

Publishing: The art of making public

"This is a perfect day for bananafish."

—J.D. Salinger, *Nine Stories*

NOTE TO THE READER

Many names in this nearly true story have been changed. Dialog has been unabashedly recreated, and characters scrambled and obscured where the rendering might have been too damning. The passing of time has been retained in years, if not its order, in terms of months. Otherwise, memory and storytelling have partnered well for the most part, both gravitating as they do over time to generate legends, especially within the Morgan family.

Foghorn Press was my brother's and my best co-creation, and this book is a tribute to those times and who we were. For the many players who lived this grand publishing era with me and have not been mentioned specifically, you are here in spirit.

The good ol' boys in this book are all compilations—which is to say that from the huge Rolodex of good ol' boys I've come across in my time in business, I've compiled singular characters to tell each part of the story. Such creativity has been employed from ex-husbands to authors to business associates. Each characterization reflects the traits of many Last Men. It's possible you might think you know specifically of whom I am speaking, but you might not, so artfully have I crafted the disguise. I did this not because I wish to protect these knuckleheads, but more because shame and embarrassment are vicious motivators for such men, and I wish to limit any future interactions of a legal sort.

As a last safety measure, if you happen to imagine yourself in this saga and are unhappy with the depiction, you can deny whatever you need to. I'm willing to call it fiction. The word nearly stands next to true in the subtitle, in defense of both memory and discretion.

INTRODUCTION

Y ou could say the business saved us. Foghorn Press, the company I originally started with my husband became the life raft onto which my brother, Dave, and I grabbed hold. Anyone without an optimistic upbringing such as we had would have realized we were bobbing above a frenzy of feeding sharks, what with the printers, the authors, the distributors, the slim margins.

But in 1987, my brother and I were young and years away from becoming jaded. Years, too, from the betrayal that would sink our family and end the company we had built.

The vocation of publisher was one I wrapped around myself so closely, it became my skin. Looking back, I see that as the eldest child and the only girl of three, I was perfectly positioned to be the boss. I had worn the mantle of authority from the beginning—out of necessity, it felt, given how young our parents were. As a big sister, I had the best answers and the practice required to inflict those answers on others. But more important to all that came later with the publishing company, it seemed I was sustained by an overdeveloped sense of the possibilities, an entrepreneurial edge that was born—almost with consciousness itself—in kindergarten, when I lay on the rough rug during naptime, eyes shut, listening to the recording of *The Little Engine That Could* "I think I can I think I can I think I can."

I always knew I could.

PART I

START-UP

SAN FRANCISCO, 1987

Published: 3 titles
Partners: 2
Employees: 0
Annual sales: $90,000

The American Booksellers Association (ABA) trade show floor is an epic creation—from a cavernous room of concrete and open space manifests the theater of publishing, the sum total of the most creative concepts publishers and their marketing directors are capable of. New York publishers claim entire aisles, their huge banners descending from the ceiling, authors enlarged to gods in their territory in the sky. The spectacle on the ground is that of a busy marketplace, encompassing publishers, distributors, wholesalers, and remainder dealers representing every type and genre of book and bookish artifacts. The bookseller is king in this environment, discovering what to place on their shelves for the Fall season, and placing orders. As the hordes of booksellers pass, the publishers press catalogs and books into their hands, issue invites to parties, direct them to autograph lines, and provide proximity to marquee authors in cordoned rooms built within their show real estate.

To this suburban bookworm from California, afloat in my little skiff next to the big mother ship, it was breathtaking.

As I peered in from the much more sparsely populated Small Press area at the trade show in D.C., I felt a quickening. A resolve. I wanted *in* to the bigger show. I felt it emphatically and completely, unlike anything else I had ever wanted before. I looked back at the booths lined up in ten-by-ten increments, ours with the other small presses. We were a feeble rendition with our makeshift signs over the pipe-and-drape, six-foot tabletops with standard white tablecloths and thin carpet beneath our feet. At the Foghorn Press booth sat Sully, my soon-to-be ex-husband—though he may have been oblivious to that campaign—behind the few remaining copies of the football guide he had written and I had hawked to booksellers just twenty minutes prior. The brawl ignited from our drinking in the hotel room the night before did not match my view of myself nor my ambition. From the marriage, I desperately wanted out.

So upon my return to San Francisco, I quickly secured an office in the City's South of Market at the Townsend Building. I told Sully it was necessary for our growth. It was small, without windows, but the brick wash of the walls made it hip enough, the freight elevator to the fourth floor transporting me out of that insular drunken world we lived in and off the kitchen table where I had worked in our house in the Sunset District.

Not a month later, I moved out of that house. Both were part of the same motion—a preemptive strike for better, for myself, and for this burgeoning vision I was fanning that Sully had no part.

My youngest brother, Dave, arrived at my door in that same interval, straight from his breakup with his girlfriend of six years, still new to the City, unhinged and ready for something. He helped me transport the two fifty-dollar heavy wooden desks from the used office-supply shop down the street by borrowed dolly and haul them up the freight elevator to the office. I gave him Sully's desk because, now that I had moved out, Sully rarely showed.

I assigned Dave the task of shipping out individual orders. He hunched over the new computer I'd managed to procure, hunting-and-pecking the shipping labels on his keyboard, readying them to print on our dot-matrix printer. It was his third week and already I was feeling better, less tremulous, like my plan to take the company could happen.

At my desk, I worked on a description for our distributor of our next camping guide, a continuation of my big idea to build a spring list. Our professional sports books were all Fall releases, and that meant that the rest of the year, nothing happened and no money came in. I knew that publishing the sports books at all meant an unholy dependence on Sully who wrote them.

When I signed John Aberdeen, a writer for the national magazine, *Get Outdoors*, it was an opportunity to go a different way. I reminded Dave about that now.

"Explain it to me again." Dave looked up.

"Publishing in two seasons stabilizes things. We build that list."

"But a lot of money goes out first, before we know it will be successful," he countered. Dave had no publishing knowledge, but he did have common sense. Our financial situation was a big worry for both of us: Dave, because he was looking for stability since he agreed to join me; me, because I was looking to build the company and, right now, we could barely afford the rent in the new office.

"Yes, but this camping guide will sell just like the last one, and when it does, more money will come in." I nodded at him emphatically. "Believe me.

"You don't know anything about camping." He grinned slightly, looking over his glasses. "I mean, you've never *camped*, have you?"

"Yes, I have camped, of course I have!" I thought back to when. High school, ten years ago? Camping wasn't my favorite thing to do. Too much wrestling around in the dirt. "But that's the glory of it. We don't have to know anything about it. Our author does!"

The phone rang and I picked it up cheerfully. "Foghorn Press, this is Vicki Morgan speaking."

Sully's voice tumbled through the line, and I knew immediately that he was drunk, very drunk. His words were unintelligible, but his anger radiated through the phone, hot and dangerous.

The familiar tension rose in my gut and my mouth went dry. *Come back, little Sheba*, I coached myself. I distanced the phone from my ear, and that simple act shot through me like an exclamation point on the never-ending sentence the ten years of living with this man had been. I pushed the receiver up in the air, my arm fully extended, and let his attack find its proper proportion as a mere buzz of fury that I no longer had to endure. *Buzz, buzz, buzz.*

Dave stopped typing as he watched me at my desk, obviously dismayed at my approach to customer service. But this wasn't a bookseller. *Buzz buzz buzz.* I grinned at Dave as if I had just completed the Korbut backward release off the uneven parallel bars. I raised my other arm in victory to match. God, how the Morgan family loved the Olympics—any test of athleticism, really. The receiver burped and buzzed.

I nodded at Dave, wondering if he recognized how I was sticking the metaphoric landing in this Olympic moment. But then I felt myself toppling sideways; the memory of the morning I had left Sully a shot of recrimination in my throat. I dangled the receiver in front of me and Dave stood to snag it from my upheld hand. In an instant, he realized who it was and barked a few expletives into the phone before hanging up, shaking his head, perhaps debating the wisdom of becoming my new business partner.

Dave and I had shaken hands on it that morning. The magnitude of what I was trying to pull off by running a small press had already escalated my insomnia, making it clear that I needed someone—and not just anyone, but someone like my brother Dave who, as a bonus, liked and appreciated me. My husband had never been that man.

"Vic, let's do the big thing." He grabbed the tape gun and pointed it at me. "Let's move. Move the whole damn business, inventory and all. And we'll move with it. We won't tell the bastard where."

I considered this from my desk, savoring the resolve so epically apparent in his stance. It was a resolve I wanted, but could only manifest in stops and starts, a state I attributed to my decade with Sully, obvious in the more than two years it took me to leave him.

I stood and grabbed Dave's shoulder and squeezed it. My mind started to churn, skimming San Francisco's neighborhoods for a place to move, someplace that Sully, an Irish Catholic City boy most comfortable with his own kind, wouldn't venture. The Mission. The Castro. Bernal Heights.

I murmured *okay*.

"Okay!" I repeated aloud, hope jettisoning through my body.

It was decided.

As Dave whipped his tape gun over the boxes we were shipping out that day, we formulated a plan—one steeped in the mathematical certitude that had been our father's gift to us. We'd find a new place where we could both live and work, ideally at a fraction of what this office, Dave and Julie's old studio, and my new apartment in the Richmond District were costing us.

Dave's eyebrows bounced with a few conspiratorial Groucho Marx lifts. "Okay, we'll start looking for places."

"Let's find one today so we can move this Saturday. That way, Brian can help. It's the perfect use of that PhD!" I said, shuffling my feet in a small dance where I stood.

He shook his head. "That's pretty quick, Vic."

I went over it for him, step by step. If we moved in a single day, we'd have our brother Brian's help since he'd be here this weekend while he was interviewing at UCSF. Plus, we could conserve the amount we'd need to spend on the U-Haul. It also would provide us the necessary stealth. After all, Sully continued to show up at the office, still believing what I'd told him—that we were merely separated, not divorcing. And, best yet, as far as Dave was concerned, the one-day moving plan was the kind of action that satisfied the Morgan need to climb only the tallest mountains.

I leaned over to smack Dave's hand with a high five and he grinned, all in.

"We are figuring this shit out, man!" I said.

For me, it meant the promise of my two brothers here with me in San Francisco. I felt a surge of our old solidarity, like an embattled warrior on the front lines with reinforcements charging down the hill.

* * *

My first memory was of the three of us, me and my brothers, all under age five, in the back seat of our young parents' Buick. Bouncing along, pre-seat belts, loose as puppies. It was 1963. They were defying their parents' advice in moving their small Morgan family from Washington to California, and the glee of that, the grass-is-greener freedom of that, was the air we breathed. Tracking us the whole way was the largest U-Haul trailer they could rent, packed with all we owned, including the secondhand furniture that had served them while my dad completed college. This was my first exercise in the Morganization ritual that would become our defining family legacy— breaking everything down to begin again.

We drove south from Cheney, Washington, through the desert of Oregon, then scaled the mountains, dropping a day later to Interstate 5 in California. Adventure streamed in the windows in warm blasts as we made our way down the long straightaway before we finally reached the Grapevine, the steep and windy threshold to a new and richer life.

We began the climb upward. As we neared the top of the long grade, the Buick doubled down, revving dramatically, Los Angeles waiting expansively on the other side. As we hit the peak, the protective mountain walls fell back and we began our descent, accelerating. My dad turned to grin at my mom, and she glanced back at us and returned his grin, dreams awakening.

Then a forceful wind struck the Buick hard, jerking us to the right. My dad pulled hard to the left and suddenly the car broke free, unmoored, swerving right and left again. My head swung back, my brothers and I in full tumble. In those seconds, my mom screamed my father's name, stopping abruptly as our front hood turned to face into the oncoming traffic. Behind us, the U-Haul staggered before it tipped, hanging there on its two right wheels before careening onto the pavement, then with a reverberating boom, the trailer bounced, throwing us kids against the side door, the force yanking us back and sideways with a metallic groan as it dragged the Buick greedily to the highway's graveled edge.

Everything stopped. I heard the rush of other cars passing on the pavement. *Shi-lop, Shi-lop, Shi-lop.* I rose to my knees. My palm found the smooth glass of the window, and I peered out. The trailer lay on its side, a third of it perched over the cliff, still connected by the chain of the hitch, an anchor ready to drop. My heart scampered, a small rabbit in my chest. I heard the deep canyon call our names.

I scooted into the center of the play area. My brothers lay toppled against the door. I dragged them over to me—first Brian, who was three, by his arm, and then Dave, age one, nude but for his diaper, my hands slipping under his armpits. We sat hunched together, our breath coming in small puffs, the only other sound inside the car against the clock-like ticking of the motor. I peered over the seat to see our mother's face convulsed in fear and our father's hands clutching the steering wheel. On one side, cars flew past.

Growing up, the tight and exclusive world of our family included our young parents, but there was our true circle, created that day, consisting of Brian, Dave, and me. I dropped my arms around my brothers' shoulders, pulling them closer to me, our heads touching, and we cemented our conclave. Our bodies still jittery, the quiet of that gaping canyon vibrated through the car and, without words, without understanding, we were imprinted: the world could be a dangerous place and to make it, we three would have to band together.

* * *

That weekend, Brian appeared in the open doorway of my studio apartment an hour earlier than expected. Tall and gaunt at twenty-seven, sporting his UCLA T-shirt and jeans, he already managed to look the part of a science professor, with premature gray fanning his temples in careful strokes. I hugged him, the thin rail of his tall body so familiar, my throat ached.

I glanced around at the mounds at my feet. It was time to start stuffing. Color-coding boxes, my original plan, was definitely out.

Dave swung through the doorway and commanded the room as only he could. His eyes met mine with that intense intelligence that delighted in disagreements, that relished the vault over mediocrity to greatness, and that suffered no fool gladly. He was ready. And to demonstrate it, he'd shaved his head for the occasion, an obvious ritual for the Morganization that lay ahead.

Brian and I glanced at each other, grinning, and then back at our brother.

"What's on the Va-genda?" Dave's gaze darted across the room. He was wearing the same Oakland A's shirt he'd worn all week, and I had a sudden inkling that maybe he'd been sleeping in the office. A faint grin pulsed at the corners of his mouth, but as a master of the deadpan, he never let it surface. "And more importantly, how's the color coding going?"

"I should never have told you that plan." I scowled at him.

His eyebrows arched. "And miss a good mocking?"

"Mockery is an art form and Dave the artist," Brian commented, motioning for Dave to join him in folding up the futon. They hauled it out as I stuffed garbage bags with the clothes piled knee-high on the floor.

I loved the apartment, having signed the lease the day I left Sully. It was the first place as an adult I had ever lived without him. It had drawn me in immediately with the hopeful charm of the exterior Victorian appointments, and inside, the carved wood framing on the doors, the antique doorknobs, and the wood floors fanning out from the entryway, illuminated by the light coursing through the bay windows.

But at night—already my worst hours—I kept my legs tucked up on the futon that doubled as my bed, listening to the whisper of rodent feet in the kitchen as I read my new copy of *Codependent No More*. In my head, the title ran altered as "Codependent ever more" with sinister insistence and the same finality of an Edgar Allan Poe poem. It didn't help that Sully knew where I was, and I often stared outside, imagining his car cruising, shark-like, past the building and down Geary Boulevard.

My brothers filtered back in the door, Brian wandering the compressed loop of living room and coming to stand in the kitchen where I stood pouring Ajax over the counter, the bleach sharp in my nose. I was holding onto the idea that even though I was breaking my lease after just a month, the landlord might return my deposit.

Dave strode out of the bathroom into the kitchen, and I turned to look at him. His bald head, combined with his glasses, gave him a Gandhi air. His hands were overflowing with condoms.

"How about these?" He plunked a handful on the counter, where they rolled toward me in gleeful abandon, and then he held an aquamarine-colored one to his right eye as if to inspect it. From Gandhi to Inspector Clouseau.

I stood and hit my head on the cupboard door. "Jesus H. Christ, that fucking hurt."

"Take a breath, Vicki Morgan," Dave laughed. "You're never going to make cheerleader with those moves."

"Where did those condoms come from?" I had an idea, though.

"Here's a concept. Throw it all away," Dave said, throwing his arms up in the air. "Toss everything. Come on, Vic, do it." He chanted a moment before Brian joined him.

"Toss it, Vic-ki. Toss it, Vic-ki." Their hands cupped around their mouths as if I were coming down the basketball court in the big play of the game, the crowd roaring while the last syllable of my name arched through the air for the net. This is what comes from having brainy jocks for brothers. Mockery at every turn. I registered it as love.

* * *

Three-quarters of the truck was still vacant when my brothers and I drove down to the office to clear it out. We spent the next hours loading the truck, up and down the ancient freight elevator, finally descending to the cool brick basement for our inventory of books. By the time the elevator staggered to street level with all three of us, clammy with sweat and perched atop our final cargo, the sky was darkening. The cool winter evening wind provided relief as it swept through the empty streets en route to the Bay, loose pieces of garbage somersaulting out of the gutters like the fanfare of a private party where we were the only guests.

We formed an assembly line, each box handed from one to the other, bucket-brigade style, huffing with each swing, until we were done. Dave latched the door of the truck and climbed in to go get food. As the vehicle chugged away, Brian and I stepped back into the elevator to ride up for a final look.

"I hope to God he doesn't bring us Brussels sprouts soup," I said, pushing the button for our floor. It gave a small ping.

"Why does he love Brussels sprouts so much?" Brian said, his voice rising over the rickety ascension. We both remembered the Brussels sprouts soup Dave had fixed us during Brian's last visit, Brussels sprouts bobbing whole like apples we had to wrest from the broth with our teeth. The lift crashed to a stop at our floor, sending an echo.

"Why did Julie leave him, anyway?"

"She hated Brussels sprouts?"

I heard the phone ringing in the office as we approached, I tensed. Sully.

"There's always Nietzsche, too," Brian said, pushing open the door to the nearly vacant office.

"Nietzsche is the Brussels sprouts of philosophers, an acquired Dave taste," I said.

The room was nearly empty by then. In the back corner I spotted a sleeping bag, a flashlight, and Dave's backpack. He must have tucked it into his desk where I wouldn't see it when there was still furniture. To the right of the door, the room still held Sully's computer, a pile of computer paper, and a few floating copies of our bestseller, the outdoor guidebook that had delivered the first hopeful deposits into our bank account.

Prior to the move, Dave and I had set up a new business account without Sully as a signer, though Sully—even as recently as Friday—had tried to make withdrawals from the old account. When he discovered we closed it, he called the office all day, the phone jarring me each time, though I never picked up, the answering machine absorbing his rage.

I shivered as the phone rang again. I didn't want to think about his reaction when he discovered we'd moved.

"Got chili!" Dave strode through the open doors, handing one bag to Brian, who was sitting on the box of printer paper. "May all your gastric disturbances be pleasant ones."

I sat on the floor, my legs stretched out in front of me.

Brian picked up a battered book and waved it. "What happened to these books, anyway? It's like a dog gnawed on their covers."

I glanced at the scuffed cover. The top section with the title had been ripped off the spine and the pages curled like an overused phone book.

"PGW, probably," I offered, and then for Brian's benefit, "our distributor." I was still proud of the fact that I—as a new publisher—had gotten Publishers Group West, the biggest distributor of independent presses, to represent Foghorn to bookstores and other retailers.

"It was Sully, actually." Dave regarded the mangled book. "He's rabid, you know."

"Yet strangely, I was the last one to know. Spoon, please," I said.

Dave turned to Brian, "*Strangely*, she says. And does she even know now? Will she still put her hand into that dog's mouth?" He peered into the bag. "Spoons. They didn't give us spoons." He took out three sodas, then flipped the bag over and shook it. "Son of a bitch. I hate that."

Dave grabbed the beat-up copy of the guidebook Brian held, ripped off the cover, and tore it into strips for makeshift spoons.

"When did *you* know?" I asked, accepting a cardboard sliver of a red tent.

"That he was an asshole?" Dave pretended to contemplate, his forehead crinkling before his eyebrows shot up. "Ten years ago. Isn't that when you met? Remember when he insulted Mom and Dad at Christmas that time by making fun of the flannel shirt they gave him?" Dave mouthed the word "asshole" in slow motion, his lips ending in an O which he held dramatically, his eyes wide, until Brian emitted a chuckle.

I didn't.

"Why didn't anyone say anything *before* I married him?" I looked at Dave, then at Brian. Ever the diplomat, Brian kept his eyes down, popping off the lids to the chili and unleashing the sweet smell of cooked onions.

Dave snorted. "Look, no one has ever been able to stop you from doing anything. And Mom and Dad just don't operate that way. They're 'live and let live.'"

"Live and *let die*, in this particular case."

Dave squinted at me. "Is it crowded on that cross or can I climb up, too?"

"Get your own," I said. I faked a punch in his direction. Brian chuckled.

I thought about Sully while we ate. It still baffled me that I could be such a horrible judge of character. But the other possibility was that Sully was redeemable, an opinion only I seemed to have held.

Just as we were cardboarding the last bit of chili into our mouths, the door of the office burst open. We all reared up. There stood Sully. How had we not heard him?

In his "Vicki!" I heard Brando shouting "Stella!" in a sour cloud of ownership and rage. My stomach tightened. He'd come to the most obvious place, tracking me, my workaholism a counterbalance to his alcoholism.

The familiar boozy scent rode Sully's skin, engulfing us where we sat. Sully's glazed eyes first darted to Dave, who picked up the tape gun and held it to his shoulder, solemn, a sharpshooter ready to engage. Sully swayed to the right and his glance flew over to Brian, who calmly looked back. Sully reached behind himself, clutching at the door for balance.

I sucked in my breath and held it, as I had been doing for the last ten years.

I considered the options. There were no windows in our four-hundred-square foot room, and it felt smaller still with Sully standing there. Normally, I'd be afraid. There was the verbal abuse, yes, but every now and then, this drunk had crossed over to something physical. For a second, I imagined his fingers around my neck. I hadn't told anyone about that.

Sully's brow furrowed. His eyes swept the room and landed where his old desk used to be, his computer still there on the painted wood floor. He strode to the machine, yanking it up with a jerk while we watched. He staggered, the cord loose and dragging on the floor as he backed out the door in a hard silence. The cord caught under the jamb, and he yelled, "Jesus Fuck."

My chest fluttered in alarm, and something close to sympathy for him jabbed at me, so I sprang forward, unwedging the cord with my foot. It whipped loose and we listened as he plowed down the hall with his treasure.

Dave met my eyes. We agreed. We could sacrifice that machine.

The elevator down the hall clanged open and closed, and started its creaky descent before any of us spoke.

"Looks like he stumbled across the bloodless coup. Though for a minute there, it almost wasn't bloodless." Dave smirked and returned to his seat. "Dickhead."

"Total dickhead." Brian glanced over at me and half smiled. "Okay, here's a question. How did you three ever work here together?" He asked as if that might be a greater scientific puzzle than those presented by neuropsychology, his specialty.

Dave shot me a look. "It wasn't easy. The bastard didn't like anyone talking when he had a hangover, which of course was every damn day. He wasn't happy I was around, that's for sure—though he never suspected Vic was in the middle of a coup and he was the dictator who was going down. Luckily, he didn't come in often. And I came when I was sure he wasn't going to be here. Before noon. I don't know what Vic did."

"What I always did. Pretended nothing was happening." I shrugged, trying to appreciate their efforts to distract me. I kept seeing Sully's face in the doorway. My stomach clenched again, and I dropped my forehead to my knees. I was reminded why it had taken so long to break free. It gave rise to that old angst that transferred his actions back to me as the cause, made me wonder what I could have done differently. Maybe I should have just answered his call on Friday. *Codependent ever more.*

I felt Dave looking at me. "What do you want in life, Vic?"

I exchanged glances with Brian, who was beating down a smile. Was Dave even capable of having a small conversation?

"Jesus." I said, trying to dodge his scrutiny. "How about, to build a vast publishing empire?"

Was there a right answer? I remembered my dad's saying: "Life can never be exactly like you'd like it to be." I was still trying to make sense of that pronouncement. It was the word *exactly* tucked in there that rattled me. But without the word *exactly*, it was even harder. "Life can never be like you'd like it to be." Really? Either way, there was a whole lot of settling going on. Now that I'd broken with Sully, I was no longer ready to settle for less.

The phone rang and we turned to glance at it. It couldn't have been Sully, but I pulled myself up and walked to the cord, snapping it from the wall before it could go to the recording, still trying to reclaim myself.

"He won't find us now." I threw my head back, laughing wickedly, and then I wrapped the cord around the phone and put it by the door.

"Unless you give him our new address and number, of course," Dave snorted.

"Unlikely, after all this," I said, as if that level of ridiculousness was beyond me.

* * *

By the next week, Brian was back in Los Angeles and Dave and I had established our routine for our new offices in Bernal Heights.

Supported by our lack of cash, each morning started with pancakes, though the art of making good pancakes eluded Dave and me. Making the batter the right density, pouring it in dollops on the hot pan, flipping the disks at the perfect moment—neither Dave nor I could achieve this holy state on the stove in the corner of our kitchen workroom, but each morning we tried. We took turns, but inevitably the pancakes were still creamy inside, or they were mashed into half-moons of dough, or they were pale, and occasionally too hard and tough.

Bob Dylan, as usual, provided the soundtrack. This morning, our favorite song, "Tangled Up in Blue" from *Blood on the Tracks* played on the tape deck.

"What's on the program?" Dave asked. His mound of pancakes was half devoured.

"Today we finish the camping guide so we can send it to the printer tomorrow." I took a bite of mine, the peanut butter that all Morgans loved on pancakes dissolving with the syrup and cake in my mouth.

"That's the plan, then. We need the last two maps, which I think I can whip out this morning, and then we can spend the rest of the day on the index," said Dave.

"I was thinking we should make it a killer index." I lifted my chin toward him.

Dave stood. "The index should have everything in it, not just the names of the campgrounds. I'm talking the park names, the types of campgrounds." His voice rose with authority as he raised his hands, palms together, elbows bent, in front of his chest for emphasis. "Are you hearing me?"

"I'm hearing you." I rose too, and pointed at him. "People should be able to pick up this guidebook and find the information they need in seconds. They want to go to a campground that only allows tents, next to river with a fire pit, we'll give it to them."

Dave pointed back, evangelical. "They want to find a campground in a state park with a beach and a night-ranger program, we'll give it to them."

"They want to find a campground to park their RV at midnight on Interstate 5, we'll give it to them." I blew on the tips of my fingers pointed like pistols to the ceiling.

"Hear me now and hear me later." Dave walked to the sink with his finished plate. "This is going to be an index to beat all indexes."

"I think it's indices, but your way sounds better."

*   *   *

We spent the afternoon into the evening cleaning and consolidating the index, each taking a portion on our machines. When it had just been Sully and me, we had outsourced the layout and didn't bother with editing. We didn't do an index at all.

"Can you believe people used to do this without computers?" Dave stood in front of my desk later that night and handed me another beer. He dropped into the chair in my office. We both looked out the window at the cranes lit up and visible across the bay in Oakland, the ones that had supposedly inspired those Imperial Walkers in *Star Wars*.

"That had to be torture."

"How much more you got?"

"I'm actually in the Zs now and as you probably could guess, there aren't a lot of Zs."

"I've got your Zs right here, man," Dave said, setting his beer on my desk. "Actually, I'm not that tired."

"Me neither. What time is it? One, two?"

"One. Early by our standards. We could squeeze in another whole book before morning if we wanted to." Dave's eyebrows shot up.

"Which I don't. I want to drink a beer and relax."

"We could also do some shipping," he said.

"Pass."

"Where's the ambition, man?"

"My ambitions after midnight are strictly horizontal." I sighed, realizing it was way too late now to pay a visit to the waiter I'd been sleeping with.

Dave said, "Here's a ridiculous idea, then. Let's just talk." He paused. "Philosophy or something else. You choose."

"Love. Past or present. You choose."

"Not a very promising topic." He stood. "Beer first."

While he vanished into the kitchen, I finished up the last two index edits. I looked up and Dave stood in the door, his head cocked to the side, waiting.

"Ready? Tell me something. What did you ever see in the bastard? Even on his best day, he's still an asshole."

I pondered. "Back when we met at the junior college, he was twenty-two and, because I was fresh out of high school, it seemed like he knew more about the world than I did, or at least acted like he did." I paused. "It's kind of like I latched onto him and his program, maybe because I didn't have one of my own."

I plopped onto the carpet in my office and lay there, looking up at the grooved pattern of the stucco ceiling.

"I mean," Dave pressed, "through high school, you were a pretty staunch feminist." He grabbed the beer on my desk, stooped down and set it on my stomach. I grabbed it.

"He was a Marine and very sure of himself. I was new to adulthood and so not sure of myself. You can be a feminist without being staunch, you know."

"That's what I mean. You used to be sure of yourself. Now you're *less* staunch." Dave took a swallow.

"Think about it. You know what that's like, going from the country to the city. When I got to San Francisco, I was still saying hello to everyone I met in the street. Sully was a City boy. He toughened me up." I looked at Dave like he should know this. "Our parents didn't exactly prepare us for the world."

"True. We learned things the hard way." He peered out through the front windows.

"Sully was definitely the hard way," I said, catching myself as I said it, realizing how natural it was for me to play the victim. I thought of my waiter's nickname for my name, Vicki Morgan, *Victim MoreGrim*, and I took a long sip of my beer.

"When you met Sully, you just disappeared from the family. For ten years."

I tried to make a joke. "I may have been busy drinking." But the idea that I had dropped out of everyone's life was new to me. I shifted to a sitting position. Had I left Brian and Dave to fend for themselves as they made their play for adulthood? I was used to casting myself as a victim, but now I realized I might have been a self-centered one. Maybe there wasn't any other kind?

Digging through the ashes of the Sully era was turning out to be my least favorite thing to do—lots of evidence that didn't make me look that good.

Dave walked to the window nearest the entry, then suddenly dropped down to his knees. "Uh-oh. Kill the lights in here."

I reached up and switched them off. "What is it?" I slunk back to the floor.

"Across the street. Our neighbor's house. There's a kid in front with a gun."

"Get down, Dave. Get back. Don't let him see you," I whispered. Bernal Heights felt like a fierce neighborhood, its houses set on tight, meandering streets and most fronted with dirty, barred windows.

"He saw me already, but don't worry. I'm down."

"The door is locked, right?"

Dave crawled over to the hall, and I heard him latch the front door.

"What's he doing?"

I heard Dave stand to peer through the side window next to the door.

"Just standing there with his gun in front of his house. Like he's keeping guard or something."

"Should we call the police?"

"If we do, he'll know it was us," he said.

"Then let's not." I slouched down against the wall. Thank God for Dave. Sully only looked out for himself.

"This is not a scene you'd see in Sonoma County." Dave crawled into the kitchen and cut off the music. He checked the back door, and I heard him latch it. He flicked off the lights in the bathroom and the whole house went dark. I heard the refrigerator pop open. A beer bottle hissed, and then another. My computer screen gave off a glow and I crawled over, reaching my hands up to the keyboard to save my work and log off.

Dave dipped through the doorway and set two beers on the desk. "Backup beers."

"How did we all become compensating overachievers, do you think?" Rehashing our childhood was easier for me than examining my marriage.

"You and Brian were the straight-A students in high school. I wasn't into school then," Dave said.

"Was Julie?"

"Julie was into drugs. Julie always had drugs. She got nosebleeds all the time, and I begged her to 'just say no.' I told her if Nancy Reagan could say it, she could, too." He smirked and took a sip. "Now I realize I was way ahead of my time." He rubbed both eyes with his hand. "We were stupid kids."

His voice was low. We sat on either side of the threshold to the kitchen and workroom. My office was the only room with carpet, and it was comfortable with our backs against the wall, the streetlight faint on our faces. You could never get Dave to talk about his life, so I kept quiet and let him continue.

"In San Diego, we were living off cabbage and tortillas and going to school at the time. Pathetic. I worked at Burger King, I delivered pizza, I drove a cab, I cleaned floors."

I raised my eyebrows as if to say, *Really?* and he nodded at me. I'd had no idea.

"And I was getting a shitty education, to boot. I have nothing kind to say about the university system. It is socialization at its worst." Dave cleared his throat and drank the last of the bottle. He stood it next to the other one he had finished; they clinked when they touched.

We could see out the windows, but they were high enough off the street that we viewed the night sky and the rooflines of the houses across from us. The teen gunman lurked below our sight. I thought about how unceremoniously Dave and I had both entered the adult world, armed with our power of positive thinking. Like that could stop a bullet or pay the rent.

I closed my eyes. "When Sully got fired from that city job his dad got him, we started living pretty close to the line. He was drinking more, but during the day he used the time to start writing the football book. We scraped together the money so Sully could attend a publishing program and then we started the company, because we were convinced it was a great way to make money." I snorted. "But if a check did come in, Sully would just pilfer it. You know, cash it and head to the bar."

"And he got fired for—?"

"Drinking on the job."

"That's what we thought," he said, adding, "Your house was so depressing."

"Wasn't it? It was dark and dirty, and all that used furniture smelled like old dog. We were hiding out in that little corner of the Sunset District near the zoo." I paused. "I could hear the lions roar at night, like the end was near."

"Plus, Sully made it depressing."

"Totally. Thank God that's over."

"Depends on how you define over." Dave chuckled.

"Over for me."

"Well, it's definitely over for Julie." Dave shook his head and stared out the window. "It was so strange, but I lived in San Diego for four years, and neither Mom nor Dad called me one time. Didn't visit, either."

I tried to think if Mom and Dad had reached out to me during the Sully years or if I had made sure they didn't because I didn't want anyone in my family to know what was going on.

Dave continued, "I can remember driving home one Christmas. Julie just got off the late shift and we were going to drive all night and arrive home in the morning. She gave me some speed because she knew we would never make it straight through. Jesus, man. I cried, thinking about everything. I drove, and I cried some more—through thick fog, ten hours toward home. Whatever home was. I mean, that was how stupid everything was. We were abandoned children. If anyone were to ask me to describe those years when we first moved out and, yes, even my childhood," Dave glanced over at me, "and nobody would ask, except you or Brian, of course, I would say exactly that 'it was like driving home on I-5, high on speed, through a thick fog.'"

"Abandoned children," I repeated, wanting him to go on. I had never thought of it like this, but it explained a lot—that free-falling feeling tinged with anxiety I carried most of my early childhood, for instance. I thought about the first day of school after our move to Northern California. In front of our rental, our mom watched us step into the school bus, which would take us to our new elementary school. They had just the one car and our dad had taken it to work.

Once we'd arrived, I'd shepherded my younger brothers to their respective classrooms. At recess, I'd watched for them, waving them over to the divider line between the lower and upper grades' play areas, where we hung out while the other kids played around us. Always surviving as our own club.

When Dave didn't continue speaking, I gestured toward the window. "How's our guy?"

Dave crawled forward into the hall and up to the window. "Still there. Crazy. Oh, jeez, he just nodded at me. He's friendly. It's Mister Robinson's Neighborhood, Eddie Murphy-style."

"Won't you be my neighbor?" I sang. "He's guarding the whole damn street by default. No one's stealing our inventory tonight, man." I laughed.

"Can't be too careful. I thought I saw a band of campers wearing black ski masks gathering at the corner." Dave walked away from the door, not bothering to bend down. "Let's shut it down, then."

"Yep." I turned to go up the stairs to bed, but stopped. "Dave."

I heard him at the back door, which would take him to his room in the garage. It swung open and paused. "Yes, Slim Bob?"

I chuckled at the new nickname. *Slim*, I was not. "Thanks for not being Sully." I waited. It didn't seem like enough. "I mean, thanks for being the anti-Sully."

He snorted. "The thing is, Vic, you act like that's a big deal. It's not that hard." The door swung shut.

I waited a minute on the stair alone. "Love you, man," I said softly before heading up.

With Sully, the danger had been always in the house, rather than outside the house. Dave had restored the proper order of things, and even improved upon that. No danger in, but no danger out either.

And that night, my insomnia solved itself, like a math problem I had been trying to figure out since I hit adulthood. It was as simple as Morgan squared.

SAN FRANCISCO, 1988

Titles: 5
Partners: 2
Employees: 0
Annual Revenue: $130,000

I n February, the new edition of our camping guide arrived, the first book of the Spring season. Dave and I took the delivery from the printer, who backed his thirty-foot truck up to our one-car garage, blocking the street. None of our neighbors glanced our way or parted a curtain to see why the truck was parked there or what we might be unloading. It was a code I recognized as belonging to big cities: Each neighbor would honor the privacy of others as the only defense of their own.

After we unloaded two hundred boxes, Dave shut the garage door, latching it from the inside, and when he flicked on the overhead light, the shadows of the evening were instantly eradicated. We were in the bright bloom of our own makeshift warehouse. "Ready?"

"Ready." I took the clipboard he handed me. "Nice chart," I noted.

He had developed a printed spreadsheet, with each book and its code and quantity per box. All I had to do was enter the number of boxes as Dave called out the total.

"Yeah, I kinda think we need to keep better track of everything." Dave cocked his head and grinned. "Can you handle that?"

"It's not my area of expertise, but—"

Dave's hands shot up to his brows and he rubbed them fiercely, taking a breath. "Vic, that's how Sully ran off with so much of the money. No one ever kept track of anything. Not the books. Not the money. None of it."

"Well, I—"

"No, you didn't. He didn't. You didn't."

Jesus H. Christ. I set the inventory chart back down on the desk. I was beginning to notice that Dave never gave you credit for a damn thing. You could run a decathlon and goddamn win, and he'd comment on how you should have tied your shoes or gone to bed earlier the night before. You could start a publishing company financed on your credit cards out of your home with only your alcoholic writer of a husband to help, and Dave would comment that you should have kept better track of inventory.

I walked over to the farthest pallet, my back to him. "You have bastard tendencies."

"Vic, you want me to be a bastard. It's good for business."

I didn't turn, but rather shoved a box that hung out over the others into a straight line. "Not to me, I don't. I am the exception to the bastard application rule. Never forget."

"No exceptions. Nietzsche says your best friends should be your worst enemies."

I could see a philosophical discussion was imminent. "Meaning?"

"I'll always tell you when you fuck up. I want you to do the same."

"Okay, I will," I said, returning to the desk where he stood.

"You won't." He looked at me sadly.

"I'll try to."

"Weak." Dave shook his head, resigned.

"I'll really try," I offered, laughing. It wasn't like I had a lot of practice in telling the truth. With Sully, I'd reconstructed every situation to minimize a reaction. Dave would probably call that lying. I called it survival. I doubted that Dave, as special as he was, really wanted the straight truth. I had yet to meet a person who did.

He smirked. "We'll see."

Each title had its own pallet, but with the arrival of the new camping guide, space was compromised. Above each book tower, there existed a one-foot crawl space under the garage ceiling. Dave passed through the narrow walkways between stacks of books by turning sideways. He crawled up on the pallet of last year's inventory to see what we had placed behind it, inching along the ceiling and hollering down numbers to me. I watched the bottoms of his sneakers following his body as he snaked through the shelf created by the boxes.

"We have to reorganize these books," he announced as he hopped down. A sheen of sweat covered the top of his head and, with no hair to catch them, drops ran down the waterfall of his forehead. He pulled off his T-shirt and ran it over his face, neck, and skull, revealing a chest that was paler than the rest of him, and I wondered if he had gone outside at all when he lived in San Diego with Julie.

Dave took the chart from me and looked at it. I glanced at the clock in the corner. It had taken us an hour to count them. He walked around toward the back end and reemerged a moment later.

"Gotta do it," he added with a little too much enthusiasm. He snapped his shirt in my direction as if we were victorious athletes in a locker room following a big first half, but with more game to play.

I frowned and turned down the volume on the tape player. "Dave."

"You see, Vic, the California camping guide needs to be the most accessible so it's easy to ship when the orders come in. We also have the next guide coming soon so we need to make room." The toe of his tennis shoe tapped rapidly on the cement. There was only one person I knew with more energy than me, and that was Dave.

He added, "Sully's sports books can move to the far back."

Sully's face floated in front of me, bunched up, pissed.

"We've unloaded a zillion books and counted them. How about tomorrow?" I glanced at the clock above the desk. It was only nine, plenty of time to go over and visit Casey, my waiter.

My visits to his apartment had ratcheted up from just the weekend to include some weekdays now.

Two things were guaranteed to keep my mind from reworking my failed marriage. One of those was found in Casey's king-sized bed after smoking a joint—which he kindly always had available—and the other was working a deadline with Dave.

"You go on." Dave smiled at me slightly. "I'm going to do it tonight." He turned back to the books. Jesus. I set the clipboard on the first desk. I glanced into Dave's bedroom. He had left the door open.

"Nice bed," I commented. A mattress and box spring perched on a pallet held high off the ground with a stack of last year's edition of the camping guide holding up each corner. Six or seven Nietzsche titles lay across the blanket, along with one copy of the new edition of the camping guide we'd received that morning. The rest of the room was bare except for a reading light on a crate next to the bed.

It reminded me of Brian, who, during his eight years at UCLA, managed in a ten-by-twenty room with a hot plate for a stove, a fact that Dave and I regularly mocked. But let's face it, my brothers were both Spartans. On purpose. That monastic characteristic had missed me entirely. Three empty bottles of Mickey's Big Mouth beer were stationed by Dave's door, ready for disposal, and when I accidentally knocked into them, they teetered before hitting the cement floor like bowling pins. I bent to reset them and felt the cold of the floor. My room in the attic was just the opposite, hot and stuffy.

"Jesus, how can you sleep there?" I said over my shoulder.

"I've conquered sleep," he replied absently, staring at the pallets of books before him.

"I'm going to go get us some beers," I said.

At the store, I stepped into the grimy phone booth out front to call Casey to let him know I wouldn't be there. Hanging up, I pictured his bed and sighed. When I got back, Bob Dylan's "A Hard Rain's A-Gonna Fall" was barreling full blast and furiously out of Dave's room. We worked until midnight and the beers were gone, lifting and restacking the boxes.

"Done!" I reached up on my tiptoes to shove the last forty-pound box into the upper corner of a high stack.

"Want to finish the orders for UPS for tomorrow?" Dave stood at the desk, with the orders piled up, ready to go.

"Relentless. You're relentless. God, you're just like Dad." I felt blurry with sleep and drink, but strangely willing. Dave had that effect on me.

"Dad? Think again. You're the one like Dad."

"Me? Relentless?"

"That too, but I was thinking ridiculously optimistic. Romantically optimistic." He paused. "Focused on some dream for the future far more than the scuffed-up reality of the present."

I thought of when we were little and still lived in Los Angeles, before our family moved to Sonoma County. Dad, after teaching at the junior high all day, worked nights at a liquor store, reading *Think and Grow Rich* in the breaks between customers. There may have been an inconsequential small gap there—just forming—between what was possible and what actually was, especially when our mother brought us three kids in for a visit. Our father's yearning was as tangible to us as the dank smell of the stockroom where we retreated when the bells over the door announced another customer, though we couldn't have named it.

"I scream, you scream, we all scream for ice cream," he'd sing to us when they finally left, dropping a missile popsicle into each of our hands.

After he had contracted diabetes, we watched with fascination, our mouths stained bright red and burning with the delicious cold, fingers sticky, as he administered his nightly insulin shot there in the back room, dropping the seat of his pants to reveal the top of his butt cheek, which he efficiently swabbed and jabbed. But we didn't recognize the rebellion inherent in his eating ice cream with us. I think our mom did, which we might have registered in her tight-lipped refusal of one for herself.

I said, "Optimism isn't a bad thing, you know." When Dave didn't say anything, I added, "If relentless, you'd be thinking about our brother, Brian, the Festerback."

"The Professor? As in relentlessly pursuing higher education? Those hives went away after he got his master's. When he comes back to the City with his PhD, we'll have to call him something else."

I thought of Dad's nicknaming predilection, something he got from his father, Grandpa Morgan, still living in Washington, who went so far as to call my grandma Mrs. Big Ones during family reunions. In our family, the more inappropriate the nickname, the better.

"Professor Brian Festerback. Who'd a thought? I miss him." I wiped a hand across my face. I felt a little weepy. Too many beers.

Dave shoved a book into a mailing pouch and sealed it. "Jesus, just stick these labels on."

The ripping of tape filled the room as he packaged three more books and handed them to me. He said, "Dad loves everything you do. Always has."

"Only daughter. Redhead. First born," I said, ticking off my credentials on my fingers. "I'll add 'similarly optimistic,'" and tapped another finger. I noticed his face and stopped.

"I'm sure he was the same for you."

"Remember how I went to Texas last summer, the year before I started working here?"

I nodded vaguely. The truth was I had been far too absorbed in my failing marriage and my clandestine efforts to disentangle from Sully.

"Dad told me to go. He saw the ad for oil workers in a magazine and told me I should go get the training and work on oil rigs."

"Was he just trying to get you to do something adventurous? Dad never did anything like that, traveled anywhere really, and I think he wanted to."

"He just thought I'd be happy working on an oil rig." Dave shook his head. "He has no idea who I am."

I glanced into his room at the books strewn over his bed.

"Did Julie?" I ventured.

"Nobody wants to do what it takes. They want to have a happy life. Like that means something."

I wanted to be happy, as ordinary as that was. I wasn't willing to admit that to Dave, though. In the years with Sully, definitions of happiness had been creatively morphed in my mind to mean *avoiding a fight*. Then that was happy enough, but I was beginning to sense there was more to this happiness puzzle.

"I'm too philosophical for her," he added.

"Too philosophical?"

"Too something." He shoved another set of labels at me. "Hey, keep up there, Slim Bob."

"Change the Dylan tape; I'm sick of it." My labels weren't precisely stuck on, and Dave reached over and tapped the pouch I was working on.

"You have to be willing to let someone stomp all over your heart. Have it ripped out of your chest," Dave said, his eyes fierce, staring at me or a point behind me intently.

"I am definitely not willing." I thought of Sully. Had I ever even loved him? What was love, anyway? And Casey, well, it wasn't about love, that much I knew. I couldn't believe Dave would be willing, but then I suspected he had loved Julie, truly, and probably still did.

He jerked his chin up. "Bring it on, I say."

* * *

At the Shoreline Amphitheater, Casey completed a three-point turn and then swept into a narrow spot near the rear end of the parking lot. "Turns on a dime and gives you ten cents change," he said, patting his Volvo's steering wheel. Casey was a self-described Irish import from Boston, and when he deployed his full Bostonian accent, it was a verbal reminder that life was supposed to be fun. Before we got out of the car, he lit one of the joints he had rolled for the occasion—the others were packed into his front shirt pocket, a button-down flannel—and sucked on it deeply. We passed it back and forth, smoking until I felt the night kick open. This was a birthday celebration. My twenty-ninth.

In the amphitheater, we made our way to the seats Casey had managed to get, located in the front section, maybe twenty rows back from the stage. When the concert started, Springsteen's new album *Tunnel of Love* swept over us at full volume. Casey threw back his head and sang along, unembarrassed, "We'll ride down baby, into this tunnel of love." His blond hair was cut short around his face, his cherubic cheeks ruddy, disappearing under a close-cropped red beard. The rest of him was fuzzy—how else to describe it?—and round, too, the latter due to our late-night dining.

I found Casey attractive, but most of the people I knew didn't see it. Dave didn't. But Casey had every nerve in my numb body wired, and being with him felt like the act of waking up. I could not be near him without touching him. The music soared into the chorus, and I joined in.

"Outrageous, isn't it?" He threw his arm around me as I pounded my hands for an encore. Bruce delivered. By the end, we were delirious, every note picked up by our sonar and rerouted down to our fingertips. Casey threw his arm around me, and we smoked another on the way to the car. A long cascade of automobiles had pulled out of their spaces, lining up to leave. We were trapped. We jumped into his 1989 Volvo, and he punched up his tape of Springsteen. The concert began again. We sipped wine from the bota bag and, closing my eyes, I became my body—my head and all its remnant thoughts floated away. With the nascent engine smell of the old Volvo and its Spartan black passenger seat enfolding me, I leaned forward. Our mouths joined. We slipped the tart white wine back and forth from mouth to mouth, reinventing—it seemed to me—the art of kissing. Looking up, forty-five minutes later, the last of the cars had gone.

Back at his place, we dropped our clothes by the side of the bed and hopped in. The mattress was waist high, and I tumbled over him while Casey turned on the lamp next to the bed, leaving the rest of the apartment suspended in darkness.

"Happy birthday," he whispered into my ear. Grabbing my upper arms, he swung me on top of him. The warmth of his skin on the back of my thighs made me dizzy and I dropped forward, closing the space between our chests while his hands clasped my behind. The slippery ease of it thrilled me.

With Casey in his bed, there was no space between who I was and what I was doing. They collapsed into one physical sensation and any self-consciousness I had slipped away while our bodies did this dance. There had been no time in my life when such a thing had been possible, when I could put my brain aside, except of course by drinking. Inevitably, when we were done, a minute would pass before another spark would light and my thighs would pull him back into me for more.

* * *

"Why would you put yourself in that position?" Dave asked. He stood in the doorway of my office in a white undershirt, his lean arms balancing on the door frame to either side in a vertical pushup. I looked up from my desk, where I had been reading the brochure about the American Booksellers Association trade show happening the next week in Los Angeles.

"Sully wants to go."

"So, does that mean he has to go with you?"

"He's still our author."

"He's still your husband."

"Not really. The divorce is final in November."

"Yeah, but it's bizarre to drive there with him and share a motel room."

"We have no money, so we have to drive. Plus, I got a cheap place with two beds, and the whole time we'll be at the show. Trust me, nothing will happen."

"Except everything that's happened up to now. He's going to be a total dick, as usual, and use our money to pay for it. You'll be a mess there and a mess when you get back home."

"Dave, I don't care about him anymore. I kind of feel sorry for him, really. He wants to go to promote the 49ers book at the Foghorn booth. I could use the help, especially driving down there, and you need to stay here to keep everything moving forward. It's a good plan."

Dave snorted and pushed back from the frame and then retreated into his office.

"A necessary plan, then," I called after him.

Early the next day, I drove over the hill to pick up Sully at our old house on 45th Avenue in the Sunset District. As I descended Taraval Street toward Ocean Beach, the rest of the City seemed to collapse behind me, forcing me forward and down. I hadn't been in this part of the City for eleven months. On the far outreaches of San Francisco, hugging the ocean, you could imagine that when they first built the rows and rows of houses over the sand dunes for the City's labor-ers—whose proud purchases were their first homes and, thirty years later and for most, their last—that the Pacific Ocean would be a draw. Beachfront living is how I imagined they might have billed it.

But those inhabitants soon discovered the gray sky that arched like a dome over the neighborhood most of the time. Living there, it seemed the fog had washed everything out to a pale rendition of what was possible. Only when I moved out did I discover the vibrant colors that belonged to the other districts in San Francisco.

The streetcar that glided in front of me stopped and took on pas-sengers, bringing me to a long stop at every second corner. I should have taken Sloat to avoid all this, but there was something about seeing it all again from the vantage point of my new life that had made this circuitous route seem like a good idea. I turned left onto 45th and into a long tunnel of squat two-story boxes on either side, houses that had settled into their circumscribed cement yards; they sat side by side, their pale shades of blues, greens, and yellows making them difficult for even their owners to discern which belonged to whom.

"Houses made of ticky-tacky," I said to myself, remembering the Pete Seeger song. I drove to the end of the row and slowed, and seeing no parking spots, I hesitated a minute before turning into the driveway.

I pulled my sweatshirt out of the car. As I quickly pulled it over my head, the sharp fingers of the wind jabbed at my midsection. I stood looking out at the street. Drivers had wedged their cars into every available parking space, and even the red zones at the corner as far as I could see, all encircling the Irish Culture Center that was located kitty-corner from our old house. A breakfast event was happening there. The Center was a double-story box-like boat of a structure that consumed the whole block, surrounded on three sides by homes, the fourth opening to Sloat and the zoo across the street. Just below the roofline and affixed to the windowless stucco face ran an edging of wood that looked to be family crests, communicating simply that once they had docked in San Francisco, the Irish all hailed from the same origin.

For its token culture, the Irish Culture Center offered a small room downstairs that I had never visited. I didn't know anyone who had, but I understood it had books and relics from Ireland. The main attraction was upstairs in the banquet room and bar, which spanned the entire second floor. That was where the culture fermented best. I had been to many an Irish wedding there, including, of course, Sully's and mine three years ago.

Sully appeared at the top of the stairs with a gym bag; our dog Murphy's nose bobbed out of the front door before Sully shut it. Seeing me, Sully grimaced in a kind of sidelong grin that he had perfected over the years to squelch any flair of emotion.

"L.A. or bust," he said, climbing into the passenger seat.

Ten years ago, he had been handsome—boy-like, almost—especially when you first met him. He was apt to flash a smile that triggered that dimple creasing his right cheek. He was still boy-like now, but for me, the handsome had long faded, eroded by the smell of alcohol that permeated his skin and saturated our existence. His eyes were a cocky green framed by wicked eyebrows, and his face would have been made for the movies had it not been for his weak chin. The chin, it turns out, was the giveaway. To compensate, he wore a goatee.

I turned right on Sloat, and for a moment, the great expanse of the Pacific Ocean rose in front of us, a blank page of steel gray with parenthetical whitecaps. I took a left at the light, and we drove along the water heading south before turning inland. How many times had he and I traveled this way on our way to Santa Cruz when we were going to college there, or when we were driving to South City to eat at Joe's Italian Restaurant?

Sully craned his neck back toward the water, a surfer watching the waves as long as he could.

"Choppy today. Bad surfing."

"Who's taking care of Murphy?"

He shrugged his shoulders. "A friend."

I looked over at him. "You look good. Doing something different?" His face was leaner, less puffy than I remembered. His hair was tousled on top, his brown curls in a plume in the middle of his head.

"Stopped drinking, if that's what you mean." He continued to look out his window.

"Wow, that's good, right?" Never in our ten years together had I ever thought that could be a possibility.

"You'd be surprised how many of my friends are in AA. It's like old home week at the meetings." He laughed, looked out the window, then added, "It's anonymous so I can't tell you who." The dimple shot out and retreated.

"Bad for the bars," I joked. Up and down the avenues of the Sunset District were the neighborhood bars I had visited with Sully, starting at age eighteen. There, I met his grammar school and high school classmates, a tight-knit group dedicated to drinking. Until I met Sully, I'd had no comprehension of a life in which alcohol was the central character. Alcohol was like a language I had to learn, and Sully was my self-appointed tutor.

Just as the native Alaskan has a hundred words for snow, the San Francisco Irish had a hundred words for getting drunk. So we proceeded to get heated, get a heat on, loaded, smashed, lit, and lit up. For the first two years of our ten together, I imagined myself an anthropologist, boozing it up with the monkeys to permeate their secret hiding spots and acquire important research data. If only I could have remained that detached. Even now, driving with him, I felt that old reduction of myself. With him, I was someone who could not defend her point or rise above.

I tried to think of safe topics to talk about.

"I took a ten-by-ten booth in the Small Press area of the trade show."

"Thought you didn't like the Small Press area. When we went to DC, you said you wouldn't do that again."

"No money. It's way cheaper. When we get bigger, we can be part of PGW's booth on the main floor." I immediately wanted to withdraw the word "we." There was no *we* anymore.

We lapsed into silence. I recalled the show last year in Washington DC. Our flight out of San Francisco had been delayed, and so, sitting on the tarmac waiting for takeoff, we ordered drinks. By the time we landed in DC, we were both lit up and staggering. We pushed open the door into the hotel room. I started in with my list of resentments. He picked up the lamp between the beds and threw it in my direction. It hit the wall. I retreated to the bathroom where I spent the night curled up in a blanket in the empty tub, the door locked. The rest of the trip, we were silent with each other, unable to recover.

"You've got a pass for me, right?" Sully glanced over at me.

"It's part of our booth, two passes." I bumped the tip of the cassette tape with my finger and it began to play The Eagles's "Hotel California."

"You're not going to sing, are you?" His hand rose as if to push the off button on the tape, depending on my answer. He had delicate fingers for a man, a writer's fingers. That writer's predilection was something we shared, and maybe even the reason I'd been attracted to him in the beginning. But I had given up a grad degree in creative writing to start the company, and in our staff of two, I did everything *but* the writing. He was the designated writer. And that is why our first book had been a history of the San Francisco 49ers, which, coming off the 1985 Super Bowl win, was something that people wanted. It jump-started the company, so I could thank him for that.

But I didn't.

"No, I'm not going to sing." I pressed my lips together and exhaled slowly out of my nose.

"I'm assuming Foghorn is going to pay for this trip. I mean the gas, the food, the hotel."

"Motel," I corrected him.

"A budget trip," he said.

"Not a lot to complain about if it's free," I said.

"Publishers pay for their authors. You're the publisher now." It felt like a jab, but I let it go.

"Peaceful Easy Feeling," my favorite song, came on next, but I did not even hum.

I thought we might make it all the way to Los Angeles without mention of Casey, and the night that had ended our marriage.

As we hit the uphill trek on the Grapevine, I gripped the steering wheel tightly and I stayed in the center lane, far from the canyon on the right that had almost claimed my family and our trailer all those years ago. Trucks blasted by on the right and left. One honked and gestured but I kept my course, as Ronald Reagan was known to advise. Sully had dozed off, but probably realizing his life was in peril, woke up.

"You could speed up," he said, sitting up straighter and putting his left hand on the dash.

The combination of the steep grade, the wind, and the fear gripped me, and I glanced down to see I was only going forty miles an hour. Adrenaline shot through my chest, and I couldn't feel my hands.

It was then that he brought it up.

"I went into the Cliff House last week and saw your waiter friend."

"What?" A truck gusted by, and I held on hard.

"He looked scared to see me." Sully wasn't big, but he was mean, the king of intimidation. It explained Casey's reluctance to get together this last week. Poor Casey.

"That guy is the best you can do?" Sully said.

We hit a crest and suddenly we were flying down the other side. My foot riding the brakes, I pushed all the way down, my body stiffening and nearly vertical as I tried to stay at fifty-five.

"You are a shitty driver," Sully said. I saw a gas station coming up and flew across the two lanes to take the exit.

"We need gas," I said, pulling in too fast.

"I'm grabbing something to eat. Got any money?"

I fished out a ten-dollar bill and handed it to him.

After I filled the car, I pulled to the side of the station and parked. I pushed the door to the bathroom and locked it. A roll of toilet paper lay unraveled across the tiled floor and rested in the crotch of the floor's drain. The acrid smell of urgent human biology from the hundreds of travelers who had been here before me would usually cause me to hustle and get out—and I still felt the germs mobilizing against me—but for now, I felt protected. I leaned against the door and rested there, breathing shallowly through my mouth. Sully always hung over me like the proverbial dark cloud.

I thought about that night, the night I didn't come home. I had joined the other waiters at an after-work party at the bartender's apartment across the City. I didn't call Sully to tell him I'd be home later. The odds were good he was at the bar anyway, I had reasoned.

Casey was there. There was already an attraction that I was ignoring and fanning at the same time. The attention Casey gave me made me want to go to work. Life there wasn't hopeless. People drank to have fun, a marker Sully and I had passed by our second year together.

I drank. Casey drank. We danced in our stocking feet on the wood floor with everyone else. The lights were turned down and when he bent to kiss me, we kept kissing. Even in my drunken state, I felt myself stepping out of my marriage. Casey called a cab to take us back to our cars, but instead we went to a motel near the Cliff House. Then it was done, messy and drunk, but the line had been crossed.

When I sobered up in the early morning, panic struck and I left Casey there, running to my car, my work shoes in my hand. There was a note on the windshield. *Where are you?* it read. I snatched it off and drove home across the beach highway. When I burst through a door with an explanation ready, Sully was on the couch, pale with circles under his eyes, and I thought, so this is how I looked to him all those times he came home late or not at all.

Alcohol still festered in my veins. The universe wavered, and I looked out the front window at the string of houses across from ours, all dark and still sleeping.

In my hand I held his note, my head ached, and I hoped—for a slender wisp of a second—that I could reverse the last twelve hours. I moved out of the house as the light came up, taking my clothes and books, leaving most everything else behind, Sully uncharacteristically silent as I shut the door behind me. It was a solution I had implemented in high school breakups, too: find a way to make it your fault, and that will provide the freedom to go.

* * *

At the trade show, I stood at our table and greeted the passersby who had badges from California, drawing them in. "Your readers can now find a campground in California with the most comprehensive guide ever compiled." I pressed our catalog into their hands, and they dropped it in their bags and kept going.

When it was time for Sully to do the signing, I stacked the books up on the table next to him and fished out a pen for him to use. Then for the next hour, I moved out into the aisle in front of our booth and hawked.

"Love the 49er football team? Author Sullivan Cavanaugh is here to sign copies of the history of the team. Get your complimentary signed copy."

I had a pretty good line going, and we were out of all forty books within twenty-five minutes. Sully flashed his dimple and shook hands and wrote his name with a flourish. He was always good about playing his role. I was, too.

By the end of the day, I had twenty-three bookseller business cards collected in a box under the table, a big success in my mind. We covered our table with a cloth and shuffled out with the other small-press publishers after the announcement came that the show was over for the day.

In the small motel room, both beds fit tightly with a three-foot space at the end. Cheap prints of the Southern California beachscapes hung above each bed, showing the same beach from slightly different angles. Sully's had a dog running into a wave. Mine had a child bending to dig with a shovel.

When I came out of the bathroom, Sully had the TV's sound at full volume, the sports scores pouring out of the mouth of the sports anchor, whose excitement never wavered. I heard the soundtrack to my old life play and I cleared my throat. He didn't look away from the screen.

I prompted, "Ready to go?" The Anne Rice party started in a half hour.

His brows knit and he held his hand up to shush me while he listened to the sports scores. I waited, both of us in a replay of our old postures. I grabbed my purse and rummaged through my wallet to find the party tickets and then to count, as discreetly as I could, how much cash I had left.

The Hilton in Los Angeles was an easy walk from our motel. When we arrived, a crowd waited in the lobby with their badges denoting their names and the names of their bookstores or, in our case, publishing house. Sully and I moved apart in the push to get in, following the crowd and presenting our tickets at the door. Inside, tables were mounted high with food. I spotted shrimp on a bed of ice. The open bar was set up in the corner of the room next to standees depicting the vampire characters from Anne Rice's *The Vampire Chronicles*. I scanned the room to see if I knew anyone, which would be a stretch. Since I'd been in the publishing business for the last three years, I'd pretty much operated on my own. Coming to the trade show last year for the first time was like discovering you weren't the only codependent, but of course, much better.

In the center of the room, a table was piled high with the readers' copies of Rice's new book, *The Queen of the Damned,* due out in September. Booksellers swarmed the table to get a copy.

Ferris Wiley, the president of our distributor, stood near the bar, talking to someone in a suit, and I waved. Ferris wore his usual jeans, button-down shirt and bolo tie. He nodded. My stomach fluttered as

I saw him take in Sully. I had let him know about our pending divorce, yet here we were.

I found us a seat on some benches on the far side of the room, in an enclave of palm trees that were stationed to the right of the band. Sully sat down and I headed toward the bar to get us drinks. I thought I'd start with soda because Sully wasn't drinking any longer. What I wanted was a beer.

"How much do you think they spent to throw this party?" Sully asked when I handed him his Coke. He handed me a copy of Anne Rice's book.

"More than the down payment on our house, for sure. Especially with the open bar. Look how many people are here." It was a mixed crowd of publishers and booksellers, two distinct sets of folks. While the publishers sported ties and suits, the booksellers were in vacation mode, much more casual in their attire, enjoying the once-a-year glamour of the trade show, a contrast to the long workdays of bookselling.

"What are you drinking?" Sully asked.

"Same as you."

"You can drink alcohol, you know. I'm not going to start drinking just because you drink around me." He tapped his foot in sync with the band. He was being very reasonable, which always led me to doubt our past. Knowing this weakness in me, Dave had warned me as he had helped me pack the car for the trip. "Remain staunch," he had suggested. When married, I had believed that if I just did the right thing, everything would be okay. Hoop-jumping was what it was. Sully put them up and, overachiever that I was, I couldn't wait to sally through each of them. My defect of character—to use the AA term—was *pride*, pride resulting in supreme martyrdom. I could suffer more, endure more than other people, and that had kept me stuck for a very long time. *Moregrim* indeed.

I went to the bar and ordered a beer and got Sully another Coke, too, dropping a few bills in the tip jar to demonstrate my affinity as a fellow waiter. I stopped by the food table and loaded up two plates, one for me and the other for Sully. It was eerie how easily I slipped into our old familiar way of being. He was the hero, and I, the witness to his exploits. I served him.

I should have worked the room, but I didn't know how to start. I needed my props, my booth, and my books, and then I could work it. I loved to sell, when it came right down to it, but I always waited for the right context. That was the core thing about sales, I was learning. It had to be the right time and place. This wasn't it.

Over the next hour and a half, I consumed four beers and Sully kept pace with his Cokes. We didn't talk; the music was too loud for that. Sully chatted with the couple to his right, booksellers from Minneapolis, but it was a conversation of leaning forward and half shouting while reading lips, and after the first few volleys, I gave up participating. Snippets came through. He talked about the sports books and then the camping series. I was never mentioned as the one who turned his publishing idea into reality. Who saw beyond the sports books he wrote. Who built the company. Nor did he mention his new role as author rather than publisher.

"Is this your wife?" the woman leaned forward and smiled at me. Her short gray hair crept like waves onto a full face with wide unblinking eyes.

My throat constricted, and I began to cough. When I finally stopped, I gulped my beer and managed, "No, I'm his publisher," the horror obvious on my face.

The alcohol was working on me. I felt like a gasoline leak that just needed a single match to ignite. On the way back to our motel, he asked, "Don't you have any other shoes?"

I looked down. My shoes were scuffed at the toes, but they were the only ones I had brought. They were my work shoes. I flushed, ashamed. I stepped ahead of him, walking faster.

"What? Now you don't want to walk with me?" Sully laughed.

At the motel, I turned the key and flicked on the light. Sully dropped onto his bed, closest to the door.

"You should thank me. I did your job by talking to those booksellers. They'll come by tomorrow and want to order books."

I didn't say anything. I doubted whether Minneapolis was the best venue for selling camping books about the West or West Coast sports histories. I was drunk and made a vow to not to talk at all. I kicked off my shoes and shoved them under the base of my bed and went into the bathroom with my change of clothes, shutting the door too loudly. The irregular buzz of the overhead fan went on with the florescent light and I saw myself in the mirror, with very little makeup, a dash of freckles, my hair in a ponytail, obviously still that country girl from Sonoma County. Outside was the City boy who seemed to know so much more than me about everything. I realized I hated him for seeing me this way, and worse, for never allowing me to be anything else. He always brought me back down to that.

I came back into the room and climbed into my bed. He went into the bathroom and when he came out, he turned off the light and laid down, pulling the covers up high over his neck. The light tore through the crack in the curtains, and he reached up to adjust the edges.

"Did you set the alarm?" he asked, falling back.

"Yes. Seven a.m."

It was silent a moment.

"I hate you," I said. My head, my chest, my whole body burned with it.

"I hate you, too," he answered and laughed slightly and turned away toward the window. His breath came evenly within minutes. I was awake for another hour or two, dodging the light from the parking lot that still slid in through the curtains and across both of our beds, thinking and hating, hating and thinking.

* * *

"Welcome home, pistachio breath." Dave handed me a beer as I came in the front door. It was a little after one a.m. The show had ended that afternoon and Sully and I had broken the booth down right after and drove back to the City as fast as we could. Even though I'd taken the slightly longer route, up 101, we got to Sully's place in nine hours. I spent those hours mentally going over the show, ignoring Sully who slept through it, except when he roused himself at the gas station pit stop. The show had been a success, but my hostility toward him lasted the car ride home and only started to dissipate when he got out of the car. I felt it finally slip away as I made my way out of the Sunset fog over Twin Peaks to the clearer night skies over Bernal Heights.

"Don't ask," I said to Dave.

I set my bag at the base of the stairs and went into the kitchen. "Let me just say you were right." I couldn't be too *Victim MoreGrim* with Dave. He had warned me.

He followed me in and sat down across from me. "Hold on. Let me get a tape recorder. I might need to play that statement back at some point."

"You shaved your head," I said, wondering what zealotry might unfold.

He leaned forward. "Vic, I've got new software to do the maps. It's incredible. I've been working on it all weekend and it'll cut the time it takes to do the maps by eighty percent. I kid you not. Check it out." He pointed to a map on the table.

"You learned the software in four days?" The map was impressive, lots of grayscale and detail.

"I worked all night on it for a few nights because I don't know, Vic, it was just so damn exciting."

I smiled at him. You had to appreciate unadulterated enthusiasm. I did. Especially compared to Sully and his scowling face.

Dave noticed my sudden shift in mood. "How did you survive the I'll-take-credit-for-everything-but-never-do-any-of-the-work guy?"

"I hate him."

"Who doesn't?" Dave, resurrecting Salinger's "A Perfect Day for Bananafish" story. It was always a perfect day for bananafish with us. He clinked his bottle against mine.

"He stole a hand-truck. I have it in the car."

"You didn't stop him?"

"I couldn't. It was like he was the murderer, and I was implicated already with the body in the back of the car. I just drove like hell out of there."

"You're not your best around him," Dave noted matter-of-factly.

"God, it shows." I folded forward onto the table, my chin resting there, my hands splayed in front of me. I was beginning to think codependence might be a permanent tattoo on my character. I appreciated how Dave didn't hold things against me, though. It would have been easy to do. That was the difference between brothers and lovers.

Dave reached over and flicked my beer. "Do you like the new beers I got you to celebrate your return?"

I looked down at my bottle. Heineken. My beer of choice.

"You are a man among men, Dave."

* * *

By June, with our check from the distributor securely deposited in our new business account, we could pay our bills. My brother and I celebrated in North Beach at Giovanni's Restaurant, our table pressed against an enormous glass window. Just outside on Lombard, the cars poured past, their red taillights softened through the condensation on the pane. I squinted my eyes and further blurred them into a long red line. The roar of bistro conversation beat into the temporary lull of our talk as the waiter fought his way in to lift our plates cleared of pasta, and left a rash of breadcrumbs scattered across the white paper tablecloth. I looked down, collecting them in a mound with both hands while Dave continued his treatise on Nietzsche.

"What doesn't kill you makes you stronger."

The imprints from the bases of our wine glasses swung in a wide arc of collapsing moons in front of each of us, measuring each glassful we had drunk so far. I tipped the remainder of the carafe into our glasses.

"Nietzsche said that?"

I tilted the short glass back and the sharp pepper shot up my nose. The tannins swept over my tongue and left it bitter and dry. What to do? Dave waved at the waiter and meeting his eye, tapped the empty carafe.

"We're doing good."

"You mean because of the check we got today?" Dave leaned back in his chair. His hair stood at a quarter-of-an-inch attention, framing his face, cutting around either temple. His forehead had a shine of sweat from the heat of the packed restaurant and, because he had left his glasses at the house, his eyes—free of their cages—vibrated a festive blue.

"That, and the systems we're developing. I mean, we're running a publishing company now, officially. We're making money." I swept the breadcrumbs to the side.

"I'm pretty sure making money and collecting checks are not the same concept." He laughed and leaned forward to grab the wine from the waiter, whose other arm bore three plates.

"I say we pretend they are for tonight." The relief of having cash in the bank was enough for me. I squeezed my eyes shut for a moment, blocking out the image of Sully's face, his brows darting down and his mouth open and shouting, demanding funds from Foghorn's account.

Dave said, "I'm not that great of a pretender. That's why my only friend is you. And Brian, of course. I've alienated everyone else by telling the truth."

"They're all bastards anyway. I'm the only friend you'll need." I tapped my glass against his.

Dave took a gulp of wine and I gestured for the check. When it came back, the waiter gave it to him with a "thank you, sir," and I smiled at Dave.

Who was in charge? No one could tell, but it didn't matter to us. Because I had the cash from making the deposit today, he slid the bill over to me.

Dave pushed open the door to the street and we walked out onto the crowded sidewalk. We stood a moment out of the flow of traffic. The wind slid up my sleeves, so I lowered my head and folded my arms across my chest for warmth. My hair swept across my face, and I spat out a strand. I looked to my left; the TransAmerica building marked the entrance to the high-rise cluster that was San Francisco's downtown Financial District, empty this time of night. Low to the street, a cushion of light wrapped the base of the buildings as far as I could see. We were in Julie's neighborhood and that, of course, made it inevitable.

"Damn this wind. It's brutal," I said.

"She lives up this street." Dave tossed his head back toward Columbus.

"Are we going?"

He turned and started walking and I joined him. His hands were shoved into his pockets and his jean jacket was open in the front.

"I'm freezing my ass off," I said.

"That's a lot of freezing, Vic."

"Not funny."

Dave chuckled, "You're getting more staunch is all. And staunch in your case is necessary." He took off his jacket and handed it to me.

"No, I don't want you to freeze your ass off, too." I tried to hand it back.

"Take it, Slim. I've got staunch to burn." He lifted his hands and backed up.

The narrow street slanted upward with two- and three-story flats on either side. We were silent and bent forward as we walked past the garage doors and gated entrances.

Three vertical blocks later, Dave stopped in front of an apartment building and looked up at the brick facade. He stepped into the foyer and gazed at the names. Then he hit the buzzer and held it while I caught my breath.

Julie's voice crackled through the speaker, "Hello? Who's there?"

It was slightly past nine. At the top of the stairs, she opened the door, wearing baby-blue pajama pants and a scooped necked T-shirt that read *I'm yours*. I'd forgotten how slim she was—delicate, even. I pulled out my shirt under Dave's jacket and let it ride over my rear.

"We're here to pick up my stuff," Dave said.

"Oh." She glanced from his face to mine and then stepped back. "Come in, then."

In the flat's hall, the scent of garlic from the night's dinner enveloped us. I peered into the living room. A black leather couch and chair flanked a glass coffee table. A copy of *The Wall Street Journal* lay spread across it. The apartment had the distinct feeling of being furnished, not by college students, but by gainfully employed individuals.

She beckoned us to follow her down the long strip of oriental rug into her high-ceilinged bedroom, where her new boyfriend sat propped up in bed, under the covers, his shirt missing, staring at the television set.

"This is Baird."

We gawked at him. Slightly balding with elegant-looking gray glasses, black hair triangulating his chest, and padding around his middle, he looked strangely successful, even though it was plain he wasn't any older than I was, and certainly less dressed. He nodded, turning his head back to the television, where a newscaster earnestly pointed to a chart with a jagged red line.

"This is mine," Dave noted, moving into the room. He lifted the end of an old hope chest I knew they had refinished together, and he dragged it noisily along the carpet from the bedroom to the front hall. Julie stood, watching him, but he didn't look at her. He came back into the bedroom. "And this." A plant joined the chest.

I ran my tongue over my lips. I wanted a glass of water, but I wasn't about to ask. I felt suddenly sober and hung over all at once. Funny how certain situations could do that to you. I took up the quest, and my knees buckled as I started to walk, but I kept going.

"Aren't these yours, Dave?" I pointed to the bookshelf in the hall. Shelved there was an entire set of Encyclopedia Britannica from 1965. Dave collected encyclopedias, never minding that the S book was missing or that they were dated. To him, the dated sets were a bonus, representing a culture arrested at a point in time, caught as if in a spotlight, a bug on a pin, and now subject to his investigation. As his appreciation for encyclopedias was not something I was sure she shared, I wondered why Julie had kept them out and so visible.

Dave knelt and walked his hand along their spines. "Yep."

I thought of my prized wall of fiction curated from my college classes in literature now on display on the plywood bookshelf in our kitchen office, Dave's Nietzsche and Greek classics occupying their own row along the bottom, and our shared Salinger zone in the middle. These belonged there.

He stood suddenly. "Vic, check out the kitchen. I think I have some plates here." His voice had an efficient business tone that he rarely used, even at the office.

Julie followed me. A dishwasher, holy shit. This place was very different than the studio she and my brother had shared in the Richmond District only months ago. Her devotion to my brother—since they were sophomores in high school—had gotten her into the inner Morgan sanctum. We all knew my brother was a bit tricky for outsiders to appreciate. But now she was out.

Dave was done, too. Last week, when taking out the trash, I'd found a dismantled photo album that she had created for him. It was buried at the bottom of the plastic can we kept in the garage, but when I inverted it and dumped it into the street can, the pages, unrestrained, came floating to the top, each featuring Julie with her stunning oval face framed by her long blond hair, full of love and looking into the camera, holding up a handmade sign that read *I love you* in bold red marker. I stood on the street looking at each one before fitting the metal lid on the can. I could see it was missing tonight—that look.

I boldly opened the pine cabinets. "Does he mean these?"

"Yes, uh. Let me get them down for you." Julie stepped around me and lifted out four plain blue plates. I took them, my hand brushing against hers for an instant, and then I turned back into the hall, avoiding her eyes.

Our pile was high in just fifteen minutes and included the chest, bookshelf and encyclopedias, two plants, four plates, a toaster, a throw rug, and one of our grandmother's crocheted blankets, which had been perched at the base of their bed.

"I'll go get the car," I offered. Dave nodded. I couldn't imagine what he would do in that situation until I got back, but I could see a perverse enjoyment on his face.

I wasn't sure where we had parked the Toyota. In North Beach, the sidewalks were jammed with people, and I coasted along at the back of a big party of revelers out celebrating a birthday. I crossed Lombard at the light with them and headed north until they finally dipped into a bar. I kept going, wandering around one corner, then another, until the car magically appeared. No ticket either.

When I drove up, the pile had been transferred to outside the apartment building door, Dave sat on the curb, all goodbyes ostensibly said. The bedroom window was closed, but a white curtain opened briefly, a halo from the television screen illuminating Julie for a moment before the curtain dropped back.

"Where's the hope chest?"

"Left it."

I lifted the back hatch, and we loaded the car.

"A bastard," Dave noted as we sped away. "A total bastard."

"Was he?"

"A complete and total asshole bastard." Dave looked stoically ahead. "Did you talk to him, then?"

"No. He was too busy watching the news. He actually turned the TV up with his damn clicker while Julie and I were getting the blanket off the bed. Julie told me he works for a brokerage. In the closet he had a million ties. Bastard."

"Bare Baird the Bastard Broker," I said, waiting a moment for any humor that might be mustered. Dave didn't turn to take it. "She looked a bit surprised, though," I added.

"She did, didn't she?" he said quietly. He tapped his fingers on the door and looked out the window at the Broadway Tunnel which arched over us, its filament of lights directing us forward to the side of the City where we belonged.

* * *

There was one major season in book publishing, and that was Fall. We had Sully's two sports books for Fall. But, as we were now outdoor guidebook publishers, Spring became our season. As early as August, we had to declare our list to PGW for the following year so their sales reps could start selling it. That meant writing descriptions, creating mock-ups of book covers, committing to formats and page counts, and submitting those to PGW for the production of their catalog. It's the way guidebooks are born, often imagined in full before a page is ever written. Scheduling was a process of counting backwards. Long before the books were declared, authors had to be signed to contracts.

For us, it was simple. What other books could our star author John Aberdeen write?

Sitting at the table in the kitchen, we pondered our options. John had informed me that his expertise in the outdoors extended to the entire West, and had suggested a camping guide covering Washington and Oregon.

"He also said that we could redo his self-published book if we wanted." I set it on the table, and Dave flipped through the pages of a glossy four-color book called *101 Outdoor Outings in the Bay Area*.

"Funky layout," Dave said. "But the idea is good."

"He loves us. I think we're making him rich, so he'd be happy if we redid it."

"At least someone is getting rich." Dave smirked, tipping his head back to take in the ceiling. "How many good ol' boys can we support, Slim Bob? Between Sully and John, I think we're doing more than our share."

"I have another writer, rock climber, who I'm reaching out to." He was probably a good ol boy too. Dave scowled.

I added, "Dave, don't be mad about Sully's new book. We need that for our Fall list. He's sober now, so that should help." I watched as his lips compressed.

"Even sober, he's a bastard. And we can't rely on Sully for our whole Fall." Dave was expressing an opinion he'd already shared with me a million times. Two million times. He shook his head, then leaned forward in his chair. "What happened when you called that golf writer? Did he say he could do a golf guide?"

That had been our big brainstorm: a guidebook that would work in the Fall season and describe every golf course in the state, some eight hundred and fifty in all.

"Yes, he's interested. He's busy, though, so we might have to do more of the work than we usually do." I hesitated. Sometimes it was best to not to share everything with Dave initially. "I'll go ahead and sign him, okay?"

"Bring on the good ol' boys." Dave pulled his chair up to the table, his face deadly serious. "Did I tell you about the new series of books I was thinking about?"

"No." I sensed a joke. "Tell me." I took a sip of coffee.

"It's called *California Good Ol' Boys*—subtitle would be something like *500 Dickheads Vicki Supports.*"

I snorted the coffee through my nose. "Jesus!" It stung.

"The guides could have icons, you know, one for whether you just give them money, another if you do their work for them."

He leaned back in his chair, his hands fanning out in a giant circle. "And we'd have to expand on the series, Foghorn-style. It's just a matter of adding the state to the title. We could sweep the nation with them. *Florida Good Ol' Boys*, *Kansas Good Ol' Boys*, you get the picture."

"Unfortunately, I do. So many dickheads." I shook my head, still smiling.

"Think of it as a public-service series, helping the rest of womankind identify and avoid them. You'd be kind of an anti-hero, a study in what not to do."

* * *

"Okay, we've got the books figured out. Now let's see how much money we need to print them," I said at our next meeting.

It was evening, and the Bernal Heights house was dark except for the ceiling bulb above us in the workroom situated between our two offices. Dave pulled his chair closer to the heavy wooden table that anchored the room. The painted clapboard floor spread under our feet, an ocean of muddy brown lapping sloppily against the baseboards.

"How do you propose to figure that out?"

"With the camping books, we can predict how many to print because we can go off last year's sales. The new books are trickier. We can do a short print run to play it safe, but that means it will cost more per book to print. And what if we sell more?" I tapped my pen on the table, thinking.

"Jesus, I don't know, Vic. How are we going to pay to print this list?" We both stared at the list of titles on the table. Five books were planned for the year, three for spring, two for fall. Between Dave and me, that would be more than enough to produce, let alone market.

"We'll send out the printing for bid to three printers and ask for sixty days to pay them. Anything we ship in February, we'll have the money by May."

Dave looked up at me. "That's ninety days. So you're saying we won't be able to pay in sixty days."

"Right, so we can do one of two things."

Dave sat up and leaned his chair back so he was balancing on the rear two legs. "Let's hear them."

"We can pay the printer late.'"

"I reject that approach." Dave, unlike Sully, stuck to his integrity, which could be annoying.

"Or we can advance on our sales from PGW. I found out at the last trade show that some of the PGW publishers do that. They go in with their sales projections for the season, and PGW looks it over and gives them money to tide them over. Then they deduct it when the sales come in."

Dave was frowning. "Do they charge us for that?"

"I don't know." I was calculating how much we should ask for.

"I was looking at their reports and they charge us for everything. Not only are we paying them a large percentage of our sales, but we're also paying every time they move the books around. If we move books from our inventory to theirs, they charge us. If one of their crew picks his nose while leaning on a stack of our books, they charge us." Dave massaged his head like it hurt.

"If they advanced us, we could hire that marketing person we were thinking about at the start of the season, and that would make a big difference in our sales numbers."

"How much would you want to ask them for?" Dave asked.

"Enough for the printer and the salesperson."

"We have other costs, too. I mean, there's still the rent. We have to pay a cover designer. All that." Dave looked unsure, but he was willing to trust me on some of this, I saw. Between the two of us, I still was the veteran in publishing.

I patted him on the arm. "Yep, but it works, right?" I hoped I was right, but if I wasn't, I probably could scramble and figure it out. We pushed away from the table like swimmers off to our separate races, his to layout, mine to figure out the projections for PGW.

* * *

I had worked myself out of my marriage slowly and with great concentration.

Occasionally, Sully demonstrated some care or concern, which had slowed the process. Alcoholics are like that—they step toward you once in fifty times and they want to be rewarded for it, like that should be the defining moment, not the other forty-nine times where they rejected or harmed you. For years, I erased the chalkboard of infractions when he did finally make an effort. In these rare moments, he was transformed. He showered me with affection, creating such a mind-splitting dichotomy in me that I nearly keeled over from shock.

How does a woman who is daily ignored, spurned, and ridiculed adjust when the day breaks on an attentive husband? Of course, he is easily enough waited out.

It was strange, then, that several weeks before the divorce became final, I became gloomy for the good Sully. Our trip to L.A. just six months ago had conveniently faded in my memory and I longed for him or what I now, with the benefit of a year and a half apart, perceived he had been.

Hadn't he once said to me in a moment of tenderness, "I want you to be the one to slice my tomatoes forever, Kahoona?" That phrase metastasized into a two-week tomato-slicing depression. I couldn't function, unable to rise in the morning, to leave my bed except for necessities like the bathroom and occasional bites of food. A new, improved Sully was circling my brain and starting to roost.

Dave stood at my closed door on the third morning.

"Vicki." Dave's voice was low but insistent.

I tried to sit up.

"Are you all right?" He rolled the handle of the door.

He pushed the door open and found me huddled under the blankets, weeping. Compassion was not one of Dave's best traits, and after hearing the sorrowful, "I miss Sully," he stalked off to complete the maps for the new edition of the camping guide.

He ran the business alone for two weeks, during which time the new edition was prepped for printer, inventory taken, and other business conducted. I heard Dave moving around downstairs, but even the guilt of not working couldn't get me out of bed. I called in sick to the Cliff House and sold the same story of illness to Casey.

In bed, I scoured through each year of my marriage from its start to end, reinventing it without alcohol. He was sober now; that opened possibilities, it seemed. There could be a different script because of it. Then I crafted a letter to Sully. It mentioned my desire to be the one to slice his tomatoes forever, that I had made a terrible mistake, that he was what I wanted in life. I signed it, *Your Kahoona*. It was lengthy at eight pages. I mailed it, then waited in bed for a reply.

It came four days later, informing me that while he would always hold a place for me in his heart, he had a new friend now who had stuck with him during this last year, the worst of his life, and he wouldn't dream of hurting her. Wouldn't it be best if we just kept to our business relationship? He—like me—obviously had little capacity to be single.

It was a careful letter on his part. I was still his publisher. As part of the divorce settlement, I had kept the business and he, the house, a deal that matched our personalities perfectly, although at the time, the business was mired in debt and financially was not the house's equal. I was banking on the possibilities. I always did.

I resumed my post at my desk the next morning.

Dave peered in at me. "Coffee?"

He handed it to me and settled in across from my desk. I could see a speech was coming.

"Look, I don't think we should do these sports books anymore. We don't know how to promote them. We have to deal with Sully. They don't make any money."

I looked at him blankly, sipping my coffee. It was my favorite mug, it read, *Drink your coffee, people are sleeping in India.*

"We have to, Dave. What will we do for our Fall list? We can't just cancel it—it's the Raiders. That team sells, no matter what."

"Who gives a shit? It's going to cost us a fortune to print and promote and it's going to eat up all our cash. I say we cancel it," he returned forcefully. "I don't think you can handle working with the bastard either. He's just going to walk all over you."

I hadn't told Dave everything. In my most victim-ridden moments—and now they were coming back to me—I had enough shame and often collusion in what had happened with Sully to keep quiet about certain things. Publicly, I was always ultimately implicated, simply because I chose Sully. But in my own head, where the war raged on, I was implicated again ethically because of how I "unchose" him.

My story to Dave was that my indiscretion with Casey was born of drunkenness and desperation. And it was justified to the degree that Sully was an asshole of the highest order. But I wasn't proud of it. And there was a part of me that felt I owed Sully something because of it.

"Maybe you can deal with the bastard?" I took a sip of my coffee. I still believed in the sports books, even though I realized I should let go of Sully redeeming himself, at least for me personally.

"I can't stand him and he's afraid of me. He'll want to deal with you, and you know it." Dave retorted, getting up to leave the room. "He already cost us two weeks when you went down. And you went down hard. We're trying to run a publishing company here, in case you haven't noticed. They don't run themselves."

"Don't worry about that. I'm back, man. In full force. No man will ever stop me again. That's a staunch-as-hell promise." I knew it to be true, too. I felt up to the publishing equivalent of a thousand push-ups. Bring on the deadlines.

"Jesus," he said. "Do you ever listen to yourself? Less bluster, more work, and maybe"—he paused in the doorway, looking at me—"just a little less smoke blown up my ass. Are you hearing me, Slim Bob?"

"Testy! You're testy as fucking fuck. Put on some Dylan, man, and get to work."

He turned toward his office and I called after him, "And don't tell *me* how to work."

"Are you still talking?" he called back from his office, clicking on the tape player. Bob Dylan's harmonica drowned us out as Dave kicked up the volume.

* * *

In business, unlike in personal relationships, Dave and I were dedicated to getting it right. I made an appointment with Ferris Wiley, the president of PGW, our distribution company. Dave had yet to meet Ferris, so I coached him in the car on the way over the Bay Bridge into Oakland.

"Ferris runs the show. We let him lead. We explain what's going on and then we let him decide to solve it."

"I hate this," Dave said. "I hate going to them for help."

"Hate it all you want. Just don't hate it in the meeting," I said curtly, parking in front. It was an Art Deco building with a ribbon of small windows on the second story. Glass bricks like enormous ice cubes flanked either side of the front door.

Dave held open the door for me. "There have to be other options. Scaling back on the Spring list, for instance."

I shot him a look, motioning for him to not discuss it here.

I approached the receptionist and gave her our names. Her nose was pierced and her hair was cropped very close to her head. They were always the epitome of cool over here.

I sat down next to Dave to wait. Thirty minutes later, Alex, the marketing director and Ferris's right-hand man, came galloping down the stairs.

"Sorry to make you wait. Meeting ran over," he said. Dave stood and Alex reached to shake his hand.

Alex whisked us into the meeting room and plopped down across from us. "Great list this Spring, huh?"

"It's a big one for us. Biggest yet," I replied. I started easing the worksheet that I had put together out of my folder. "Is Ferris coming?"

"I'll go check on him." He got up. "Coffee, soda?"

We declined.

"Unbelievable." Dave groused when Alex left the room.

"What?"

"Making us wait like this."

"Par for the course. But we'll get what we want. Just wait."

Ferris burst into the room, Alex trailing behind him. "Vicki!"

"Dave, meet Ferris. Ferris, this is my brother and partner, Dave." I nodded in Dave's direction.

"Glad to meet you." Ferris always gave the rodeo impression that he was riding a much bigger animal than he could handle and that he was thrilled to death about it. Like there was no way he was going to let go. He was in jeans with a white shirt and his signature bolo tie. His hair meeting his shoulders, he was handsome, young, and brilliant. For the moment, we were the next animal, and he was looking for a way to hop on.

I laid out the list and went through each of the books. Then I went through the print runs for each, and the dollars required.

"How much do you need?"

I pointed to the number.

"We'll advance it on their Spring sales," he said to Alex and got up to leave.

We waited in the lobby for them to cut us a check. Sandra Lippy, their marketing coordinator, came down the stairs and stopped before us. Her auburn hair was bluntly cut at her shoulders, with swatches of pink streaking through it, and she looked down at me through her 1950s retro frames.

"I need to talk to you, Vicki." Her voice was stamped with humor and a kind of desperation—or maybe exasperation, I couldn't tell. She looked at Dave, then back at me, and eased backwards up the stairs, out of the view of the receptionist, mouthing the words, "Call me."

Alex came down twenty minutes later and handed me the check.

"Thanks." I took the envelope. Once we were outside, I held it aloft a moment, pretending to calculate its heft. I chuckled. "Do you know what this means?"

"I don't know about this," Dave ventured.

"Know about what?" I handed him the envelope and started the engine.

"Know if we should be so reliant on these guys."

"Look, with the orders coming in from Costco, our sales will be high enough to cover it. We'll be clear by the end of the year. And we won't have to do it again." I drummed on the steering wheel as I slid the car through traffic and into a lane to pay the bridge toll. This was what happy felt like, I was pretty sure.

I pushed in a tape of Dylan and "Shelter from the Storm" came soaring out. I laughed and sang a line, but Dave didn't.

He dug in his pocket and handed me the cash to pay, and then we charged out of the gate and up onto the Bay Bridge. As we crossed, the vista to our right was clear to the Golden Gate Bridge, the water in the Bay sparkling with the sun like the fleet of quarter slot machines in a casino that I had glimpsed once when in Reno with Sully.

Dave popped in another tape and forwarded it to a different Dylan song, "Gotta Serve Somebody." He leaned back in the passenger seat and glanced over at me.

"Very funny." It wasn't.

* * *

My divorce was final in November. The morning it was official, I explained to Casey (he traced my thigh with his fingers as we lay in bed) all the things the divorce signified. I had broken free and it felt like a miracle. I gestured with my hands. I was a circus performer who had let go of the bar where I dangled from my husband's slippery perspective and somersaulted across fifty feet of the open air to clasp my own bar at last. My hands simulated the somersault. The rubbing stopped.

"I got it," he said. His face bunched into a wince.

"Got what?"

"I'm going to call you Metaphor Woman now." He hopped out of bed and made his way to the bathroom. As I threw on my clothes, I smiled to think that Casey finally might relinquish *Victim MoreGrim*.

Metaphor Woman, I liked. Heroic. Able to create far-reaching connections in a single bound, hauling on my back the linguistic tools for any occasion, ready to spar, formidable in my aptitude, dramatic in my approach. Plus, metaphor-harvesting was a frequent pastime with Dave and me, Bob Dylan aficionados that we were.

When I kissed Casey goodbye at the door, he didn't give me his usual hug. I poked him in the ribs to see if I could get him to laugh. I realized that was his job—he usually bolstered my mood—but now he didn't need to. I had gotten there myself.

He shooed me away. "Off to your business, Metaphor Woman."

As I drove to work, I thought about it. Casey and I had a singular pastime: sex. Sex in parked cars. Sex in his apartment. Sex with food appetizers. Sex with alcohol relaxers. Sex with wall-pounding neighbors as a backdrop. We were blissfully in a full tumble most of the time. Sliding from party to party and ultimately into bed and into each other. He never wanted to hear about Foghorn, but maybe I could do without all the talking. I had Dave for that.

When I arrived home, I heard Prince's "Little Red Corvette" at top volume, vibrating out of the garage. I parked in the driveway and sang along, "Baby, you're much too fast."

Just then, the garage door flew open a foot in front of my hood, and Carmen, the waitress from the Cliff House I had introduced Dave to, came storming out. I liked Carmen immensely for her capacity for swearing and telling it like was. Most of the other servers gave Carmen wide berth as she loudly chided the cooks for any mishaps with her customers' food or slammed drinks down on a table when a customer had been too demanding. She was an inspiration to me, and I was trying to be a bit more direct now, post-Sully, part of my new "staunchness" that Dave noted.

Dave stood there, both arms extended above him, grasping the bar, leaning forward as she stalked out into the middle of the street. Ignoring me, she turned and screamed at him in Spanish, her mouth commanding most of the real estate on her face, both arms extended above her head and swinging back in wide, maddened circles, and her purse, propelled by her arm, jerking wildly. I watched her out of my rearview window and then glanced at Dave. His face was puzzled. I popped open my door slightly to hear better.

"Little Red Corvette," an exuberant festival of sound, swept over the neighborhood. Frustrated, she finally turned, charging down the street to Cortland to catch a cab.

I got out and looked at him.

"Prince has to be played at full volume, Vic."

I nodded in agreement, perplexed. He explained that he had turned it up when she demanded it be turned down, not quite believing that she didn't love that song as much as we both did. But obviously, she did not. More evidence of the gap between the shared sensibility that he and I possessed but no one else did.

To compensate for the mismatch, later that week I introduced him to a new hostess at the Cliff House, Sandy Green, who Dave loved in principle even before he met her because of her name and the fact that we were publishing the golf guide.

As I was heading out to Casey's and he was going out to see her, he grinned and said, "Gotta get your greens every day."

But her sweetness began to wear on him, and after just three weeks, he broke it off and rededicated himself to his computer at the office. She had inspired him, though. He created a series of alter egos for himself, and rather than crediting himself in the guidebooks, the production credits appeared with pseudonyms: Sandy Loam, Anon Lee, and the one that really stuck, Luke Thrasher. We were both disasters at the complexities of relationships, but we always managed to salvage a business application.

SAN FRANCISCO, 1989

Published: 6 titles
Partners: 2
Employees: 2
Annual sales: $200,000

P GW's ex-marketing coordinator, Sandra Lippy, was our first paid employee, hired that spring to kick up our sales numbers. Dave's and my workweeks had shot to eighty to one-hundred-hour odysseys of book deadlines based on our Spring list. We weren't paying ourselves yet. I had my tips from the restaurant and Dave subsisted like the Spartan he was. Occasionally we made a draw from the business. The business continued to pay the rent. To make Dave less nervous, I agreed he should be in charge of the money.

As a former key employee of our book distributor, Sandra knew the book buyers in all the chain stores personally. We believed we stole her from PGW, but in fact, she was on her way out, just launching the series of monkey-bar career jumps—one hand always reaching—that eventually would land her a corner office in the high-rise of a New York City publisher. Smattered in freckles, she wore billowy Berkeley-style dresses. Her fingers interlaced and rested on the shelf created by her breasts if she was conversing and, when making a strong point, she was liable to seize them in hand-to-breast combat from below.

I discovered the confidences she had shared with me in the past had nothing to do with me. She was a universal sharer, a personable sales representative who revealed the most intimate details of her life with whatever buyer she had on the phone. She was forever in mishaps, from car crashes to unexplained rashes, yet she was so smart, she managed those mishaps into humor, which begot sales. She amused, cajoled, and charmed, setting up alliances that were hers alone, but that we got to claim while she worked for us. Often the calls would go on for an hour, and only at the end would she ask for the order, an afterthought. But the orders came—from Waldenbooks, Crown, Barnes & Noble, and Costco.

Sandra was a wonder to watch, and we never questioned how much we were paying her. She logged twenty or fewer working hours a week, was paid for forty, and accomplished what I never could have in eighty. Surprisingly, Dave, usually a stickler for value based on money paid for hours worked, was fine with it. Sandra was the perfect sales-person, as far as we were concerned, and we were more than a little proud to have taken her from PGW.

Sandra created a contest for Girl Scouts to secure a badge by dec-orating Waldenbooks store windows in camping themes using our books. The Scout troop with the winning window received a check for $150 and a free camping trip to the site of their choice picked from our top-selling camping guide. The store with the winning window scored a month's supply of Girl Scout cookies. I was watching Sandra's brilliance closely, taking notes. Waldenbooks bought three times their normal quantity of Foghorn outdoor titles for the promotion, and we were off to a bold spring.

* * *

One March morning, Sandra arrived, late as usual. Rumpled in a print dress that rippled with tiny blue flowers and a wide ruffle at its hem, she pushed in the front door, staggered through the arch into my office, and threw herself into the armchair before my desk.

"I almost had an accident on the Bay Bridge," she said in deadpan voice that fought off the urgency crackling around the words.

I stopped loading to-dos onto my yellow pad. "You're kidding."

"Yeah, no kidding. I fell asleep at the wheel and I almost hit the railing." Her hands were clasped above her breasts, her freckled arms eking out of her sleeves.

Her eyes, now that I looked at her more closely, were puffy, and her eyeliner—usually boldly drawn across the bottom of her lower lid—was missing, giving her a much more wholesome appearance than she normally was comfortable with.

"Aren't you sleeping?"

"I'm sleeping. I'm sleeping all the time, my friend. Occasionally with your brother."

I paused a minute to see which line of questioning to pursue first. Shock value was her specialty. I made a note to grill Dave. He was listening to all this from the next room, I was sure.

"Narcolepsy. When you can't keep your eyes open, it's narcolepsy," she informed me, self-diagnosing, leaning forward confidentially.

I paused to see where she would go with it. I tried to look at her objectively, but it was almost impossible—her charms had won me over as well. But I was having a hard time picturing Dave with her. Dave and Sandra seemed complete opposites to me, psychologically, and, most importantly, philosophically.

"Shit," she said. "I was supposed to call Waldenbooks this morning. Did they send in the order yet?"

Dave peeked his head in the door, his eyebrows reaching for his hairline, his mouth twitching, trying not to laugh. I looked at him, wondering how I could have missed this liaison. Usually he was rooted to the house, working. Obviously when I was at Casey's, he was doing more than figuring out new book-production software programs.

"What?" she said, swiftly whipping around to face him.

"What the hell?" I mouthed at him.

"Vicki and I tried to save you a doughnut, but you never came, so we had it for lunch."

She held up her hand, blocking her view of him. "Don't say anything more. I just got here."

He glanced at the clock above my desk, which read eleven thirty. He and I had started the day at seven a.m. "Your fax from Waldenbooks came."

She snatched it from him and teetered up the stairs, clutching the railing as she went. We had put her office across the short hall from my bedroom, the last available room in the house.

Dave looked at me and grinned, waiting.

"First rule of business. No sleeping with employees," I said.

"I'll put it in the new employee handbook. Or hmm, maybe you should write that document," he said. "More coffee?"

I heard her start her calls. "Yeah. I almost hit the rail on the damn Bay Bridge. Narcolepsy."

* * *

"Look at the Costco order! Waldenbooks! Barnes & Noble." I could hardly contain myself. "Orders from the independent bookstores are off the charts."

Dave, Sandra, and I sat in the kitchen and pored over PGW's monthly distribution report, which detailed the shipments of our titles all over the state and the country. It was late in the day and Sandra usually went home by this time, but Dave had invited her to stay for an Old Milwaukee beer, his idea of an upgrade from his usual Mickey's Big Mouths.

Nearly twenty thousand books had been shipped out from PGW to bookstores the past month, constituting the biggest month in the history of the company.

"You guys. You guys did this." I looked first at Dave and then Sandra.

"Well, you might have had something to do with it, too," Sandra joked.

"Fellas," Dave said, his finger pointing at the bottom line. "We're thousandaires!"

"Thousandaires," I repeated with delight.

"This calls for music!" Dave said, springing to the tape deck.

"Not Bob Dylan, God help me," Sandra pretended to wail.

"Bob Dylan goes with anything," he reminded her, pressing a tape into place. " 'If Not for You,' winter would have no spring."

When Dave came into the business, he brought with him the Morgan pride and code of humor—corny as it was—that I had deserted in my preemptive strike for adulthood. He reinstalled it like a piece of software that I had stopped using somewhere in my tenure with Sully. Ten years of not dancing. Not laughing out loud. Not playing Dylan. *Not* after *not*.

"It's time to do the *Yes Shuffle*," he called out, laughing. He grabbed each of our hands and pulled us up from the table. Sandra resisted at first, too hip for this kind of display, until he threw an arm around her. He reached out with his other hand and pulled me to his other side, gripping us each around the waist. His back hunched forward and then rocked back while he raised his knees like a perverse can-can dancer.

"Yes! Yes! Yes!" he crooned. We joined in, laughing, too. Sandra kicked out her sandaled feet, her freckled knees peeking out of her dress, and I swung my legs out to match Dave's as we whirled around the kitchen.

"If not for you," we all sang, Dave's voice, off-key but strong, leading the way.

"Yes, yes!" Sandra and I sang, clutching him back.

* * *

Giddy and fueled by optimism, Dave and I attacked our next guide to great outdoor adventures with every ounce of creativity we had. As we began to work on it, it began to differ from the description we had submitted to PGW. The more we worked on it, in fact, the less the resemblance. Although it still had the touted three hundred Bay Area outdoor outings, it now had a slew of other marvelous features.

"Fellas," Sandra said diplomatically when we first told her of our concept. "PGW won't know what to do with it. They won't get it and if they don't get it, they won't sell it."

But we were entranced by an idea. Our author, John Aberdeen, hadn't sold many as a self-published guidebook, and so we were free to redesign it as God Himself might, in Aberdeen's image.

The guide featured a black-and-white drawing Dave had done of John's head with his trademark cowboy hat. Using our new copier, Dave and I were able to attach this drawing to a variety of bodies we'd pulled from free clip art, coordinated with the adventure featured in that chapter. For fishing adventures, John came in a boat, hiking adventures in his big boots, and so on. Our jubilation, and even a renewed will to live, came from the entertainment we derived from attaching his head to as many drawings as possible. We worked for three weeks until two or three a.m., laying out the pages. I didn't think of visiting Casey when we had deadlines like this. And Sandra steered clear of us. After shouting hello each morning from the front hall, she headed up the stairs.

Sandra found us the final morning, delirious over the copy machine after an all-night vigil so we could FedEx the book to our printer that day. She snapped off the tape, cutting off Dylan's "You're Gonna Make Me Lonesome When You Go."

"What? What is it?" she said, working her way into Dave's office where we were leaning over the copier, chortling. She set her coffee on Dave's desk and squeezed in between us. She lifted her breasts and placed them on the copier.

"My God," she said, turning the pages we had resting there.

"This is the one," I said, flipping forward to a page that had consumed us for nearly two hours.

John's head had been placed on the body of a butler whose coattails and white shirt were elegantly portrayed and who held up a platter. A balloon issued from some unseen speaker: *Yo! Butler! Bring us some adventures.*

"You've gone too far, my friends." Sandra giggled. "Obviously, John will love it."

Every crevice the rebel herself, she added, "PGW will freak out."

"You think so?"

"They've got a sense of humor, don't they?" Dave said, proudly stacking the pages.

Sandra's mouth twisted to the right. Now, outside the tight, hip circle our distributor had created for itself, she harbored some ill feelings toward them. There had been that incident where a sales manager, a little drunk, had eased her into a corner at the annual Christmas party and forced himself upon her. There had been no sympathy from anyone in charge in the matter. Everyone was too young and too hip. That was the incident I had heard about in detail at the publishers' party when we first met, again during her job interview, and then again after we hired her and as she broadcast the particulars to her accounts during her calls.

"They'll freak out," she said again bitterly, but Dave and I were already wrapping the box in packing tape, anxious to ship it off to the printer.

* * *

In May, Dave and I set out with John Aberdeen to the Pacific Northwest for our first media tour. We were doing radio and television in both Seattle and Portland. I had contracted with a public-relations specialist who had snapped the tour together in days for what Dave considered an outrageous sum, but I convinced him it was worth it. We left Sandra to mind the publishing house. We knew she was a negligible anchor given her lack of accountability, but it was only two days.

We rented an economy car at the Seattle airport and Dave drove. I sat in the front seat, negotiating maps and streets, while John played celebrity in the back seat, which was too small for his sprawling physique. He had wedged himself sideways and his knees were level with his chest. He had trimmed his beard, but still looked the mountain-man part. His wide-brimmed hat set off his mustache, which curled out on either side of his nose. His plaid shirt was buttoned to the top, and his jeans had his wide belt touting *Yosemite*. He had icy blue eyes, which you only noticed if negotiations were getting sticky.

Otherwise, he looked genial and calm, a master of the outdoors, come down from the mountains and trapped willingly for the time being.

"Well, I guess I'll just hunker down back here while you folks get us to our destination." John talked like he wrote.

Dave looked at me briefly. He had become markedly silent, the only way he knew to withhold judgment. He would rather be at his computer, creating the maps for our next book. I was the one who wanted him to come. My defense against John.

"It's a ways yet. We have to go into downtown Seattle to reach the station," I told him evenly.

John was holding forth, Dave his new audience. They had talked a few times on the phone to discuss the maps for two of the guides this season, but had yet to meet.

He launched in. "I knew Vicki was going to be my publisher from the first time I set eyes on her. I've heard it a hundred times, people calling me at the newspaper and asking about writing a book for them. When Vicki called me and said she'd be interested in publishing a book, I heard her out. Then I told her to call me next week. Next week, there she is, calling me, like she said she would, when she said she would. That's when I said to myself, 'This is worth checking out.' I told her I'd meet with her. As soon as I saw her, I could see the fire in her eyes, and I knew she was the real thing. Not many people have that kind of fire in their eyes. Yep, I knew when I saw her."

Dave met my eyes again, looking for the fire perhaps, his mouth bemused.

"Can you please turn the air conditioner off?" I said smartly. "Aren't you freezing?"

Dave flicked it off. "I've conquered cold."

"You know what makes a good book? A book that sells?" John paused for effect.

"The maps?" Dave ventured. I would have laughed if we were alone.

"The maps are important. No doubt about it. A year ago, I was driving to a campground in Desolation Valley and the car in front of me stopped. So I stopped. I was about to get out of my car when something big and red flew out of the passenger's window. They drove off. And I was curious, so I hopped out. I walked over to where they had stopped, and there, lying by the side of the road, was a copy of our camping guide. It was our first edition, remember, Vicki? Before you figured them out, Dave, the maps were terrible. I learned that day that the maps have to be reliable."

"So, what makes a good book, John?" I said, leading him back to where he started. I gestured to Dave that the exit was pending. John was trying to win Dave over. I wondered if Dave would be won. Dave's bullshit detector was big, and rote stories like John's were not going to help.

"It's a book you can trust. A book on which you know people did the work and have been to every one of those spots and checked them out for themselves." John was always writing marketing copy when he spoke, selling us our already-spent investments like a hypervigilant broker with more stocks up his sleeve.

He continued, "The outdoor adventure guide is the best book yet. We totally reorganized that book and it's going to pay off in sales. Plus, I put in all those new adventures." He paused, then added for Dave's benefit, "And Dave redid the maps."

"This is the exit," I noted. We all watched for it. I wondered if John had any idea how transparent he was.

* * *

The interview went well. John turned on his full drawl and captivated the host with a description of a little-known campground within a few miles of Seattle that very few people knew about. John always did his homework. They flashed the cover of the camping guide on the screen after the interview. I gave Dave a high five where we stood watching behind the cameras.

Dave drove us to the next TV station, and it went equally well. The morning show gave John a full five minutes.

John presented a copy of the camping guide to the female host on the air, who enthused about how much she loved to camp, which was hard to believe looking at her perched on her high stool in her short skirt, her makeup intense. She probably liked to camp the way I liked to camp—in theory.

After a half-hour radio show, we were off to Portland. Dave drove and John talked and I nodded. John had an arsenal of canned anecdotes to which we listened. He had climbed Mount Shasta and heard and reported on the Lemurians and Yaktavians, elfin creatures who lived in its interior. He had been paid to search for Bigfoot for a big feature story by the outdoor magazine he worked for. He had hiked the John Muir Trail at least four times, and traveled the rivers of Canada. By the time we were crossing the Columbia River into Portland, Dave had the glazed expression of a person who had accidentally picked up Daniel Boone as a hitchhiker and was beginning to long for the twentieth century, when you could wrestle a computer to the ground and be called a man.

The car had become unbearably hot. "Turn on the air conditioner, would you?" I asked Dave as I dug around my feet for the Portland city map.

John got quiet. "I thought you didn't like the air conditioner," he said, puzzled. Apprehensive, even. I looked at him for a moment.

"I only like it on when it's hot. When it's cold, I like it off." I felt I had clarified once and for all my position on air conditioners.

"Ah." His eyes grew sorrowful, as if this were indicative of much more. John preferred things black or white. In past negotiations, anything left unclear generated a barrage of calls until the matter was settled. Consistency was a must; even, it seemed in the matter of air conditioners.

Then, perhaps because I had dared to venture into the gray area of life, John decided to do so.

"I don't know if I ever told you this, Vicki."

I waited. I had heard all John's stories at least five times during book signings, interviews, and publisher meetings. It was unlikely to be anything I hadn't heard, but I was always polite to John, so I nodded for him to continue.

"I moved to Mount Lassen last year, you know. I did it mostly because of what happened to me in Point Reyes at the house I had there. You know, the one I sold last year?"

I nodded and began watching for the Portland exits. The directions had warned that if you missed your exit in Portland, you had to go another half hour sometimes before you could find another to come back.

"I was asleep when a noise in my house woke me up. I could see someone in my room. I jumped up and must have scared him, because he took off out the door. I lit out after him. I tore into my yard. Next to the woodpile where I had been chopping wood that day, he stopped and grabbed my ax, and that was the last I knew. I was in the hospital for months." He paused for effect. "That's why you should always treasure each day."

John liked to sum up the meaning of any anecdote, lest it went misunderstood.

"He hit you with an ax?" Dave was incredulous, waking from his stupor.

"Yes, in the head."

"In the head?"

"You're lucky to be alive, John," I noted, wondering why I had never heard this tale before. It suddenly made a kind of sense to me that John was the way he was. I always had the feeling I needed to be especially explicit and clear when I talked to him, which was puzzling because he was certainly capable of writing great guidebooks.

I looked over at Dave, who kept glancing in the rearview mirror at John.

"There goes our exit," I said as we whipped by.

* * *

The outdoor store where John was speaking was packed that night. At the front entry, there was a placard with a cover of the book and John's head with his trademark hat. Every fifteen minutes, someone announced the seminar would begin at seven p.m.

To an audience of more than eighty outdoor enthusiasts, John ran through his slide show, sprinkled with anecdotes for which Dave and I had been the rehearsal. Dave sat in the back of the room, and I sat in front, alongside the seminar coordinator who introduced John, who then began as usual.

"I'm in the outdoors two hundred and sixty days a year—"

"Going on a camping trip can be like trying to put hiking boots on an octopus. You've tried it too, eh?"

The audience was enthralled as slide after slide depicted John atop a mountain, beside a lake, hiking a trail. John sold the outdoors like Mother Nature was giving him a commission. I loved it.

At the end, John stood over the autograph table, signing books and answering people's specific questions about what kind of fish the Columbia River had and how and when to make reservations for the national parks. Dave stacked the chairs and I helped the coordinator pack up the projector. We'd sold fifty-six copies and she pumped my hand in thanks, gushing about John, who had already wandered back into the store to peruse the sleeping bags.

* * *

The motel room was stuffy when Dave and I came in, and I went to the air-conditioning unit to turn it on.

"I thought you didn't like air conditioners." Dave shut the door.

I knelt and ramped up the AC. "You're right. I've always had something against them."

"I wish you'd give them a chance, Vicki, they're just trying to do their job."

"Maybe if I hadn't had that ax in the head, I could let go of my prejudices, but I just can't." I plopped down on my bed, relieved to be done with the day.

Dave snorted and we broke into laughter.

"Air conditioners? The philosophical debate continues to rage. What will she want tomorrow?" I wanted to hear him laugh again.

"That's what we needed, a belly laugh. I believe in a belly laugh a day! And today, we can thank John." Dave was rooting through the mini refrigerator for a beer.

He handed me one and dropped onto his bed, flipping the bottle cap onto the nightstand between us.

"Listen to this," he said, settling back after producing a book from his pack. "This is from *Ecce Homo*."

"Nietzsche?"

"Of course." He began reading. " 'Reality has been deprived of its value, its meaning, its veracity to the same degree as an ideal world has been fabricated—' "

I heard the television next door in John's room, tuned to the late night news.

"Hmm," I said, a little lost. "You're unimpressed, then, with the tour circuit?"

"That's the world of publicity, I guess. I just don't want any part of it. I want to work on the books. For me, that's reality."

We sat a minute, mulling that over.

"That works, I suppose," I said. I took a long swig of my beer. "So what's going on with you and Sandra? She seems kind of, I don't know, reserved or something lately."

"Tell you the truth, it was just kind of a one-night thing. She invited me over and one thing led to another."

"She seems a little more invested than that."

"She shouldn't be. I don't even know why I did it, really."

"Lonely, maybe?" I ventured.

"Ah, as Nietzsche would say—wait a minute." He found the passage. "'Philosophy, as I have hitherto understood and lived it, is a voluntary living in ice and high mountains—a seeking after everything strange and questionable in existence, all that has hitherto been excommunicated by morality—'"

The look in his eye, the way his mouth worked all around an idea. I was transfixed. He could still surprise me with his intelligence, so sharp. Mine felt dull, like a tool I had been lugging around since high school that I'd forgotten I had. I had to pay attention, I realized, or I'd be lost.

I put my beer down on the dresser. "Read it again," I demanded, gazing at him still absorbed in the book.

He ran his finger across the page as he continued to read to himself while chewing his lower lip. Brian once told me that Dave had read *Ecce Homo* at least eight times. Even as an English literature major, I hadn't ever read anything eight times, with the possible exception of Salinger's *Nine Stories*, which both Dave and I loved and revered above all other literature.

"Especially that excommunicated by morality part," I said.

* * *

We flew out of Portland at noon, arriving at the Oakland Airport shortly thereafter. We dropped John at his truck so he could make his way back to Lassen, and we fled to the bridge.

Downtown San Francisco loomed on the right, the buildings imperious and royal, evoking the feeling of approaching Oz. I pointed it out to Dave. I loved it. Always had. From the first time our parents brought us to Fisherman's Wharf after our move to Northern California, the City had already captivated me. But I was exhausted and told Dave as much.

"I'm exhausted, too, and no clichés about Oz are going to help that. Hey, watch the railing, Slim Bob. We don't want any incidents of *narcolepsy*." Dave looked over at me. "I wonder if Sandra came into the office at all."

As we drove up, we could see her at her desk through the second-story window, her head dropped forward onto her arms. We looked at each other. Dave sighed.

We climbed the stairs to her office. She lifted her head and yawned. Her thin hair floated around her head. Sandra never hid her actions. If anything, she strutted them, like she dared the world to call her on them.

She picked up a pile of purchase orders from Barnes & Noble and handed them to me.

"Wow," I said, flipping through them.

"You're in early," Dave said, attempting to be funny.

"Listen, fellas. I'm giving notice. Mountain Top Books has offered me a job as their sales manager and so I'm going to move to Denver." She nodded her head sadly, looking at me and then, for a longer time, at Dave. She pushed back in her chair, her hands crossed and resting on the top shelf of her breasts.

"Sandra—"

She interrupted. "I'll be gone by end of day. I already called all the accounts and let them know."

I glanced over at Dave, and he was looking at her closely, a puzzled expression working his face. I glanced around her office, which hadn't changed at all in the short time she'd worked for us. She'd occupied the desk and that was all. This small-time setup on the top floor of a fake Victorian probably appalled her, and I thought of all the mileage she would get from dragging us through her stories. I felt a small hit of shame.

Then I took a breath and let it out slowly. I felt my engine starting to rev, defiance and pride wrestling for control. We didn't need her. Or maybe we'd have to learn not to.

"Oh, and I called PGW like you asked me to do, to see why the outdoor adventure guide isn't advancing, and they told me they don't like it. They think the cover is terrible and the whole book needs a redesign. They also said we need to hire an editor. Too many typos."

Sandra smiled at us sweetly where we stood, crouched forward in her small attic office. I turned and walked out, my steps coming down hard on the stairs as I descended to my office, and Dave followed.

We drank a six-pack that night, looking through a copy of the adventure guide and debating what to do now that Sandra had left. There was *Neveda* in sixteen-point type where Nevada should be flanking the map of eastern California. The typos leapt out at us, Dave's spelling unchecked on the maps and my inconsistencies popping up in the text listings. We'd need an editor, that much was clear. And with Sandra gone, I'd have to take over sales. Maybe we needed a business manager, too, so Dave could concentrate on laying out the books.

Dave popped "Little Red Corvette" into the tape player. It was just him and me once again. I turned it all the way up. We moved the desks around in Dave's office. Before long, we'd changed around my office, realigning my desk before the front window and then reorganizing the meeting room as well, which simply meant pulling the table over nearer the stove and shuffling the bookshelves on either wall. We did the shipping for the next day, stacking the pouches containing our books inside the front door for UPS.

When we were done, just before two a.m., Morganization, our go-to strategy for hurt and disappointment—for every downturn, really—had prevailed. Everything had been moved to form a new office and a new beginning.

Dave looked around and proclaimed, "Publishing, Smublishing."

"Yo, Butler, Got any adventures?" I replied.

* * *

That year, the American Booksellers Association trade show returned to Washington D.C. and Foghorn was moving to the big room, housed in the Publishers Group West block of publishers for the first time. Dave couldn't understand my excitement, expecting me to document how the show was tied to sales, especially now that the costs for the booth and drayage had gone up dramatically.

"It's tied to relationships," I told him. "From relationships, come sales."

He looked at me warily.

"And being in the PGW group, we'll learn all sorts of stuff from the neighboring publishers."

I had an idea, born of my observations in previous shows. As a small press, we could never command an audience like the bigger publishers, with their Anne Rice parties and in-booth hospitality. But what if we banded together? I shot out letters to twenty-eight small-press travel publishers, inviting them to collaborate on a party that we'd throw together. For a nominal amount from each publisher, we could rent a boat in D.C., cater the party, and invite travel booksellers and media to come aboard. With twenty-eight immediate yeses, I put together the invites to the first Booked for Adventure event, and reserved the boat and caterer.

At the show, I gave tickets to the participating publishers to hand out to accounts. The buzz in the air about the party was palpable.

Alex from PGW shot across the aisle to request a ticket. On Friday afternoon, the Costco buyer showed up at our booth.

"Did you get your ticket to the Booked for Adventure travel publishers party for Saturday night?" I asked. I waited. She had the kind of authority that belonged exclusively to people who hold the fates of thousands of publishers in their hands.

"I'm definitely coming." She nodded. She stopped in front of the golf-guide cover mock-up.

"What is this?"

I described the guide to her, picking up one of the camping guides to illustrate the descriptions, maps, and indices.

"I want this for Fall. Call and remind me when you get home from the show," she said, picking up our catalog and unfolding it.

"There's a show special through PGW," I told her.

"We already get that discount." She winked. "I'd probably order ten thousand to start for all the California stores." She glanced over at the table where the 49ers and Raiders books were featured. "And I was thinking about bringing in your sports collectors' editions for Fall, too, in our Bay Area stores. Especially after the Super Bowl win. We could test them and see."

I couldn't wait to tell Alex at PGW.

He was gobsmacked. "You know that means they are taking every one of your titles this year. That's unheard of. But your books are perfect for Costco."

"What makes a successful test?" I asked him.

"If that first week they see good movement, say thirty titles or more per week, then they order up big. Once they order big, the books sell themselves because they command so much space." Alex grinned. "Hey, could I have another ticket to the travel party? Ferris wants to come."

On Saturday, I left the booth early to go set up the party. D.C. was humid and the moment I stepped out of the air-conditioned show, the hot air assaulted me. Sweat ran down my neck as I flagged a cab. The small wood ship lolled in the water, and I dragged the boxes of publisher catalogs over to the gangplank and up. A walkway ran the full circumference of the ship around the party room. Inside was a bar, a table for food, and another two tables for the publishers' display books. On the roof were benches so guests could survey the bay. We weren't taking the boat out—it would be docked through the three-hour event so partygoers could come and go.

At six p.m., the party was officially open. By six thirty, it was packed. *Travel & Leisure Magazine* sent a reporter. *Publishers Weekly* came. Book chain buyers from Crown and B. Dalton Booksellers were there, plus independent booksellers from Tattered Cover to Books Inc. I stood at the door and greeted them all. I realized I could stand in my booth all day and not meet half as many people critical to our business.

At the end of the party, Alex shook my hand on the way out. "Home run, Vicki. Home run!" Was that newfound respect I saw?

It was two a.m. D.C. time when I got back to my room, but I was still keyed up. I called Dave from the hotel to report.

"That's great, Vic," he said absently. I heard Bob Dylan's "Mr. Tambourine Man" in the background.

I paused in my excited recital of the day's events. "What are you doing?"

"I'm trying to figure out how to load the golf book into a database. Imagine if we had our books on databases. I'm going to test it. It'd be super simple to keep it up to date that way." He cleared his throat. "I almost got it, but not quite."

"You heard what I said about Costco, right?" Marketing and sales never interested him. But then production and logistics never interested me. That's the reason we were a good team.

After I hung up, I tried Casey's home phone. No answer. I tried the Cliff House and he picked it up on the third ring. As a waiter, Casey had often swooped in at the host station, intercepting calls just to stand next to me when I first started as a hostess, collecting customer names. He'd brush against my backside as he did it. Remembering that, I felt a little shiver up my legs.

"We're all going out to Rockin' Robins after we get out of here," he told me. Then I heard him address a customer. "Thanks for coming."

"Sounds fun," I said. I didn't bring up any of the accomplishments of the day. If anyone was worse than Dave in thinking these things mattered, it was Casey. Any time I ventured into a discussion about the business, he simply changed the subject.

"What are you wearing?" He issued another thanks for coming and then quietly whispered into the phone. "I'm missing my sex maniac."

"Me? That's you." I laughed.

I heard him reply to another customer, "Thanks for coming."

Then, "Oops, gotta go. My food is up. Last customers of the night." I pictured him looking over to his left at the chef's window where the food stayed hot. "And Vic"—his voice dropped to a whisper, his voice husky—"thanks for coming."

I hung up, laughing.

* * *

That summer we researched the new Fall golf book. I had already called thirty golf courses one morning to discover their tee times, course lengths, and fees, then painstakingly put it into my computer with the appropriate golf lingo. Golf courses "dogged left" frequently, for instance.

Dave was up to the same in his office and he'd been muttering about it all morning. Occasionally, he'd shout, "Why are we doing the author's job?" and later in the morning, it turned to a few loud bursts consisting of a one-word philosophical inquiry: "Why? Why? Why?"

I was on my third cup of coffee and my head was hammering in my temples, making me regret the three a.m. arrival back at Casey's from a party we'd hit. I wasn't regretting the rest of it, however, and I lifted my hands from the keyboard for a minute and pictured Casey again as we tumbled across his king-sized bed.

"When does our bastard author arrive?" Dave hollered from the next room.

"His name's Gary Hedge," I shouted back, feeling my voice ricochet through my forehead. I put my hand to my head to steady it. *God, let it go quickly*, I said to myself.

Gary sauntered in moments later wearing a polo shirt, his sunglasses atop his head. His face was pudgy but tan, reflecting a weakness of character that was obvious only to the laborers of the world such as Dave and me. As the golf columnist for a national golf magazine, he used these credentials like all good ol' boys do. I thought those credentials might be useful in selling the book.

"Is my car okay out there?" He gestured out to the street, and I peered in the direction he was pointing. About a block down, I saw an obviously out-of-place white BMW. I thought of the friendly drug dealers who lived across from us and how much they might like that car.

"It's fine, I'm sure," I replied.

Dave came around the corner and shook Gary's hand warily. Dave could never understand people who didn't really work or want to. I was subjected to many Nietzschean passages on mediocrity in Gary's honor after he reviewed the signed contract Gary had mailed back to us. I didn't much like Gary, but Sully had been a good ol' boy wannabe and I still hadn't relinquished his viewpoint that ingratiating oneself was how you got ahead.

"Gary, you remember Dave, my business partner." I hesitated a moment. "And brother."

Gary nodded noncommittally. He sized up Dave's jeans and T-shirt and dismissed him.

He turned back to me. "Here's the stuff." He slid a folder onto my desk and looked around the room. I looked around for a minute, too. I expect he was used to offices that weren't situated in faux Victorians on the "bad" side of town. I picked it up and handed it to Dave, who stood by my desk and began to thumb through the contents.

"I'm heading down to Pebble Beach right now. You know, the AT&T golf tournament is in January. Will the book be out by then?"

I nodded. "You're covering the tournament in your column for the magazine?" I asked.

"No, actually I'm playing in it." He grinned and then, as if he knew this would impress us, "I have a 7 handicap." He added that he was assigned a celebrity golf partner each year.

I sat down at my desk and, taking my pen, leaned forward. I asked him for the name of the tournament director. I felt Dave, with the folder in his grip, pacing to my left.

"Sure. What are you going to do?" he said genially. He sat down in the armchair across from my desk.

"I don't know, but it's worth calling. Are there media there?" I probed.

"Hundreds. From all over the world. I suppose you could get it promoted in the press room." He looked doubtful.

Dave spoke up. "There are only ten pages here." He looked down at Gary's folder and then up again at Gary.

"Well, I wrote what you guys asked me." Gary glanced at me for help. "That's all I have time for."

I saw Dave's jaw working; a faint flush came over his cheeks.

"For ten pages, he gets his name on the cover of the book like he wrote it?" Dave was incredulous. He tossed the folder on my desk.

We paused a moment, Dave standing over us.

"Gary's providing the marketing, Dave." I smiled at Gary reassuringly, but I could see Dave wasn't going to let it go.

"This is total bullshit. At least the other authors do the work."

Gary started, and then sputtered, half words tumbling from his lips. Writers never liked to be compared to other writers. I opened the file and looked. Not only were there just ten pages, but two were double-spaced and obviously quickly written. Less attention than he gave his monthly column. The rest were recycled columns he hadn't bothered to retype—he'd just lined the portion to use in yellow marker.

"Tell me why you think this is something that we would even think of publishing." Dave faced Gary, who slowly rose to his feet, but I knew he was talking to me as well.

"Look, you guys called me. That's what I have time for. I was clear from the start." His face was losing its benign expression. He was used to having things go his way.

"No, I don't think you *were* clear from the start." Dave's voice was rising.

Dave turned to me and then back to Gary. "Jesus, we're researching the golf courses in the book. You can't even put together articles that have any more substance than this?"

Gary took a step back, knocking a moment against the chair; his hand flew to the armrest to steady himself. He replied angrily, "That's all I can do. We have a contract. I followed it."

I thought of Sully. He would have defended himself the same way.

"We publish this, we look stupid." Dave glowered at me.

It was getting way out of hand, but I was paralyzed. This was one of those good ol' boy inequities that offended Dave the most.

"You need to get out of here. Take this crap with you." Dave strode toward the door, pushing past Gary, their shoulders colliding as he did. "If you can take time away from your golf game to come up with something else, let us know."

"Hey, you can't do that." Gary had gone red in the face, he was puffing.

Dave opened the door and gestured toward the stairs leading to the street. "Wrong."

"You're throwing me out?" Gary squeaked, stepping back and glancing at me.

I stood transfixed, unable to help him. Not daring to.

Dave slammed the door after him. I peered out my window, watching Gary jog down the street to his car and climb in, his BMW spinning away with him as he hit the gas.

Dave glanced at me and then quickly strode to the back door, which bounced in the door jamb in his wake. I heard him pull the cord to charge the lawn mower our landlord had left in the backyard hoping we'd use it, and when it roared angrily to life, he began to mow.

At dinner he told me, "All I ask is that people do the work." His voice was even and low as he dished up a bowl of soup from the stove for each of us. It was minestrone of Dave's own creation; all of the leftovers of the week had gone into it.

"He's only getting half the royalty," I countered as we sat.

"Half is ninety-nine percent too much."

"The contract's signed, Dave. It's too late to change all this now. I can get him to write more," I said, recasting it best I could.

"I mean, he's not even a good writer," said Dave. "I don't know how the magazine even publishes his stuff. I want to publish books we can be proud of, not books by bastards who get everything handed to them."

"Now we're talking about Sully, too?"

"We're talking about the Bastards of America Club. All of them. Nietzsche had the perfect derogatory term for these guys—the Last Man. Happy to follow, no talent, no passion, yet arrogant that his lifestyle is the chosen lifestyle—that he's got it all figured out. You know, if you could physically mesh all the stupidity at high school, you would end up with a Gary Hedge. And I ask you, do we want to go back there?"

He looked at me as if he was considering letting me answer. "The Last Man is the embodiment of the American status quo. He is the best argument against democracy. God, and to think the law allows him to procreate. If Americans can't figure out why they have a major crisis on their hands, I might have to remind them."

He spooned up a mouthful of soup and looked at me. "I'm beginning to think you only choose these Last Men."

"I chose you," I retorted. "And you're no Last Man. So you are wrong there, mister." But in my head, I conceded that Casey was probably such a man. And you don't *choose* your brothers. I wondered then—other than my brothers—if there were others who weren't Last Men. It made me wonder about my future.

He cocked his head at me as if I were a specimen. "God, you're the perfect woman, just like Nietzsche described. Hostile to truth, more concerned with how it looks than anything else. I don't know why I fight with you. You can't even help it."

"Less Nietzsche, more publishing," I said, figuring that might fix the situation. I gathered our bowls.

"Nietzsche would never have survived this kind of publishing." He sighed, defeated. Then after a moment, he stood. "You're probably right, Slim Bob. What else can we do?" He disappeared into his office to work on maps.

Later that week, I called Gary. I mediated a solution. Increase the number of pages to twenty, I said, and everything will be fine.

* * *

Around six p.m. on a Monday at the start of football season, I received a call. It sounded like it came from a bar, which the speaker confirmed.

"Who are you?" I asked.

"Someone who can make you big money on your sports books."

"Do I know you?" I returned tentatively, but I was listening.

"You should know me. In fact, you should come down here right now so we can talk about this. I have all the connections to make it happen."

Dave frowned as I slipped on my jacket and explained the call. "Wait. Where are you going? You don't even know who he is, Vic."

"Dave, he said he could make us big money on the sports books. It won't hurt to check that out, will it? It's a crowded bar and I promise not to leave it with him."

Dave shrugged. Long shots were not his method of operating. He was much more of the plug-away-each-day-and-build-it-yourself mindset. But I liked the home runs.

"By the way, Alex at PGW just let me know about the test order from Costco for the Raiders book and he said another's coming for the 49ers. These sports books are starting to work. All we have to do is promote them. This could be part of that promotion," I assured him.

The waterfront bar was packed with sports fans watching *Monday Night Football*, screens mounted every five feet throughout the mahogany room. My anonymous caller saw me come in and shoved off the barstool where he was perched. He was a tall, heavyset man with broken veins across his cheeks and an inflamed nose that told me he was a drinker. Ten years with Sully had taught me something.

"Lyle Cousins." He shook my hand jovially. "Come on over and let me buy you a drink, pretty lady."

I attributed his comment to my youth. Not many people expected that I might own and run my own publishing company. I often felt tested when meeting new people, as if I needed to prove something, demonstrate my intelligence in some way. But I let him talk while I sipped my usual vodka-Seven.

He unfolded his plan. He was a professional sports promoter, and as such would get the Raider quarterback great Ken Stabler for an autograph session featuring our Raiders sports book. I would provide the signing venues and the money to pay Stabler's fee. I said I'd handle the publicity as well, and on the way home, I began to write the press release in my head.

I explained it all to Dave, warding off his pessimism, and two weeks later, Dave and I rented a limo in the East Bay. We were going to pick up Ken Stabler at the Oakland Hyatt in the East Bay, a former Raider haunt where we were hosting him prior to the event, then drive him to the book signing. I told Dave we needed to define our roles before we set out, another necessity of small-business ownership. Today, Dave was the driver and I was the publicist.

Lyle Cousins had told us to meet him at the hotel suite and he would have Ken Stabler ready to go. When I pushed open the room door, there were about a dozen people whom I didn't know milling about the suite. On the table sat a platter of hors d'oeuvres, consisting of shrimp and cocktail sauce and another with steak and horseradish. There were some suitcases in the corner of the room. I looked for Lyle.

Lyle saw me, waved a drink in acknowledgement, and grabbed Ken Stabler's arm and brought him over. Stabler had the grizzled, lean look of an old football player who had spent most of his football career partying. But I heard that when he retired, he yanked himself free of the nightlife and had dedicated himself to his family.

"This is the lady from the publisher I was telling you about." Lyle beamed. I smelled the alcohol on him. Stabler smiled wanly, disentangling his arm from Lyle's grip.

"We're going to Modesto, which is a couple of hours away," I told him. "We'd better get going."

"I have my flight for later tonight. You can drive me to the airport?" Stabler replied.

I looked at Lyle and he shrugged. I had a jolt of awareness.

When we reached the hall, I asked the star, "You're not staying here?"

"Nope, just in and out for the day," Stabler returned quietly.

"Of course, our driver can take you to the airport," I said, walking him out to the car and pointing to my brother. "Go ahead and climb in. I'll be right there."

I walked back to the room where Lyle was saying goodbye to his friends who were bottled up around the door, shaking his hand. He raised his drink to indicate he was coming. I waved back and turned into the lobby of the hotel.

"Excuse me." I stood at the counter. The clerk smiled professionally at me. "Room 121. How long has Lyle Cousins been in it?"

He scanned the computer. "Oh, let's see. Are you Ms. Morgan?"

"Yes."

"It says you are the payee on the account."

I nodded. I caught my breath and held it.

"Two weeks."

Two weeks! I couldn't believe it. While I had thought I had called my credit card into the Hyatt to put up Ken Stabler for the night, it appeared I had actually been housing Lyle Cousins and his assorted friends for two weeks with room service.

"I need to close that account out now," I said, my voice shaking. "No more charges are to be allowed."

"I understand. Let me do that for you now, Ms. Morgan."

I staggered out to the car with a receipt for close to $3,000 in my pocket and launched myself into the passenger seat next to Dave. He was wearing a cap like all limo drivers do. Ken Stabler was stretched out in the back. The glass was drawn. I breathed deeply, trying not to hyperventilate.

"Where's Lyle?" Dave asked suspiciously.

"Closing up the room. Let's go without him."

Dave looked at me closely and started to drive. I opened the glass that divided the driver from the passengers.

"Mr. Stabler. Lyle isn't able to come with us. I hope that's okay."

"Who?"

"The guy who arranged for you being here. You know, Lyle."

"I don't know him. I just heard through my agent. That's fine. Mind if I sleep while we drive?"

I shut the window to the back. I pointed to Stabler sleeping in the back and that was reason enough for Dave and me not to talk. I found myself calculating how many books we'd have to sell to cover that bill. One hundred and sixty-six books at thirty dollars each. Then we had the limo cost, Stabler's fee, the ad I had taken. Two hundred and sixty-six books. We had brought just two hundred books, which at the time had seemed reasonable, and even showed a healthy amount of optimism.

At the Sports Cave in Modesto, a line of a few hundred people weaved through the mall. A cheer went up as we approached. Ken waved, smiling for the first time since I'd seen him. I directed him to the table that had been set up with our books. About one in eight bought a book; the rest had him sign their memorabilia or purchases they had made from the Sports Cave. I had guaranteed the manager that he could sell memorabilia and that we would collect money from our book sales. I hawked those books through the line, but memorabilia was cheaper, and we sold just forty-two books by the end.

We drove Ken Stabler to the Oakland airport. I paid him $1,000 cash in hundred-dollar bills through the open window. He took it and didn't look back as he exited the car and strode without luggage through the spinning doors. We returned the rental car at the airport and walked to our car.

Dave unlocked our doors and said to me over the roof top, "How much?"

"How much did we sell?" I pretended to clarify.

"How much did we lose?"

The $8,000 loss pounded in my head, but I couldn't bring myself to say it aloud.

"The books we sold covered Kenny Stabler's fee," I said. I slid into my seat.

He climbed into the car, sitting in the parking lot, looking forward, the ignition off, his hands on the wheel. "Vic, you have to tell me."

I put my hand on his shoulder, but he ignored it. "Dave, we'll make it up with Costco order if the test works. One order for three thousand books will generate three times what we lost." I leaned forward, twisting in my seat to get him to look at me.

"Right now, all I want to know is how much we lost. How much?" His voice was cool, detached. He looked over the steering wheel rather than at me. He kept track of the money, there was no way to keep it from him.

"Dave. I can't." I started to cry, sick with what had happened and how I had let it happen. "I should have checked Lyle out. I know I should have."

Dave was never influenced by tears. He said, "You made a bad decision, face it. Now the business has to pay for it. And it's not like we have the money to throw away like this. If we had worked together, we could have avoided this."

He sighed deeply, hurt as much as he was angry. "So how much?"

"Eight thousand dollars," I mumbled. I explained the hotel bill and Lyle's deception.

He listened carefully, turning finally to look at me as I told him we'd never find Lyle or get the money back.

"Eight thousand dollars," he repeated, and he started the car to drive us over the bridge and home. His hurt was a thousand times worse than Sully's anger. I couldn't counterattack with my own anger; I had to sit in it, feel it.

And I didn't want to, so I began to plan for my redemption.

* * *

I was off to drive sales at Costco. I had a plan to make that test order for our 49ers and Raiders books to the Bay Area stores lead to a bigger order.

Dave hadn't talked to me about anything but the production schedule since the Lyle debacle. Nothing personal. Standing in the door to my office, he now looked incredulous. "You're going to go to Costcos throughout the Bay Area and do what?"

"I'm going to give people money to buy our sports books." I had a printed list of the Bay Area stores and addresses on a clipboard. I was planning to start in the East Bay and work my way to the Peninsula, then hit the North Bay.

"And why is this a good idea?"

"They base their ordering on sales from the test week. If sales are strong during the test week, they order a big quantity and the big quantity sells itself because it's such a massive presentation in the store. Can you imagine an order for three thousand or more on the sports books? It could translate to three times the loss we had with Lyle, or even more, at this time of the year when we need it the most. And the price we pay for that? Two thousand dollars," I explained. It was a calculated risk and after the $8,000 fiasco, I could see that he was reluctant. But I had thought it through, and I was determined to make it work, even if it meant me hitting every Costco in the Bay Area over the next three days.

"It's probably not something most publishers do," he countered. "Hand people a twenty and the book you want them to buy with it. Some might just keep the money."

"Nah, they'll buy it." I smiled at him. "If you want to be successful, you gotta do the big thing." I was using his own lingo against him and he knew it. "I'll start in the East Bay and get the check from PGW and deposit it. Then I'll take two thousand in twenties and leave the rest in the account for the bills."

"This is definitely the big thing." Dave walked me to the door. "Listen, I think we're both in over our heads, Vic. I'll get the bills we need to pay ready to go. But we still need to work on the list for next spring, you know, and figure this financial stuff out."

"Okay. I've got some ideas." I pulled on my jacket and grinned at him.

Dave puckered his lips and blew out. "That's what I'm worried about. All your big ideas have big price tags."

Two weeks later, Alex from PGW called me to report that the tests went well and that three thousand of each the 49ers and the Raiders books were being ordered. I didn't tell him about my recon trips to the stores. I didn't want PGW to know how far I was willing to go. All they needed to know was that the books sold. When I hung up, I put my head down on my desk and thanked God. I didn't run into Dave's office, either, but walked in calmly to report the sale.

"But they can still return it, right?" Returns were possible in the book industry. My brother was a glass-half-empty guy now, and I was pretty sure I was the one who had caused that defection.

* * *

On 580 North, I pulled over to examine my tires, thinking I had a flat. I had just crossed over the Bay Bridge on my way north to the Silverado Golf Tournament, where I had a booth to sell the new California golf guide. When I got out of the car, I wasn't alone. The entire freeway was lined with hundreds of cars, their drivers all pulled over to the right side in one long lane, all kicking their tires. We eyed each other.

"What happened?" echoed up and down the freeway.

When we climbed back into our vehicles, we turned on our radios to hear that an earthquake had struck the Bay Area, a big one. We pulled out together, resumed our lanes, plans dissolving in the wake of the news. As I drove toward Napa, the enormity of what had happened still spinning out of the dash, I realized I wasn't going there anymore; I was going home.

I drove to my parents' house in Rincon Valley in Santa Rosa with the window down, the rush of wind whipping through, providing a natural buffer against the urgency blasting from the radio. Reports of major connecting freeways falling, fires spreading, buildings collapsing, all combined to blow out the usual jumble of feelings that plagued my returns to Sonoma County.

I was worried about my brothers, who were still in the City. Brian had been in town a little more than month now, in an apartment near UCSF, and Dave was at our office in Bernal Heights. He still wasn't talking to me in the old way we had. He was warming up, but there had been no belly laughs in a month, and I missed those especially. I was trying to repair the damage my decisions had caused by working harder. I had even stopped going to Casey's during the week, doubling down on my efforts to sell books.

But as I drove north, then west, I stopped brainstorming ways to increase our sales altogether and focused on my brothers' safety. I wondered if I would sense it if something were to happen to either of them. I wanted to know if they were okay. I listened to the vibration in my chest, only interrupted by the tap of my foot on the brakes in the heavy traffic, a circular inquiry that went unsolved, repeating for the duration of the trip.

Our family home sat just outside the city limits in the open space below the foothills. Similar ranch-style houses sprawled luxuriously in the open space in either direction. I pulled in to witness my father's latest, achieved since I'd been there last: Two enormous boulders had been brought in and now sat in the half circle of yard created by the scoop driveway. I pushed open the front door to the detonating television news. Both of my parents were watching it, a cribbage game abandoned on the counter. I felt a jolt of hope seeing the cribbage board, evidence that my parents still played that game together.

"Oh, my God, Vic." Both of them stood, then rushed forward to hug me. My mom still wore her work clothes from the bank.

She pulled back but held onto my shoulders. "How did you get here? Where are Brian and Dave? We couldn't reach anyone..." She trailed off, her arms dropping to her sides.

My mother had a fresh farm-girl face, everything in petite proportion to everything else, her ears delicately framed in the circle of her short haircut, but now lines rode her forehead and she pressed her lips together, trying not to cry.

My dad drowned me in a big bear hug, rocking side to side as he did. "I was worried about you, baby doll." His beard scraped my neck.

Over my dad's shoulder, I saw the screen on the television with a video of Bay Bridge's upper deck giving way. A car perched on the gap.

"I just crossed that bridge," I said. I sat down and watched the clips of the destruction.

My mother uttered, "I wish I knew the boys were okay." Brian and Dave, always *the boys*.

"They're okay. If there was anything to report, they'd be on the news," Dad said. Strands from his beard jutted out randomly where he had worried it with his hand. When he'd contracted diabetes at twenty-six—a hospital visit none of us kids now remembered—he'd returned to us white-haired.

Yet over the years, he retained his handsomeness and exuberance. By the time I entered the junior high school where he taught, girls my age, exiting his math class and seeing me in the hall, felt the need to comment about his Paul Newman blue eyes, which had made me blush red in confusion over how to respond. And then there were the rumors that circulated about him and my English teacher, which I pretended not to hear.

The television played the same images again. The newscaster said that you couldn't get into San Francisco, and you couldn't get out. The phone lines to the City were down as well, congested with worried relatives all trying to get through. They warned of aftershocks. There was no way of us reaching Dave or Brian, or them, us.

My mother leaned into me on the couch, her head resting on my shoulder as we watched the stories and images as they flooded the room. I tucked the blanket around our feet and held her hand. It was comforting to not have to hide my life and feelings from her anymore. Another post-Sully benefit.

The phone rang. My mom took it in the den, and we could hear her voice rise and fall with emotion as she relayed her anxiety to the neighbor.

"We got Costco to take the sports books," I said.

My father glanced from the television to me. He sat at the kitchen table, correcting his algebra students' tests, running each paper against his answer key and then recording the grade in his binder. It was a schoolteacher's tribulation to always have papers to grade at home; the scene had not changed in twenty years.

"That's great, kid." He grinned, both of us suspending our earthquake concerns for our usual Foghorn exchange.

Foghorn confirmed my father's long-held beliefs about what was possible if you put your mind to it. Growing up in the '70s, we had been conditioned to believe that we were only held back by our concept of ourselves. Our dad's self-help books commandeered two entire walls of his den, paperbacks with the titles: *How to Be Your Own Best Friend; Jonathan Livingston Seagull; How to Win Friends & Influence People, I'm OK—You're OK*. Now that we were all in our twenties, Dave and I—strictly speaking—were not okay, but all three of us kids believed that hard work could conquer anything, as evidenced by both of our parents, who preferred to bank vacation time rather than take it.

My mother was sacrificing, but my father, it always seemed, was stockpiling for some glorious future. He had worked two jobs since he was an eighteen-year-old father, even now: teaching math at the junior high that was walking distance from their house and umpiring on the weekends for adult league softball.

He tapped his pencil on the table as I described how we had gotten such a big order. The publishing company's existence represented a resurgence of optimism, definitely for Dave and me, but also for my dad. Foghorn provided a focal point for the whole family, it seemed, spurring a reassembly of the family puzzle pieces that had been in a box for at least ten years.

"You and Dave are really making things happen," he said.

At the mention of Dave, we both turned back to the television.

* * *

That night, I slept in my old room. I rarely returned to Sonoma County, not at all during my marriage, and rarely now since Foghorn absorbed one hundred hours of each week. Casey took the rest. I shut the door gently against the unexpressed quarrel I felt emanating from the opposite side of the house where my parents' bedroom was located.

My room had been converted to a guest room, but the windows were still framed by bright blue plastic shades with dangling blue balls made of yarn—designed for me before I hit high school. As I pulled the shades down, I remembered climbing out this window and trekking across the field at age seventeen to meet my boyfriend in his van parked where the road bent back into town. At the rear of the van, his lean torso forward, he waited, his feet dangling onto the road. And when I strode out of the field, he looked up and grinned. I crawled in, the doors shut, and the magic began.

I threw myself onto the soft bed and burrowed under the covers. I thought about Casey. With the earthquake, I imagined the Cliff House tipping from its cliff perch into the ocean, *Titanic*-like. But even knowing it hadn't fallen, I imagined Casey in his waiter black slacks with the white shirt, telling jokes while he inflated rafts and loaded customers into them. I wasn't worried about *him*; his gregarious nature was an odd but effective shield.

But my brothers—I was worried about them. I pictured Brian at the university. Dave was most likely by himself across the City in Bernal Heights. As the crickets roared outside, my chest churned with that urgent coupling of imagined responsibility and ultimate lack of power that rules an oldest child. I had abandoned my post. I required action, the only remedy for so many feelings. But there was none to be taken. I steeped in it while the hand of the bedside clock ticked off the minutes into the early morning hours.

My parents' house had open fields on the east and south sides, and in the morning, I woke to the crowing of the neighbor's rooster and the birds funneling through my dad's trees, planted along the fence line. I tugged on the shade and it flew up. In the tall, wet grass, there stood a deer, and behind the deer, a small row of ranch houses, and farther, the lushly green mountain that had framed my view growing up. Picture perfect, a metaphor for the way I'd always managed to see my childhood.

I wasn't the only one who saw it that way. Right before I started seventh grade, we settled into this ranchette home on its one-third acre, and became part of the community. My brothers and I shed our timidity, finally finding friends other than each other. Our parents morphed from the isolated and tentative young couple starting out in Los Angeles to the cool parents, now stabilized by maturity, increased income, and a nice home. Our dad was the jokester, our mom fun-loving, both still younger than any of the other parents, both beautiful. Our family became the one our friends wanted to be a part of.

There was a time when our family played card games together, kidded each other, hung out together, and rooted for each other. As we kids got older—into our high school years—it shifted again. This is what Dave felt, perhaps, calling it abandonment. It may have been simply that they had found their own lives, my mom starting to work at the bank and my dad rarely home. But they were stuck emotionally, too; unprepared for teenagers, I think. My dad still interacted at the level appropriate to the junior-high-age kids he taught, unable to track up, and my mom preferred not to witness our emerging sexuality.

When I came into the kitchen the next morning, the room ached with an uncomfortable quiet. I recognized the icy stillness that was periodic but pervasive throughout my teen years. My dad huddled over the stove, stirring his pot of oatmeal, and my mom sat at the counter with the newspaper.

"Good morning," I crowed, my voice high, like I could lift them both up and out of their state with my good humor. I glanced down at the newspaper my mom was reading. The headline read: *Hundreds Dead in Huge Quake*. My mom pointed to the line that read 7.1, the strongest since the 1906 San Francisco earthquake. I went to the television and turned it on, the incessant reportage sweeping the silence away.

My mom had on her robe and slippers. The phone hung on the bright yellow wall to her right.

"No work today?"

"I want to hear from the boys first." She looked up at me. Without her makeup, she looked more vulnerable, more her age.

"I'm taking off in a minute," my dad said. "Want some oatmeal?"

I shook my head. "Still no phone connection this morning?"

But just then, the phone rang. My mom snagged it and after uttering her hello, her shoulders dropped in relief, and then she started to silently cry, her face buckling. She didn't say anything more and I understood it was Brian and Brian was safe. Brian was making her feel better with whatever he was saying. The downturned ends of her pained mouth returned to their place.

"Do you want to talk to anyone else?" she asked, regaining herself. "Okay, that's good, I'll tell them." But as soon as she hung up with Brian, she dialed Dave. I came over and stood by her, and she turned the phone so we both could hear. Dad stood across the counter listening, his bowl of oatmeal steaming.

"Hullo, hullo?" Dave's voice, distant and thin, bounced into the dining room.

"Oh, Dave, we've been so worried. We kept trying to get through. We just talked to Brian and he's good. We tried—" My mother's voice cracked.

"I'm good. I'm good. Where's Vic? Have you heard?"

"Here, I'm here, Dave." I took the phone and nestled it into my neck.

"Whew. When I heard about the bridge and I knew you were crossing it, I got worried. I didn't know where you were after the earthquake hit."

"Here, I've been here. We've been trying to reach you. You and Brian were the ones we were worried about."

"No need to worry. Bernal Heights is the only place that didn't get impacted by the earthquake—they told me at the store. I guess we're on solid rock. The electricity is out, that's about it. Can't work, so I've got my Nietzsche books out and it's giving me a chance to read. Got out the candles. I'm reading *Ecce Homo* again and it's blowing my mind."

"You're a philosopher at heart," I said, grateful to hear him talk to me so readily again.

"Philosophers always survive, one way or another." I heard him laugh quietly.

My chest heaved and I turned my face away from my parents' view. "I'm so sorry, Dave. For all of it. I'll make it up. I will."

"We'll figure it out together, Vic."

"Thank you for saying that. Really, Dave. I don't know what I would do without you."

The magnitude of that truth hit me hard. I took a step away from my parents and said as quietly yet as forcefully as I could, "I love you, man."

I wanted that to register with him, to fortify him somehow. I wanted him to know he was exactly what I admired most in the world. I wanted to declare my complete loyalty and affection in a world where there were no guarantees, where the earth shook, bridges collapsed and fires raged and people died, or even worse, it seemed to me right then—standing in the room with our parents—stopped loving one another.

"I love you, too, Vic."

My mom took the phone from me to talk to Dave again. My dad slid his empty bowl in the sink. My mom turned on the stool facing the wall, her head lowered and her back to us both.

"Will you be here when I get home?" my dad asked.

"I'm heading back now, I think," I said.

He nodded. "Be careful, doll." He gave me a quick hug and a wet kiss on the forehead, and went out the front door without glancing at my mother. I turned to the television set, where once again the film ran showing the car that nearly drove off the Bay Bridge.

* * *

A month later, the City was slowly starting to stir itself out of its state of shock, and so were we. Dave answered the call in his office and then hollered at me to pick up.

"Vicki, Alex at PGW."

Alex at PGW rarely called me. I was the initiator in the relationship with our distributor. So I instantly suspected it might be bad news, but I tried to ward it off.

"Alex?"

"Vicki."

"Alex!"

"Vicki!"

Laughter at both ends.

"Let me guess. Costco will order our outdoor books for Christmas because they worked so well for Spring." This was our first year with Costco and I hadn't learned the game.

"Uh, no. But it *is* about Costco. A large return from Spring, actually."

I hung up and lay my cheek on the cool of my desk and tried to breathe. The Costco return wiped out our gain on the sports books and left us in the hole. I knew that without looking. I thought about Dave and my plan to start paying ourselves in the new year. I thought about having to continue to work at the Cliff House. I thought about how Dave would take it.

Dave, who never believed in good news until I persuaded him that he could trust it. It was real, I had said, waving the sales reports.

I guess it wasn't real.

I staggered into Dave's office. It was crowded with another desk and the copier up against the wall. The one narrow window was covered by a curtain and cut off any light. He was bent over his machine, peering fixedly at a map page of the new edition of our California camping guide for the following spring.

I explained the situation.

"Pardon?" Dave had a way of scrunching up his brows when he sensed a disaster.

I waved off explanations. I could hardly speak. "Spring titles are coming back. I need Salinger."

He grabbed the copy of *Nine Stories*, which we kept with copies of our guides on the plywood bookshelf in the kitchen, and up the stairs we went. We didn't glance into the room housing Sandra Lippy's empty desk. We passed through my bedroom, dipping our heads as we approached the window. Dave pushed the sash up. Outside, it was sunny and piercingly bright compared to the rest of the house, and the roof was hot to sit on in a delicious, San Francisco-sun-starved way.

I sat down and placed my hands on the black rubber shingles, soaking up the warmth. Dave sat down next to me.

"Did you take the phone off the hook?"

My brother nodded. "You want to read it or me?"

"You."

The two-story houses formed a kind of castle around the courtyard of our backyards. Looking down, everything was visible to everyone, the broken tricycles and laundry that hung from the second-story clotheslines. When I first moved to the City to be with Sully, I was amazed at the closeness of the homes, so contrary to the ranch-style housing where Dave and I had grown up. The Bernal Heights yard had been overgrown and neglected most of the time Foghorn had been here, until Dave mowed it with vengeance following his fight with Gary Hedge. Now our yard was the neatest on the block.

I reached for a joke.

"Gary's is the first and last BMW to ever park on this street. He must have flipped out when he found he couldn't park right in front."

Dave made a face of disgust. "Look, it's a perfect day for bananafish. Let's not wreck it with a Hedge-ism, okay?"

"Or returns," I added. "Okay. Read, my friend."

Dave and I identified with Seymour Glass, J.D. Salinger's martyred character. I don't know if Salinger provided us the training for humor, or if it was a match we recognized deep in our funny bones. We knew every story, every line from his *Nine Stories*. The little girl in *A Perfect Day for Bananafish* corrects him with, "It's a yellow," when Seymour compliments her on her blue bathing suit. We were Seymour, the ones in life suggesting it was a blue, when it clearly was a yellow. We thought that was hilarious, but most people didn't appreciate the humor of it when we reprised it. So the joke felt private to us.

Like Seymour, we were the ones whose feet were being stared at in the elevator while everyone else sat in the hotel—miles away from our sensibility. But, unlike Seymour, we weren't alone, and, unlike Salinger, we had no capacity for sad endings.

* * *

All through Christmas 1989, Tracy Chapman played heavily on the tape player. When she finished, Dave or I hit the rewind button to start again. We wanted to get into her fast car and ride. The Costco hit had sunk us further in a year that had already tested us. It had only been the one in a series of business trials that led to pervasive gloom in our office. That gloom was echoed throughout San Francisco in the aftermath of the earthquake, and we felt it as we drove through the City, in the rubble at the base of the freeways and the damaged, tilted homes.

Personally, it wasn't much better. The week before Christmas, I invited Casey to spend Christmas with me at my parents', and that was too much commitment for my self-described "flinchy" lover. He disappeared for the final two bleak weeks of the year into work, where the unrelenting number of tourists who made the Cliff House their holiday destination, despite the earthquake, created a natural distraction.

That left Dave, Brian, and me sitting around each evening, trying to find some humor in our childhood memories. Brian's new place in the Inner Sunset had room for both of us, so we took refuge there. I moved into the other bedroom and realized I was going to remain there. I need a separation of church and state, business and home. Dave claimed the futon in the living room, pulling the shutter doors shut for privacy. But most of the time, we three camped in the family room next to the fireplace. The bare floors of the house were cold, and we bundled up with our grandma's crocheted blankets around our knees in front of the fire we built. We were all single.

Christmas Day, we would all drive home together and assume our old beds, but I knew Sonoma County wouldn't be any brighter.

* * *

Optimism arises out of a number of factors. For most people, it comes from a night's sleep or a meal or a connection with someone who reminds them they are loved. The brain, thus armed, recalibrates and begins anew. Optimism for me, however, was a fundamental part of my being, needing no external stimuli. Instead, it was always amassing in my blood, like its own type of carcinogenic cell, rushing from limb to limb, gaining momentum before settling in my chest. The physical sensation accumulated, until at full force, it nearly danced against my ribs. I felt the excitement rise with each breath, warming my throat before exploding into my brain. It was what allowed me to shake free from whatever held me down, to forget my part in it and any blame that fell my way, and rise again with a new and better plan. It was what kept me in my relationship with Sully so long and it was what allowed me to survive the first three years of publishing before Dave came into the picture.

With the Costco return at the end of the year, I was appropriately downtrodden. But when the new year broke, I started feeling the early sensations of optimism returning as a tingling in the tips of my fingers. Dave wasn't having any part of it. He had his head down over his computer, working on the next edition of the camping guide for California. I developed a financial worksheet for the Spring that I took to PGW for an advance, depositing the check when I got back to San Francisco. I trotted up the stairs and threw open the front door of our Bernal Heights office.

Tracy Chapman still played like a dirge on the tape player. I clicked it off and went in to see Dave.

"I have an idea." He looked up at me and I could see him prepare himself to hear it, his hands lifted off the keyboard, his fingers spread and stretching up like defensive sea anemone, his wrists still planted on the coral reef of the desk. He looked at me. "Do you want my full attention?"

"Yes, let's talk."

He stood and came into the kitchen. "Shoot, Slim Bob."

I grinned at him, happy to hear my nickname after all these months of not. Maybe he'd be open to my plans again.

"We can't keep working like this, these crazy hours with just you and me. We can't be spending our time proofing, *Mr. Neveda*. I mean, I'm not good at it either. Obviously."

He shook his head to contradict my thought. "I just don't want to pay for something that we can do. If we can do it, we should."

"Would you agree we can't do everything if we are planning on growing the company?" I said.

"I don't agree."

"Honestly? Dave?"

"You want to do more than work. That's understandable. I don't think we should make company decisions based on our love lives, though. I don't have anything else. I'd just as soon work."

I sat up. "I'm not doing this because of Casey. You know he's flinched himself off the property, anyway."

"Temporarily, until his trousers get tight again. What was it this time? You accidentally left your toothbrush there and the commitment overwhelmed him?"

My face flushed at his accuracy. "I want to talk about the business."

"Okay, get to the point, then." His hands flew up in the air in exasperation, then descended to the tops of his thighs. "What's your plan?"

"Testy, testy. Too much Tracy Chapman for you."

"You don't really want to talk about the business. You just want to keep initiating your ambitious plans that we cannot afford and then you want me to agree to go along with them," he said.

"I do not. I want you to be happy about them."

Dave snorted. "How is that different from what I said?"

"Employees," I blurted out. "We need some employees to do some of this work."

"Then we'll have a bunch of people in our space who will drive us both crazy." Dave looked around the kitchen as if it were a sacred vestibule that he alone treasured.

"Dave, we don't have to have them here all the time. They can work part time."

"And how do we pay for them?"

"It won't be much. Part-time editorial. And maybe someone who knows business. You want that yourself. I worked it out. We can afford it."

Dave looked at me. "Do what you want. I know you'll be complaining about them being here, the same as me."

"Do what I want? That's nice. We're a team. We should decide together." I eyed him carefully, trying to determine if he was mad or just being contrary, his newly acquired attitude.

"Go, team," Dave retorted. "You just threw Tracy off the team, right?" With that, I thought he might have let me off the hook. It wasn't agreement, but it wasn't disagreement either.

"That's right. No more Tracy Chapman." I popped in a new tape, Don Henley's *The End of the Innocence*, and turned it all the way up.

PART II

THE GREAT PHILOSOPHY CRISIS

SAN FRANCISCO, 1990

Published: 7 titles
Partners: 3
Employees: 2
Annual sales: $350,000

Allison Crew walked into our publishing company in response to an ad we ran for a business-manager position. She was devastatingly sophisticated, from our point of view. She wore a fitted red dress with no sleeves and black high heels that propelled her nearly to the cracked ceiling of our Bernal Heights publishing house. An Amazon of a woman, she was blond, plainly beautiful, Stanford-smart, and extremely capable.

She sat in my office for the interview. I peered at her résumé while Dave, who had dragged in his chair, peppered her with questions about inventory management, budgeting and projections, cash flow—all terms that we had begun to sense were important.

"What's your view on profitability?" Dave asked her. He always asked open-ended questions that bordered on the philosophical. I waited to see what she'd do with it.

"Profitability is important," she said, meeting him where he lived. He nodded to me, his part taken. "But very often, start-ups are not profitable in the first few years because of the expenses involved in getting the business started." I nodded back to him, my part taken.

She understood us perfectly.

Dave glanced at me, signaling that she was it. I nodded my agreement and asked her about salary.

She let us know her salary range was normally way above what we wanted to pay, but she was willing to work as a part-time consultant to help us with the business aspect of Foghorn. When she left, we were both enamored and, I think, a little amazed that she wanted to work for us at all. Plus she would work at home, not here—another bonus for Dave.

"Remember the one rule in the as-yet-unwritten employee handbook, Dave?"

"It's not that. I just think she knows her stuff," Dave replied. He was right.

But it was more than that. When she said "absolutely" yes, we were grateful. We wanted to believe that finally, someone did know something absolutely—a rarity in the small-press world we inhabited. Dave turned over the books, such as they were, and Allison Crew took over.

* * *

Carol Luft sang in a choir. But she also sang through the job interview, which should have been a sign. We had her proofing the books and fact-checking at the table in the kitchen. She emitted a constant hum, a melody playing in the back of her throat and in the front of our consciousness.

Dave came into my office and looked at me.

"I know," I mouthed.

She was twenty-one and new to San Francisco, living with her boyfriend. She wore her long blond hair in heavy, loose ringlets that swayed from side to side when she walked. A small person, she chirped cheerfully upon entering each room. "Hellooo." Her chin pointed out and her lips enunciated each word as if it were a note of a song: "Just fin-ish-innnnng," the *ing* resonating.

I pulled her into my office.

"We need a little more quiet when we're all working. It's close quarters."

She smiled. "Not a problemmm."

I smiled back.

A knock came at the door. Carol got up and let Tara Terlot in. I was interviewing her for the editor position. We needed to get the California camping guide to the printer, and it needed a quick professional edit first.

Carol evoked the *Lone Ranger* melody and announced, "Here you are," and gestured Tara into my office to potentially save the day.

Tara and I had met at a book-trade event and she had attached herself to me after she heard we needed an editor. She grinned broadly and sat down on the edge of the armchair in my office. Her frizzy brown hair rose like a cloud around a face that had big, round glasses and enormous lips that only partially hid her equally enormous teeth. A shawl covered her shoulders.

Qualifications, I thought.

"I'm so glad you invited me to interview for the editor position," she said. "I've been taking editing classes through the community college, and I really can't wait to use my skills."

"But you have work experience?" I asked. I remembered her telling me that she had.

"I'm getting top grades in every one of my classes and all I need is a chance, and I'll be the best editor you could ever hope for. I brought some of my assignments, if you want to look at them." She placed a folder on my desk.

I reached forward to take it. Opening it, I discovered a number of edited sheets with the teacher's comments in the right-hand corner that read in red pen, *Nice work! Good job!*

"Nice," I said. "What job experience do you have?"

"I was a dental hygienist before I decided to make this career switch." She broadcast her teeth for me, and I noted that they were indeed very well cared for.

"Hmm. We're really looking for someone with editing experience." I looked up at her and watched as she batted tears back.

"I can do this job. You have to let me have it. It's everything I've been working for, everything I want."

"You want to edit guidebooks? That's your dream?" I chuckled, but she didn't smile.

"I am an editor. I will be an editor." She took the folder back and opened it. She looked down at her work, and mouthed the words, "good job," then went silent.

Jesus. "We don't pay well," I said.

Her face lit up and out came the teeth. The front two hooked on her bottom lip and I thought she might sob.

"Oh, I don't mind. I'll work for anything. I need this first job in editing to get in the door."

"Okay, okay. You can start tomorrow."

She rose and approached the desk as if to hug me. I stood up and stepped back.

"Carol, can you let Tara out?"

Tara beamed. "You won't be sorry." She clutched her file to her chest and backed out of the room.

"Goodbye," said Carol at the door, reprising the *Sound of Music* song in which the von Trapp Family Singers waved their exits.

Tara was diligent. For the next week, she sat in Sandra Lippy's old office upstairs and edited the California camping guide. No questions. No concerns. Just quiet. On the fifth day, I made my way up the stairs to see her and make sure it was all going well. On her desk were a Random House dictionary, a thesaurus, two grammar books, and a slew of red pens. She was bent over the pages we had printed out for her. I walked into the room and she looked up.

I took a step closer. "How's it going?"

"Fine, just fine." I could see the page she was working on, and it was covered in red ink.

"What's this?" I pointed to the sheet to the left of the document.

"This is a style sheet," she said. "I'm having to create a style sheet for the whole book. The author has quite a vocabulary, and I think some of it he might have made up himself."

"Sounds like something John Aberdeen might do. He likes to hunker down, for instance." I laughed. "Oh, wait, hunker is a word!"

Tara looked at me blankly. "That's the least of it, really. I took it to my teacher yesterday to see just how to approach it."

"What did your teacher say?"

"She said to put the invented words on the style sheet and make sure they are spelled the same throughout the book, which is what I was doing to begin with." She cleared her throat and looked down at the page.

"You know, this book has been printed in four editions with no editing, or hardly any at all," I told her.

She gasped.

I turned the knife. "Yes, and nearly one hundred thousand people have bought it."

"The commas alone—"

"We're not big on commas at Foghorn," I said, striving for levity.

"Not big on commas?" She furrowed her brow.

"Nope, we're kind of against them, actually. Dave took them out of all the other books, but John liked the few we had in the California guide, so we left them for his sake."

"For his sake—" she mumbled.

"Look, I think the thing to do is not to get too bogged down with overly zealous punctuation and grammar. What we were hoping you'd do is really make sure that the spelling was correct and that there is consistency from listing to listing. You know, so we're covering the same features, the same way for each campground." I paused and looked at her. "You can do the style sheet, but remember on the first day when I said we published guidebooks?"

"Yes." She nodded solemnly.

"Guidebooks that are seven hundred pages and packed with information?"

"Well, yes."

"How that information is presented is a bigger deal than trying to inject commas into everything."

"The English language has rules we have to follow."

"Not necessarily," I said. "You know I was kidding about being against commas, right?"

"Oh, right." She smiled weakly.

"Yep, we're actually against semicolons and colons. Anyway, think about it. I think you might be getting a bit carried away. We have deadlines and really can't make this many changes."

"I—"

"You might be losing sight of the forest for the trees or, as we like to say in publishing, the book for the commas," I continued. "How about we meet later this afternoon and work together on what the priorities are?"

I went downstairs and into Dave's office and shut the door behind me.

"Tara is obsessed with commas," I reported.

"Really? She looks like more of a parenthesis kind of gal."

"I told her that we strictly forbade the use of colons and semicolons, of course," I said.

"Yes, we don't like anyone, especially dogs and editors, near our colons." Dave looked back at his computer screen.

"She doesn't have a sense of humor, which is a bad discovery."

He sighed. "Yesterday she seemed frustrated, so I asked her if she didn't want to have a bit of a change from editing and punch the wall or bang on her finger with a hammer for a while. Now I'm thinking I should just build her a ball and chain for her ankle."

"She'd probably like that."

"Carol doesn't seem to have a sense of humor, either," he said. "I told her I couldn't handle the singing unless she knew some Bob Dylan tunes, and she got very offended."

"She doesn't like Dylan?"

"Apparently not. I tried to talk to her about Wagner, but she thought I was making fun of her, which I wasn't. I just thought if she knew music she might want to talk Wagner."

"I hate to say this, because it's my fault, but remember when it was just you and me?"

"I remember." He shook his head. "Those were the days, my friend."

"No song lyrics, I beg you."

I heard a knock on the front door of the house and waited to see if Carol would get it.

The knock came again, so I pushed open Dave's door and peered out. The kitchen was empty, so I walked to the front door and opened it. A man stood there, on the second stair, looking up at me.

"Do you have a delivery?" I asked, looking at the street for a truck.

"It's me, Rob!" He tapped his chest with both hands.

"Rob?"

"The landlord."

Dave came up behind me, joining me in the doorway. We both stared at him. He looked totally different to me, but of course it had been two years since we signed the lease and two years since we had seen him. I tried to remember what we had told him in the beginning. Did we tell him about the business?

"It's me, Rob." He tapped his chest with both hands again for Dave's benefit.

Dave stepped out of the doorway. "Yes, Rob, what can we do for you?"

Rob climbed up a step and tried to peer around us into the kitchen.

"I'm thinking of selling the house and I wanted to talk to you about buying it. When you first moved in, you thought you might want to buy it someday. That's what you said."

"We might be outgrowing it," Dave told him.

Carol came out onto the step. "The printer's on the phone for you, Vicki," she sang, her arm sweeping out in front of her in an operatic gesture. I motioned for her to take a message.

Tara came down the stairs. "I'm ready for our meeting."

Just then Allison came driving up, pulled to the curb, and put on her emergency brake with a loud grind as she turned off the engine. She jumped out of the car and came up the steps.

"Hi." She turned and gave Rob a big smile before going in.

Rob turned to his left and leaned into the window into my office where Tara now sat waiting across from my desk.

"You've got a business here," he said uncertainly.

UPS pulled up and the driver leaned out. "Got a pickup today?"

"Yep, let me open the garage for you," Dave said.

"Oh no." I glanced at Dave.

Dave walked down the steps past Rob, glancing up at me before opening the garage. The books were stacked to the ceiling, of course, and the UPS pickup was set on a table.

Rob dropped back a step and took it all in. "What kind of business?"

"Book publishing."

"Book publishing—hey, my brother wrote a book. I should have him talk to you." When I didn't immediately reply, he added, "So all these people aren't living here, just working here." He smiled as if that discovery was vital to his well-being. Then he interrupted himself by wincing as if something terrible had just occurred to him.

"You know, I don't know that this area is zoned for this." His voice came out tentative and reluctant, and he leaned forward as if the neighbors might overhear. Or maybe he feared the city ordinance workers who populated the neighborhood streets, searching for zoning crimes.

"We are considering buying it," I quickly countered. "Is the price the same as when we first moved in?" Dave stopped just below the stairs and looked up at me.

Rob grinned, reassured. "Well, I was going to list it for another ten thousand dollars, but if you are interested, I won't. It saves me a lot of grief."

"We'll think it over and get back to you," I said as he pressed his business card into my hand and pointed to his name and said, "Rob."

"Yes, Rob." I repeated, feeling like Tarzan's Jane. He backed down the steps and left. The UPS truck followed him down the street and Dave walked up the stairs. A dog trotted down the street in the direction Rob had just went, and Dave turned back to eye him from the stairs.

"Colon eater," he pronounced, a little fearfully.

"Rob, dog, or both?"

"Dog. Rob is a definitely a parenthesis fella. We should marry him off to Tara."

"Yeah, they can have their doubts and asides all day long and never give birth to any conviction."

I closed the door and we stood inside the hall, afraid to go back into either of the rooms. I could hear Allison talking to Tara, who was explaining her comma dilemma, while Carol hummed "The Battle Hymn of the Republic" in time with the copier as it spat out its sheets.

"Now you want to buy the house?" Dave looked at me, amazement flitting over his face.

"No. Do you?" I said, lowering my voice so only he could hear me.

"Absolutely not. If we had the money, I would not spend it on that. Better computers, I say."

I whispered, "Because I want to get the hell out of here and get a real office."

"We're going to have to move if he's selling it," Dave replied.

"Let me ask you something. What in the hell was that whole thing about out there? How come he kept repeating his name?"

He whispered back, "Let me ask you something. Who in the hell are all these people in here?"

I shook my head. "I don't know, but I wish we hadn't let them all in."

He nodded. "Agreed. Allison is good, but the rest have to go."

"We'll just move and neglect to tell them." I laughed, imagining how long Tara would continue to plug away at the California camping guide, her style sheet at her side in her room upstairs, before she noticed that everything and everyone was gone.

Thank God for Morganization.

* * *

The American Booksellers Association trade show was in Las Vegas that year and we reprised our Booked for Adventure event with the theme "See You in Rio," to take place at the Rio Suite Hotel, which had sandy beaches and waterfalls. We booked a bus from the convention center that included on-board entertainment of a Latin singer with a guitar. My partner-in-crime, Anna Termine from Globe Pequot, booked B.B. King's daughter, Shirley King, as the musical entertainment for the event itself, and that hit all the dancing notes. We also produced a catalog of our participating publishers, with a floor map for the show on the back cover and interior info about each publisher that could also serve as a directory throughout the year. This time PGW and BookPeople both helped sponsor.

* * *

When I got back from the trade show, Dave and I met Allison on a Saturday at the Whole Earth Café near the Kabuki Theaters off Geary. She had purchased a condo nearby and suggested the location because she was working on it over the weekend. She came in old gray sweats, the sweatshirt torn on both wrists. Around the collar, a black aerobic top peeked through on either side of her neck. Her blond hair was pulled back into a ponytail. She also taught aerobics at the USF campus, she said, explaining her attire. Dave and I exchanged looks.

Even though we'd worked together for the last four months, Allison was still a mystery, and each new piece of the puzzle surprised us. But she knew her stuff. Allison had been a significant addition to our team of two. She knew business. She knew finances. And apparently, she knew something about hiring employees. For the first time, we had the comfort of knowing our financial situation and even though the previous year had been a loss, it wasn't a significant one, she assured us. She also understood how to file business taxes. She described the new condo and the work she was doing to renovate it. We waited for our tea to cool, and I dug into a carrot muffin.

"But who's doing the work?" Dave asked.

"I am." She smiled.

"You're putting in the wood floor? You're retiling the bathroom?" Dave popped the last of his blueberry muffin in his mouth and waited before chewing.

"It's cheaper if you do it yourself."

"I understand that," Dave started. "But—"

"Dave doesn't believe anyone could be as insane as he is about doing everything himself. He taught himself a database program, a map program, and a design program all in the past year."

Allison laughed.

"Listen, fellas," I began. "I've been thinking about this business and how far we could take it. I think we are on the brink of having an actual publishing house."

I paused to see if I had their full attention. They both nodded.

"So, what I want to know is this: Are you in?"

Dave opened his mouth to reply, but I jumped ahead. "If you were both partners in the business—I mean, yes, you're not being paid so far, Dave, and you're being paid very little, Allison—but we could build this thing to the point where we'd all be making a decent living, and it would be worth it to all of us."

"You're asking if I want to be a partner?" Allison said.

"Yes. I could give you both a percentage. Dave's already a partner but we haven't made it legal. We're still operating as a sole proprietorship. We could incorporate. I'd keep fifty percent, and then give Dave forty percent and you ten percent."

Dave said, "I'm going to do the work anyway, whether I'm a partner or not."

"I know, but wouldn't it better to be official about it and have you as a partner, legally?" I learned something from Sully. Having it in writing was better.

"Dave, you can handle the book production, I'll do marketing, and Allison will cover the finance. That way, we have everything important accounted for."

I addressed Allison. "Dave and I can't do this by ourselves anymore. We need you to make it really work. We need to make these big decisions together."

Dave shifted uncomfortably. We had discussed how much we needed Allison plenty of times, but not the partnership idea. I could almost hear him thinking, *Like this big decision, for instance?*

But then Allison laughed. "I like you guys. I'm having more fun at Foghorn than any of my other jobs. I like the business." She turned to Dave and said, "I agree—that is, if you want me, Dave."

I continued before he could speak. "What I'm looking for, though, is for all of us to commit to making this our main goal in life. I want to give up my waitressing job and put all my energy into this. We need to take salaries, all of us."

"Like what? What can we afford?" Dave shook his head.

"We can work it out. The point is we all need to get paid the same, and we use the money we already have coming to pay ourselves."

The business was already Dave's and mine, but I was trying to get Allison's commitment now.

"And we have the advance from PGW to put into the rest of the publishing company."

"You're sure about this, Vic? The money part?" Dave said.

Allison jumped in. "From a financial perspective, it can be done, if that's what you mean. Vicki asked me to review the salary idea, and I did. This year, the advance sales on all the titles are way up. Plus, because you'll have me full time, I can do more and that should lead to better financial decisions."

She stopped and regarded Dave. "You know I wouldn't go along with it if I didn't see that it worked."

Dave drank a sip of his coffee. "It's a conspiracy, obviously, but I'm in."

"I'm in, too." Allison grinned and sat back in her chair.

"We need to get another office," I said. "We need room to grow. Allison needs space. And maybe we can do a better job with a new crop of employees."

Dave said, "Hold up there, Slim Bob. I know we've got to move, but employees? We're just getting ready to shed some."

"Let's do the first books on our Spring list and see how we do with just us." Allison nodded at Dave. "If we need help, we can bring people in, but only then."

"Okay. Looks like we're doing the big thing." Dave looked at me. "We're all in, Vic. I guess that means you can give notice at the Cliff House."

"Hallelujah!" We clinked our coffee cups together and drank.

I couldn't wait to start looking for office space. And I couldn't wait to stop waiting tables. I could still see Casey after hours. The possibility of serving as someone's waiter while simultaneously trying to do a deal with them as the publisher of Foghorn was starting to worry me. Sooner or later it would happen; these two separate lives would converge and embarrass me.

I couldn't have that. I had a publishing empire to build.

* * *

We found our new office space on DeHaro in the Potrero Hill District, one neighborhood removed from South of Market. We were part of a vacant three-story building that had on its main floor an 800-square-foot room with an old boiler, a boiler that historically had provided steam heat to the neighborhood. The Boiler Room lacked the stylish nuances required by the architectural firm that had preceded us, but was a perfect for a burgeoning publishing company. And it was next door to the Anchor Steam Brewery, which elevated its attractiveness even more in our eyes.

Picture the enormous hulking boiler lying like a thirty-foot red whale, consuming half of the room we were leasing, its rounded back nearly breaching the twenty-foot ceiling. Windows ran around the top of the white cement brick walls on two sides. We were dug into a hill—one of many in the neighborhood—the windows high above us at street level, like the viewing glass in a museum that showcased the whimsical great red beast, if anyone should peer down. We had all the elements of industrial chic twenty years before its heyday.

My office was tucked into the front, a master cave surrounded by red pipes, an octopus under the whale. It had room enough in the opening just outside for the conference table we'd brought over from Bernal Heights. Dave and Allison claimed the two built-in office cubicles in the open area next to the boiler. On sunny days, the light poured in, flooding the room, obscuring the reality that we essentially were operating in a basement. When it was foggy or overcast, the space had a chill, a dampness that nothing could dispel, and so we covered our laps with Grandma's crocheted blankets and went on working.

We'd said goodbye to our two employees at Bernal Heights. They hadn't gone quietly into that good night, Dave joked, but they'd gone—Carol a little hurt that she couldn't come with us, and Tara wanting more editorial miles on her résumé before she gave us up, but instead settling for a letter of reference. We'd relinquished the keys to Rob, the landlord, who also expressed his disappointment that we weren't buying the house after all.

The shift precipitated a personal move, too. While I had already moved into Brian's Inner Sunset flat over Christmas, Dave now followed, making Brian's living room his permanent bedroom. He appreciated the light from the triad of Victorian windows, something his Bernal Heights garage bedroom had lacked. Plus, with the bougainvillea obstructing the view from the street, Dave had his privacy, too. A perfect reading room, he declared.

With so many brothers in residence, it was impossible to get Casey to come to my new place, so I still spent weekend nights at his apartment. But as my Foghorn plans ramped up, even those weekends were less frequent.

All I really wanted to do was build Foghorn.

SAN FRANCISCO, 1991

Published: 10 titles
Partners: 3
Employees: 2
Annual sales: $500,000

Allison, Dave, and I convened for our weekly organizational meeting in front of the boiler. Dave held up a binder and then laid it on the table, unclipping the rings and handing each of us a sheet.

"Okay, fellas. This binder represents every step in the publishing process. From the moment we sign a book with an author to the moment it lands in a bookstore."

Allison and I exchanged glances.

"I've given you an example of one of the sheets in the binder," he said, looking down at it, as we did the same. "When you accomplish one of the steps in the process, you fill out a sheet and sign your name."

He tapped the page. "The way I figure it, there are fifty-three steps, fifty-three sheets that we need to sign off on. Feel free to look it over and add some if you'd like, but you need to do it soon, because I want this up and running so we can track everything."

I took the binder from him.

"We'll keep the sheets in the binder and that's how we'll all know where a book is at any given time," he said as I opened it. "From the time we sign the contract with the author to production to marketing."

I looked through his steps. "You probably could put these two together."

He glanced at me and then the sheet. "No, they're separate tasks."

"In marketing, we don't do all these steps for every book."

"Why not?"

"Because every book is different," I said.

"Every book is not different," he countered.

"Dave, you're kidding, right?"

His cheeks started to flush. "I'm not kidding." His voice rose a notch.

"Dave, it may not be possible to follow every step for every book," Allison interpreted. She leaned forward on the table.

But he was addressing me. "It's not impossible. Don't mix up the fact that you don't want to do it, Vicki, with whether it's impossible or not." He waited a moment, before glancing at Allison. She smiled at him.

"It's necessary," he said.

Dave and I both were experts living the Morgan maxim that "he who organizes it, controls it." This was his way of controlling the whole company, not just his department, I realized. The steps outlined what I had to do, what Allison had to do, and in recording our progress, we were answerable to him. He was reining us in—mostly me, I felt—the only way he knew how. I could stomp it out or tolerate it for the time being. I realized his premise was right, a system of some sort was necessary, and as yet, I didn't have a better solution. So I waited.

* * *

We met weekly to go over the 53 Steps and the finances. Dave was on a mission. The next week, he had assembled a stack of phone books.

"What's all this?" Allison asked.

"I want you to picture our guidebooks for a moment on this paper."

"No, Dave. The paper's too thin," I argued.

"It's more transparent, but it's actually bulkier. Plus, printing them on this paper will cut our printing bill by forty percent. And since we do new editions every year or every other year, people don't need them on nice paper. They may actually appreciate that the paper is recycled. And, the best part is, they're fatter and that creates more value."

The next week he introduced the grid system.

"Our books should be easy to use. They're guidebooks. The maps need to be much better, so campers can find a location on the map and then easily find the description in the text."

Allison and I nodded.

"I've developed a grid system that will change how the whole book is organized. People are going to love it."

The following week, he came with icons.

"Icons will allow people to immediately see if the campsite matches their needs. If it has picnic tables, we'll use this one. If it has showers, we'll use this one. If you can go horseback riding, we'll use this one."

His industry tired us both. His standards were higher than both of ours combined.

"I need to call PGW and update the catalog copy. These books are much more user-friendly now. We have to market that," I told Allison.

"I came in last night, late, and Dave was still here," she whispered. "He's working night and day."

"I know. I came in at six a.m. today and he was here. I think he slept on the couch in the back side of the boiler."

At the next meeting he said, "You two have been talking about hiring again. Here's the thing about employees. We need to interview them carefully and give them job descriptions, so they know exactly what they're here to do. I would also add that they definitely need to be computer literate."

Allison volunteered to develop the job descriptions and set up the interviews.

"Should we have an employee manual?" I asked. Dave and I exchanged glances, remembering Sandra Lippy.

Allison volunteered to put that together.

It was my turn to talk. I outlined the promotion plans for each of the Spring books. I had recreated Sandra Lippy's Girl Scout Display Contest for the independent bookstores in the Bay Area, with John Aberdeen as one of the judges.

"Genius. You're a marketing genius." Dave exclaimed.

By the time Allison reviewed the numbers, including a new profit-and-loss report for each book, the meeting had gone two hours. We stood up and stretched.

"Dave, you're looking different," I said. He looked much thicker around the middle.

"I change one hundred percent every day," he answered absently.

Allison grabbed me by the arm at the end of the meeting while Dave was in the restroom. "Come here," she said, taking me into Dave's office. "Look."

A large vat of protein powder sat on the shelf above his computer. "What is it?"

She took it off the shelf. "This stuff has a million calories in it."

At the next meeting. we studied him. He had gained about twenty pounds, I estimated. His waist protruded over the top of his pants, causing his T-shirt to buckle around his midsection. He was pale from never getting out of the office, and a kind of blue patina emanated from his face.

"Dave, you need to take some time. You're working too hard. It's not good for you," I said.

"I'm trying to bulk up. After the Spring list gets out, I'll take a few days. I've got a lot of books to reformat and lay out. I have to redo every one of the maps."

"Hire someone quickly," I told Allison. "He needs help. Worse, I can't keep up."

"I can't either," she said.

* * *

Our new employees were a twenty-two-year-old woman named Caren with a C, a recent design school graduate hired to assist with book production, and a twenty-year-old man, Jimmy, an all-around assistant and shipper. Quickly, they formed an alliance and shared lunch hours. Allison gave them their paychecks and seemed to escape the deadpan looks and eyeball rolls Dave and I elicited from them.

I consulted with Allison about strategies for dealing with them, but more and more, they both checked in with Allison to get their duties for the day, which ultimately suited Dave and me just fine. Their help was negligible, I thought, but it was still better than no help, and I hoped it would only improve the more they learned their jobs.

Our biggest Spring list ever was coming up and suddenly there was a tremendous amount to do. Dave put Design School Girl—as he started calling her to me because she brought up these credentials nearly every time we spoke—on designing all the final book covers per our format. The tearing of tape and prepping of books for shipment by Jimmy sounded throughout the Boiler Room in the daylight hours now, work Dave and I had done ourselves in the evenings back in Bernal Heights.

* * *

Six guidebooks were being published that spring, five authored by John Aberdeen and one, hopefully the first of many, by our new rock-climbing author Harrison Wolf. Harrison was a big catch for us because of his celebrity in the rock climbing world but he had been difficult from the beginning, negotiating hard. In addition to more regional camping guides, and a new hiking guide for California, we planned to revamp John's outdoor adventure guide into a more traditional-looking book for the Spring list. We tamped down our wit and removed the illustrations that had so delighted Dave and me, but apparently no one else. John's seasonal meeting was scheduled for the end of the week, and this time I would be joined by both Dave and Allison. But first we met with Harrison.

Our mission at both meetings was to lower the royalty rate we had initially given. Our rate was substantially higher than most royalty rates given by publishers I discovered in my mingling with other PGW publishers and the travel publishers I had met at the last trade show. This was affecting our bottom line because we had so many titles with John. And we didn't want to make the same mistake with Harrison.

The moment Harrison strode through the door, I saw there would be trouble. He looked like he just came in from rock climbing, an undershirt exposed his tanned and muscular arms and he lithely threw his leg over the back of the chair and slid into his seat. He offered us all a big grin and then his eyes lit on Allison and for the rest of the meeting he never looked away.

Halfway through, I said, "Harrison, could you and Dave discuss the maps for the guidebook a moment? I need to discuss something with Allison."

"Fine, fine." He looked at Dave. Dave looked at me.

Outside in the hall, I whispered, "Allison, you have to be the one to show him the numbers and back him off the royalty rate."

Her eyes grew wide and she gnawed at her bottom lip. "Okay. Any recommended strategy for that?"

"I think all you have to do is ask him. If I asked him, I'd need a strategy."

We returned to the room and when she bent over Harrison and pointed out the numbers, Harrison was starstruck, nearly swooning, it seemed. Dave and I watched.

"Holy shit," Dave whispered.

Harrison tucked the papers into his folder and looked up at Allison. "I'll give it a look. My lawyer will have to look it over, too." His eyes had snapped back into some semblance of professionalism. She smiled at him.

"Absolutely, you should."

Beautiful women often don't realize their impact on those around them. Allison was one of those women. For her, simply being polite registered as much more in the heart of the receiver. Harrison was smitten. That was clear.

"I'm sorry, Allison," I said after Harrison had finally gone. I felt guilty to use her that way. I was hoping Dave hadn't noticed I'd fallen off the feminist wagon by using Allison's looks as my strategy. He was more of a feminist than I was, with his lack of tolerance for anything that smacked of feminine wiles. It was part of an integrity that was second nature to him, but eluded me. I did whatever worked.

I felt sorrier the next day when Harrison called Allison directly.

Ever polite, she asked him if he'd decided yet. No, he told her, but he'd call back.

He called back each day to talk with her, longer talks that always ended in a request to go climbing together. I listened from my desk across the hall as she redirected him—again and again—to the topic at hand.

"Vicki, I don't think I can deal with this," she reported at our meeting.

"I'll talk to him," Dave said, bristling.

"No, you can't," I told him, wondering where my staunch was. "We don't want to make him mad."

"At least John has agreed to the change," she said.

"He needs to back off. Someone needs to talk to him." Dave's eyes flashed. "Allison shouldn't have to put up with Harrison's horny crap."

"Okay, I agree." I nodded. But I didn't know what to do, so I didn't do anything.

* * *

"Harrison is going to take the royalty reduction," Allison reported a week later at our meeting.

"Let's get it in writing ASAP."

Later that afternoon, dipping her head to avoid the defunct temperature gauge theatrically welded to the boiler above my desk, she handed me a fax of the new agreement with his signature.

"Do you want me to call him now and tell him to back off?"

She shook her head. "I've handled it."

* * *

In March, we found a note on Dave's computer. "Gone to the Yucatan. Design School Girl can finish the maps for the Washington and Oregon camping guide. Will do layout when I get back."

But Design School Girl begged off, admitting she didn't know anything about the software program. "He showed me, but I'm a designer," she said. "I don't do maps."

Caren took off the square-shaped black glasses that perched on her tiny nose, wiped them with a tissue she pulled from her fitted black jacket, then returned to her desk. Allison and I exchanged glances.

I was happy Dave wasn't here to witness this admission. He'd flip. Allison and I would have to do this ourselves. "I don't know how to work this program. Do you?"

She shook her head and slid into his chair. "How hard can it be?"

Five days later, I found Dave at his desk when I came in that morning, slimmer and with color in his face.

"How was your break?" I said evenly.

"Great ruins."

"Did you visit the pyramids?"

"And did some reading in a hammock. You got the maps done?" He turned toward the computer screen.

"We actually ended up printing the maps and pasting up the numbered dots by hand."

"You did?" His eyebrows shot up. "What about Design School Girl?"

"She didn't know that particular program, even though you showed her, so she couldn't do it, she said. And Allison and I couldn't figure it out."

"You pasted up fifty to a hundred dots on every page?" He shook his head.

"Desperate measures." I held up my hands as if the glue-stick residue still stuck to my fingertips.

"But it's ready for layout."

I nodded. "Where'd your protein powder go?" The tub had vanished from the shelf, and in its place were a few books by Henry Miller and a paperback stack of Anaïs Nin journals.

He glanced up at the shelf. "I'm on a new program."

"Next time, tell us when you're planning to take off."

"I did, but it's possible that you weren't listening."

"When's the last time you took a vacation? I mean we have been working eighty- to one-hundred-hour weeks for two years. I think if you said you were going to the Yucatan, I might have remembered," I countered. "What am I, totally unconscious?"

He grinned at me. "I don't want to cast 'dispersions,' of course, but on certain things—"

I blinked at him.

"I wanted to see how I'd do on my own, with no one I knew around. Throw myself out there with just myself to rely on. I wasn't too worried that you couldn't get along without me for a few days."

"Well, we didn't get along without you."

"Allison finished the employee manual," he said. "That's something."

"When did you see that?" I said. "I haven't seen it yet."

He looked at me, deadpan. "While you were doing leg lifts at Casey's, I was at Allison's."

"Dave."

He shrugged and grinned. "Must be the tan and the new relaxed persona."

"Jesus, I'm the last to know every damn thing."

After our next weekly meeting, Allison told me they were going to dinner. I worked until eight p.m., but they didn't come back, so I locked up and went home. I didn't know how to feel about it. If it worked out, two of my favorite people would be happy. If it didn't, well, I didn't want to think about that.

* * *

Our first big check of the 1991 Spring season was ready to be picked up from PGW. Vendors were waiting to get paid, including our printer, who had generously agreed to a one-hundred-and-twenty-day payment schedule. When we had moved from Bernal Heights, we debated about moving the inventory with us until we heard about Moving Books, a warehouse and shipping facility for small presses, that had opened not far from PGW. So we sent our inventory there, but continued to ship our individual orders out of our offices at the Boiler Room.

Jimmy was making a run to the Moving Books' warehouse this morning to pick up some inventory. He stood in my office, awaiting instructions. Most of his long hair was bound in a ponytail, but along the top ridge of his head, he wore a short Mohawk.

"I need you to go by PGW and pick up our check. Ask for Alex and he'll have it ready for you," I told him. I handed him a sheet of paper with the address and the directions.

Allison had the bills waiting. We'd be clean and ahead for the first time since last December. It was Friday, and the first weekend this year we had agreed we all could take off guilt-free. I'd even managed to pin Casey down for an actual date after he got off work.

My plan was to go to a late showing of *Thelma & Louise*, a safe choice, I thought. It'd be the first movie we'd been to together, chosen with the knowledge that when he'd seen *Fatal Attraction* at the beginning flirtation stage of our relationship, he had for several weeks ignored me, swearing off women in publishing as though we all—though terribly sexy—brandished knives and loved to fillet pet rabbits. We couldn't help ourselves.

Dave and Allison had plans to drive down to Big Sur for a look at Henry Miller's old haunts.

Later that afternoon, Dave popped into my cave in the Boiler.

"Did you know that Design School Girl knows *nothing* about designing on computers? She's telling me she wants to lay out everything by hand, if you can believe that! When she started this job, she told me she preferred to do book covers that way and I let her, but the whole book?"

"What? I thought she said she had computer-design skills. We had Allison ask that, right?" I said.

"She lied." Dave leaned over my desk, like a lawyer making a damning point to a judge.

"Maybe she misunderstood. She's only been here a month."

"No, she actually lied. And when I mentioned this to her, she got offended, like it was my fault she lied."

I waited.

"She's got to go. It's ridiculous. This is the age of computers. She's so old-school, I can't believe it," Dave said.

"Is there any way we could make it work? We have another book cover she can work on." Why I still needed to smooth everything over for everyone was a mystery even to me. Only Edgar Allen Poe knew.

He shook his head. "We are on a hairy deadline for the Washington and Oregon camping guide. It has to go to the printer next week and I was hoping to have some help with the layout."

"We've got to get Allison in on this," I said.

"We're fucked. I can't believe she'd lie like that. She walks in here with her design school attitude, and this is what they taught her in design school? She acts like I'm being ridiculous. *You* could be a better designer, for God's sake." Dave couldn't stand still.

I heard Jimmy come in the front and hollered, "Yes! Bring it in here, please."

He came into the Boiler where Dave and I stood, looking at me blankly before holding out the shipping request form, signed at the bottom by the warehouse manager at Moving.

"Got the books so I can finish the shipping," he said.

"Do you have the check?"

His eyes rolled up to the Boiler ceiling, pondering my question. "The check?"

"Yes, the check I sent you for. You were going to PGW first, remember?"

"Jesus," Dave sputtered.

Allison peered in. "Did you get the check?"

"Ah, I knew I forgot something," our shipper said.

"Lie down," I pointed to the ground in front of him. "I want to kick you in the ribs." I chortled. With an exasperated shake of my head, I glanced over at Dave, who snorted.

Allison eased into the room, tapped me on the arm, and whispered something to Dave.

Jimmy looked at Dave, then back at me. "Uh, you want me to drive back?"

I dropped my incredulous tone for my best estimation of an efficient, managerial one. "Well, yes. Yes, I do. I'll be here when you get back, hopefully before six p.m. so we can deposit it and everyone can get paid."

Allison shook her head after he left. "I know you were both joking, but I'm not sure our new employees do."

"They can't work here without a sense of humor. I thought you put that in the employee manual," I said.

"We've got to hire better people. Are there any?" Dave asked.

"Or we could give them more direction," offered Allison, who may have been feeling the guilt of being part of the hiring.

"I couldn't have been any more direct about the check. Did you already mail all the checks for the bills?" I asked.

Allison held up a thick stack of envelopes and waved them. "I wanted to make sure the check was in hand before I did." She was more cautious than I, thank God. I would have mailed them.

"You go; we'll wait for him, deposit it, and lock up," said Dave. He glanced at Allison. "Allison is recording herself reading *The Tropic of Capricorn* for me and we've got a few more chapters to go. We're not actually heading out to Big Sur until morning, anyway."

I felt a small prick of envy. This was what it was like to have someone who shared your interests. You could go to movies and museums that appealed to both of you. You could take trips together. On our best day, Casey and I had *Columbo* and the horizontal arts.

On Monday morning, our shipper gave notice by calling and speaking to Allison. Moving Books wanted to hire him, and he thought it best to go. Monday afternoon, after she got back from lunch, Design School Girl gave notice, also to Allison. She couldn't work with these artistic constraints, she said. A week later, the state of California sent us a notice from the Employee Development Department; a complaint had been filed that we had been verbally abusive to employees.

At our meeting, Allison read us the complaint, penned by Caren with C. "Foghorn is the most cutthroat publisher in the Bay Area."

"Cutthroat?" I echoed.

Allison laughed. "Oh, yeah, that describes you two perfectly. Especially compared to all those other publishers she knows."

Dave tapped his pen on the table authoritatively. "No more employees, I say."

Allison and I smiled at each other. "Right," I said.

* * *

Dave, Brian, and I sat in front of the fireplace in our living room, Grandma's crocheted blankets over our knees. My cheeks were hot from the fire, but my back was freezing.

"The landlord stopped by earlier and assured me he was addressing the heat issue." I told Dave.

"When he saw us here huddled around the fire, I think he got a clue," Brian said.

"If you can't convince them with the law, guilt will have to do. Thank you, Grandma," I said, referencing my mother's mother, who could have written a master's thesis entitled *Shame as a Motivational Tool*. My mom was still dusted with some of it, but had worked hard not to pass it onto us. Thus evolved, she managed to sacrifice without inflicting guilt.

I went to the kitchen and returned with three beers, which I handed off. Then I slid onto a pillow next to the fire. I held up my hands to capture the warmth.

"You've still got skills," Dave said, noting the waitress-like grace with which I had carried and handed off the beers. "Hey, Vic, have you lost weight?"

"Probably. Not going out to eat lately."

"What happened to your aerobic eating program? Where's the Casbah?" Dave said of Casey.

"Fuck the Casbah." I pursed my lips and stared into the fire.

After dinner, Dave went to Allison's, Brian went back to the lab, and I called the Cliff House. Maybe I could get him to come to my place. The hostess said Casey was busy on the floor. Could he call me back? But he never called.

The next day after work, I caught up with Casey, arriving at his apartment in the late evening unannounced. When I pushed through the front door, which was ajar as usual, I heard voices: Casey's and a woman's. Peering around the corner, I saw Colette—the banquet manager at the Cliff House, five years older than me, three older than Casey—at the table, drinking a glass of wine. She had her black hair down and it made her look younger. They both turned and looked up at me. Casey stood and asked if I wanted a glass of wine. I dropped into the extra chair and took a big gulp from the glass he handed me, an oaky Chardonnay that I had always been partial to that he kept stocked at his apartment for me.

"Did something happen at work?" I asked. The Cliff House was a soap opera and the daily show always offered up something new. If I still worked there, I wouldn't have to ask.

Casey went to the oven and pulled out a chicken. Colette followed him with her eyes, and I watched her watch him.

"What's up with Rick?" I prompted. Rick was Colette's husband, but also the manager of the bar at the Cliff House.

She looked at me. "I really don't know, and I don't care either."

"Rick is an ass," Casey offered. He set the dish down on the hot pads and expertly began to cut into it. "Colette has nowhere to stay."

My theory—developed over the last few months as I waited for him—was proving out. Casey was what the singer James Taylor had described in the song "Handy Man." It was the nature of a handyman in a relationship that when someone was fixed, he was done. I knew that meant something good about me, that somehow I wasn't so needy and desperate anymore. I didn't need him, though I had thought perhaps I had wanted him.

But here was Colette, and with a handyman, there was always someone new to fix.

"So she's staying here?"

Casey nodded slightly and continued to dish out the chicken. I stood up and walked a few steps into the living room. The couch was not made up into a bed and the shuttered doors to his room were pulled open, the bed a wild array of blankets and sheets.

"How long?" I asked.

"A week or two," Casey said. "Do you want the breast or the leg?"

"I mean, how long has she been here already?" I spoke directly to him, and he avoided my eyes.

Colette looked up at me and at the same time, reached to squeeze his hand. "A few days."

I took the last swig of wine and set it on the table. "That's clear, then." I shut the door behind me when I left and drove through the park back to the flat.

My brothers were still up, even though it was late for Brian, who liked to be at the university by seven a.m. They huddled at the fireplace—the landlord's promise still unfulfilled—in the middle of some philosophical discussion that included mention of Wagner and Nietzsche. Seeing my face, Dave stopped talking, got up and retrieved a bottle of beer, and handed it to me. I took the beer but didn't speak.

"Is it the end of the Last Man, then?" he asked, and when I nodded, plopping into the chair next to him, he said, "That went on longer than a bad movie."

He extended his bottle, and Brian and I reached out for the toast. I wasn't mad about what had just happened; I was more embarrassed about not seeing it sooner. I never wanted to be the one to chase after someone. I much preferred to be the one to initiate a breakup. Salinger might say, *who doesn't?*

But for us Morgans, it went a little further. We needed to have control. Our superiority as Morgans was supremely affronted by humiliation. That was part of the Morgan pride, something that governed all three of us, though Brian to a lesser degree. He always had girlfriends. For Dave and me, it kept us out of relationships, except, of course, with our siblings. While the fire popped and shot light into the cold room, I worked on letting go of the humiliation I felt. For now, it was enough to sit there with my brothers and let their jokes fill me up and warm me.

* * *

The American Booksellers Association was taking place in New York City, the epicenter of the publishing world, and it promised to be big for us. I was figuring it out. Rather than sit passively in my booth, waiting for buyers to come to me, I'd realized I could proactively set up meetings, which I had done with a company interested in acquiring digital rights to our content for CD-ROMs. PGW had invited me to join their meeting with Costco. For added help in the booth, I'd invited my mom to join me.

This year's Booked for Adventure event was a chartered Circle Line boat cruise around the New York Harbor at sunset. By the second day of the show, all two hundred and fifty invitations to the Booked for Adventure cruise were claimed. When people came to Foghorn's booth, asking for more, we had to tell them we were out. Our group of publishers had evolved into an organization, the Independent Travel Publishers Association, and we appointed Anna Termine our executive director.

On the day of the party, I sent my mom ahead to Circle Line via cab with the balloons and a box of Foghorn's guidebooks and catalogs. Two hours later, I cut out of the trade show to meet the caterer at the boat and put up the signs. I also changed into my white captain's outfit that I had bought for the day—a shirt designed like a white jacket with long sleeves and large button anchors down the middle, with matching pants—and that was how I greeted everyone that evening as they crossed the plank to board the boat.

When the boat left the dock for the open water, the party was underway and my job was done. I found my mom next to the sponsoring publishers' book display table.

Her hands were curled on her lap, each with fingertips in the air, like she was waiting for a manicure to dry. A nest of red and blue balloons bounced gently next to her, tied to the rail above the books.

"You okay?"

She looked up at me, surprised. "Yes, good here."

"Oh, your hands," I said, nodding at them, picturing the hundreds of balloons she had single-handedly tied. I plopped down next to her and reached over and gently rubbed her arm.

"You want to walk outside and see what we can see?"

I opened the door for her, and we walked out into a mild wind which was surprisingly warm and dry, as it might be if we were on a balmy vacation in some southern port. Most of the attendees were grouped around the railing, gazing out. The boat churned along, the sound of the engine soothing and constant, the water below us slapping against the sides of the boat.

I put one arm around my mom, and we huddled together, leaning on the rail. As I touched my head against hers, we watched the sun drop, a band of orange pooling atop the distant horizon with another layer of nautical blue hanging just above. The outline of the Statue of Liberty was perfectly balanced in the middle, and above her, the sky opened to a faint swell of yellow.

I heard the party sounds of laughter and music drift up from the lower floor. The cruise boat turned right and there it was before us, New York City, the publishing capital of the world, the towering buildings as one now, ethereal and distant, floating independently of the earth beneath them, it seemed. We weren't as coalesced on the West Coast, new scrabblers on the big board, making it up as we went along. New York City may not even have recognized us, but it felt inevitable that one day they would.

That night, after the big event, my mom and I lay in our shared queen bed in the apartment. We were just seventeen years apart in age, and at times it felt like we were sisters rather than mother and daughter.

"You amaze me, Vicki," my mother said quietly as we lay on our backs. The advantage of having a windowless room was it was completely dark except for the thin strip of light framing the door that led out to the living room where another publisher, Carla Tribetti from Sun Books and her intern, sharing the rental of the tiny apartment with us, were just coming back from a night of publisher parties. Despite their efforts to be quiet, we could hear the intern chattering away. There was no chance of sleep until they settled down and turned off the light.

"What do you mean?" I asked, turning on my side toward my mom.

"I could never do all the things you do," she said. "But you, you just do them, like it's second nature." She laughed. "Which, knowing you as long as I have, it is. You're not afraid. You just jump in."

"It's more like I get an idea, then trap myself by telling people about it, and then I have to hustle to actually pull it off," I said, laughing at the truth of it. "My ideas rule me."

"We were worried when you married Sully. But since then, you and Dave have really done so much with the company. I mean, look at all that's happened."

I realized I rarely thought of Sully anymore. He belonged to a different life and time.

"And this is so great for Dave," she added.

"Dave is the anti-Sully," I said, snorting at the joke. "I don't know how I even got mixed up with Sully to begin with. It's like I completely forgot who I was and listened to who he thought I was. Which wasn't much."

"He was terrible," she concurred. "Terrible."

"Dad didn't like him either," I said.

"Yes, your dad is your biggest fan and he never liked Sully."

"But no one said anything when I married him."

She was silent a moment. "Sometimes when people have their own problems, it's not that they don't notice, but that they can't help." She hesitated. "It's hard to know what advice to give your kids when you don't even know if you've even made the right choices yourself."

The lights around the door went out and the murmur of voices in the front room stopped. I was quiet a minute. "Like what, Mom? You mean like even getting married to begin with?"

"Oh, we had to do that," she said, "If we didn't, we wouldn't have had you." I reached out and squeezed her hand. I rarely thought about that sacrifice and the angst that might have gone into such a decision. As the first born, I'd boldly arrived in the Washington farm town of Kenko, population 650, the product of teenagers who could not resist the back seat of a Chevy parked on a rural road in the sweaty harvest month of August. My sixteen-year-old mother had not returned to her high school.

At age sixteen in the 1950s, marriage must have seemed the only solution when there was a pregnancy, though she wanted to marry my dad, she told me. It had taken courage to stand up to her mother and say so when her mother thought an abortion might be a better choice. It launched my mother into a rapid adulthood. Here I was, still growing up at age thirty-two. She had three kids by twenty-one, and when she was thirty-two, I was fifteen, just hitting the time of life in which her entire life had exploded. I remembered the struggle on her face as I started to date, and the fear she couldn't hide when I went off with my boyfriend, and why I had crept around to meet him rather than walk out the front door.

The era had flipped during the '60s to a permissive one, but her script still played the old one, where sex wasn't allowed. I felt a surge of guilt now about the trauma I had put her through. When I was sixteen, it was all about living the life I thought I wanted, a teenager on the warpath to adulthood. Thirty-two years ago, my mother had had the same feelings about her life.

* * *

Promoting and selling Foghorn's books fell to me. For each season, I'd think about the upcoming titles and where and how to sell them next. I'd propagate ideas for promotions or partnerships and then present those ideas to Allison and Dave. Allison was an easier sell. Depending on the idea, Dave would either call it genius or would challenge me, citing expenses or some other objection. But he was easy enough to veto, as I believed that if I wanted to do something, I should be able to do it. It was that simple.

I also was handling the editorial expansion, calling would-be authors at newspapers to enlist them as guidebook authors, then managing the negotiations and their contracts. We had a few options in growing our list of published titles. We could continue publishing California titles and establish ourselves as California's foremost recreation publisher, or we could expand our most successful concepts to other states and regions. Of course, I chose both. We took the camping guide concept and began to replicate it for other regions. We signed John to write a fishing guide for California. We expanded the golf series and John Aberdeen's concept of the outdoor adventure guide to Hawaii.

I wasn't the only one doing several jobs. Allison, while managing the finances, also edited and proofed the books. Dave handled the layout of the guidebooks, but also oversaw our company systems, serving as the operations manager. At our management meeting for the week, Allison proffered another shift in our organizational model. She elected herself editor-in-chief and suggested we hire a chief financial officer to fill her shoes. Dave offered to cover the financial department so we didn't have to hire, and we all happily made the shift.

As the editor-in-chief, Allison oversaw all editorial and production on the books, hiring more people to build our team, most of them young and anxious to get into the world of publishing. Dave checked out accounting books from the library to educate himself, then provisioned the right software. We assumed the positions of our greatest strengths. Allison as the filterer of outdoor information, me as the expansionist marketing guru, and Dave as the whip master and regulator.

* * *

On the West Coast, the book publishing community was growing, the newly formed San Francisco Bay Area Book Festival both a catalyst and a result. The first Bay Area Book Festival had taken place down the road from the Boiler Room, at the Concourse Exhibition Hall. I came in a year after its launch, invited as a board member as plans were being made for the second festival. Some twenty-five thousand booklovers attended that year, in a headlong love affair with books. When they announced at a board meeting that a Book Festival office was needed, I arranged to sublet the conference room on the first floor of our building.

The Book Festival provided an opportunity to mix with other small-press publishers. Up to this point at Foghorn, we'd been operating in the realm of our own made-up systems, Dave's sheets with the 53 Steps created out of necessity. We relied on PGW or the annual trade show to compare notes or ask questions. Now, with the Book Festival practically in-house, the proximity to other presses infused us with comparative knowledge about how to best run our press. That meant we could all grow faster and more profitably.

And it gave me an idea. I laid it out for the board at the next meeting. There were small presses, booksellers, and libraries all represented around the table.

"The promotional aspects are huge. We'll enlist a group of junior-high and high school kids for a six-week summer program, with the purpose of producing a book. The Junior Publishers would meet in the back room of Foghorn's offices. I'm happy to facilitate it."

"And imagine this." I paused for effect. "Each of the junior publishers will be assigned a job in the mock publishing company. They will be the ones to decide the title, edit the text, work out the book cover, get the book blurbs, and lay out a marketing program."

I saw heads nodding. "Foghorn would publish the book, distributing it through PGW to all our accounts, with proceeds going to the Book Festival. The book would publish in the Fall with fanfare and lead into the Book Festival."

The board voted unanimously yes and suddenly there was a lot at stake, my newly forming reputation for one.

The next morning, I told Dave and Allison. By that afternoon, they trooped back into my office together, their own dissenting duo.

"Tell me, Vicki, what does this Junior Publishers Program have to do with Foghorn Press?" Dave said. It wasn't a question; it was a challenge. He stood and paced my office. Allison sat and watched him.

"It connects us to the publishing community, and I'm bringing in lots of speakers to talk to the kids so we'll have those connections with experts in publishing. Plus, we'll have a book that will get lots of publicity when it's done." It was weird that they couldn't see the glory of it. I pushed my chair back from my desk, creating more space in between us.

Dave looked at Allison and she said, "But the thing is, if you do this for six weeks, then we don't have you for six weeks, and that means your stuff doesn't get done."

"I will do everything I'm supposed to be doing for Foghorn and do the Junior Publishers Program too," I countered. Jesus, did they know me at all?

"Not possible, unless of course you are a Greek goddess with powers beyond a mere mortal," said Dave.

"I have time, believe me. I can do it."

I watched them exchange a look.

Allison said in Dave's direction, "Well, she does have more time now that Casey's out of the picture."

"Exactly!" I agreed. "I'm excited to do it, too. Think about it. It's an amazing idea and a challenge: Can kids who know nothing about publishing come together and publish a book in six weeks?"

Dave shot back, "I would answer that with another question. Can they publish a book in six weeks and drive us crazy while they are trying to do it? The answer is yes."

Dave walked to my desk and leaned over it, facing me. "Vic, it's going to disrupt not only your work, but ours, too."

I rented the empty back room next to the Boiler Room to house the program, thinking a separate room would be enough to quell Dave's reservations, but on the second week of the Junior Publishers Program, Dave threw up his hands and went home to work. Allison tolerated it better, but I saw her and Dave commiserating. It was definitely too loud, but it was hard to tell sixteen teens and preteens to pipe down. They had only one volume, and it was all the way up.

* * *

When the Junior Publishers Program was over, Dave moved his finance office into the now open room and quiet reigned again. To fill it—and as a kind of balm to mend our disagreement—he and I scavenged three more desks and room dividers at the used office furniture store and moved them in and arranged them, still one of our favorite things to do together.

In addition to the Boiler Room and finance office, we now commanded the whole bottom floor of the building, including the foyer with the big metal drum reception desk and the conference room occupied by the Book Festival. For fun, Dave had set up a climbing wall on the concrete wall at the rear of the Boiler Room. Because of our proximity to Anchor Steam, the smell of sweet hops was part of Foghorn's publishing business now, especially during the hot fall evenings when we threw open the windows and happily inhaled.

I thought we were ready to show ourselves, and a party the night before the Book Festival would be the way to do it.

"We'll call it Books & Brew in the Boiler Room. We'll get a keg from the Anchor Steam brewery. Maybe we'll invite people to go next door and do a tour there if they want."

"But what's it have to do with publishing books?" Dave countered.

"It'll build our credibility in the Bay Area. We'll invite everyone in the book community: booksellers, media, our distributor, our authors and potential authors, even other publishers. It'll be part of the fanfare leading up to the Book Festival."

"How much will it cost?" Allison intervened.

"Just the keg and the printing of the invites," I promised.

We started the party at five p.m. and at eight p.m., it was still rocking. The Anchor Steam keg was a hit. Ferris Wiley had come with Alex and a few more from PGW. Ferris was perched on my desk in the Boiler Room, surrounded by a few of his distributed publishers. Allison was talking to an independent bookseller and I could see her gesture toward me, telling him I was the one to see about the promotions. Dave was somewhere in back, drinking and discussing Nietzsche's philosophy with one of our new authors, who was doing a book on river rafting for us. A reporter from the *Chronicle* stood next to me, querying about a guidebook idea for dog-owners. People were congregating around the keg in the front, and I had to push through them and down the hall in the Boiler Room to get to Dave, who stood with his back against the climbing wall.

"Good, huh?"

"I'd rather be publishing," Dave said smartly, and the rafting author laughed.

"I'd rather be drinking another beer. Get you one?" The author took Dave's cup and began to work his way to the keg.

"Jesus, when will they all go home? Where's Allison?" Dave said.

"Up front. Harrison hasn't come, thank God. He worries me."

"That guy makes me sick. Harrison Wolf represents what is sickest in our society. That self-serving artifice, put on the right hat, success. He is like someone who has told the initial lie about himself, and now has to keep on lying. He's an identity crisis waiting to happen. When it does, it's going to be ugly."

I could see he was a little drunk, but so was I.

"He is hard to like."

"Worse than that," Dave countered.

Allison slid into the back room with us.

"Harrison Wolf's here," she murmured, glancing at Dave, then at me.

"Stay with us," I said.

"Oh, he's coming back here, I'll bet. Let him," Dave said.

Harrison pushed through the crowd in the hallway, dressed in a tank top and shorts, always ready to climb it seemed.

"Good evening, folks. Looks like a good party you have here." His eyes flitted over Allison, and I could see Dave taking aim.

"Harrison, I have something I want to show you in my office." I took his arm to lead him away. He made no move to come with me.

"Harrison, do you know what the word 'lecherous' means?" Dave leaned forward.

Oh, Jesus. "Dave," I snapped.

Allison slid her arm into Dave's and gave him a squeeze.

"Just looking, Dave," Harrison countered. "Didn't know you two were together." He took a long drink from his beer. "You might have told me, Allison. I did ask."

Allison looked at me, her lips pressed together in irritation. I wondered why she hadn't told him. But Allison never discussed her love life, even when prompted. You couldn't get anything out of her, not what happened before Dave and certainly nothing about Dave.

"You're something else, Harrison," Dave said, raising up a bit. He was a half foot shorter than Harrison, whose lean limbs made him look taller.

"I am something else." His blond hair was in his eyes and I wondered how he could climb with it like that. Then he laughed.

"Well that's the crux of it." Harrison smiled. He pointed behind Dave and before we knew it he had scurried up the rock holds on wall, touched the ceiling 20 feet above us and then climbed down half way before jumping to the carpet next to Allison.

Ignoring Dave, he glanced over at me. "Okay, show me what you want to show me." And I led him away.

* * *

As we neared the end of our first year in the Boiler Room, Dave, in his appointed role as the finance manager, met me early one morning in the lobby before any employees had arrived. "Vic, we don't have the cash to do next season's list. We're short, big time."

"Can we meet with the printer and get better terms?" I turned to go to my desk in the Boiler Room and he followed me in, and when I sat down, so did he.

"They're giving us sixty days now."

"Ninety. They should give us ninety. That matches with how we get paid by PGW and it will work out."

"No, it won't, because PGW is deducting the money we borrowed from them on the first check they get."

"I'll call them and see if they can wait until the end of the year."

"You're not getting it," he said.

"I'm getting it. I'm getting it. I'm trying to think what to do." I waved him off. "Let me get myself organized and we can discuss it later." I pushed aside the stack of files on my desk, looking for my note-pad listing the to-dos I had for the day.

"No, you're not *getting* it. You think borrowing money is making money."

"Dave, *you're* not getting it. This is our chance to grow this company."

He sighed heavily and leaned forward, his elbows on his knees. There was no one else in yet, no one listening. "Vicki, you're going to grow this company this aggressively and also grow the Book Festival at the same time? Not humanly possible. You're still human, right?"

"You're still worried about that? They go together. The festival is good for Foghorn. Everything I do for the festival benefits Foghorn."

"I don't see it. I see you getting us in way over our heads. I'm looking at the bills, man." Dave sat up.

I heard the front door open and shut. Allison came around the corner and I gestured her in.

"Are we in trouble here?" I asked her. Dave did not turn around.

"Trouble?"

"Financially."

"I don't think so, but Dave would know better. He's in charge of the books." She looked at the back of his head, but he didn't turn.

"He says we are."

Allison stepped into the room, standing to Dave's left, a few feet away. "I can look it over and give you a second opinion if you'd like."

"Do it," I told her. "Let me know as soon as possible." She turned to go to her office.

"Now she's going to come in and check my work?" Dave's face was white, and his voice cracked when he spoke.

"What happened?" I realized they hadn't come in together, their usual routine for the past five months.

He spoke softly. "Allison is actually Anaïs Nin reincarnate. She's off to the next big thing in her odyssey to collect as many men as possible."

"This happened last night?"

"Absolutely. We'd reached the end of our reading program, so to speak. Lucky for me, she made me a tape." He stalked out and I heard him pass the climbing wall and enter his office in the next room, where he turned on his computer, which issued a bong that echoed through the Boiler Room.

* * *

That night I found Brian and Dave standing over the stove, poking a pan with vegetables that hissed with too much oil.

"What's cooking, my brothers?"

"I thought you were working the late shift," Brian said.

"I'm short on brother hours this month." I eyed Dave to determine if he was still upset. He'd left the office early, without saying goodbye.

Brian popped open the oven and pulled out a tray of chicken legs and breasts. "Perfect, then, let's eat."

Dave wasn't looking at me, his lips pressed together. He dished up his plate and walked out the glass door to the patio.

The patio extended twenty feet back in cross-hatched brick, and now that the weather was warmer, it was our favorite place to eat. We sprawled in the folding chairs with our plates under the neighbor's deck, which provided a natural overhang. Vines crept up each of the pillars, and for San Francisco, it was as close to privacy in a backyard as you were likely to get.

We ate silently for a bit.

"So, fellas," Dave began, setting his plate on his knees. "I'm going to rent a place nearer the office and get back to some reading I want to do."

Brian and I both turned to look at him. If he was announcing it like this, it had already been done.

"You can convert my bedroom back into a living room," he continued.

"You can read here," I pointed out. "I mean, the heater doesn't work for shit, but the place has room for you and your reading. We have all these finely crocheted blankets courtesy of Grandma to throw across your knees." I waited for him to look at me, but he didn't. "Why move?"

"I need space." He gestured with his hands, opening and shutting them like a book, like we had seen a cartoon character do in a film. It had become our newest shtick.

"He means space from us," Brian said, chewing.

"I want to immerse myself in Nietzsche; you know, really understand it. I need to retire to solitude." A smile flitted across Dave's lips.

"Are you saying we're noisy bastards?" I asked.

"We can ask the neighbors one block up if you need more confirmation. Actually, we probably have a five-block radius of affected parties." Dave took a pull of his beer.

I had kept my indiscretions to Casey's place and Dave knew that. I frowned at him. This was pure hostility on his part.

Brian chuckled.

Dave said, "Don't laugh. You're going to be alone with her in this house. The neighbors will be filing their complaints with you."

"You know he's dead to me." I sniffed. "Casey, I mean."

"Ah, but there'll be others, right?" Dave said maliciously.

"I'm going to be up at the campus most of the time," Brian said, running interference.

"Shooting up rats," I said trying to regain our playful spirit.

"Experimenting on how the brain processes and feels pain, actually," said Brian.

"I have a time-tested strategy for not feeling pain," said Dave, tipping his beer. "Beer and philosophy, mixed in equal parts."

"Maybe a little publishing mixed in," I offered.

"That's your philosophy. Not mine."

"Since when?"

"Since Allison crushed my department with her mammoth thighs."

Brian met my eye, as if to confirm that big thighs were not really the issue. He gathered the plates and went into the kitchen. Dave and I were silent. When he came back and sat down, it felt safe to talk again.

"I have news, too," said Brian. "It looks like I got that professor position in Washington that I interviewed for last spring."

"That's fantastic, Brian," I said. "When do you start?"

"This fall. I need to get up there and get a place to live soon, though, before the quarter starts."

Dave glanced at me and looked away.

"Jesus, I can't lose two brothers in a single night," I exclaimed.

"Jesus," Dave pronounced, shaking his head at Brian, mocking me.

"Well, now I'm going to have to move, too, Dave," I retorted, angry. It felt like the male defections were starting to stack up. First Casey. Now Brian and Dave.

* * *

The same week that Brian was moving out, I found an apartment in the Marina District on Octavia Street. Most of my furnishings were random pieces that I had happily surrendered to Foghorn. I called my parents for help and they arrived with their pickup truck at Brian's. Together we easily moved everything in a single haul across the City. My dad trudged up the three flights of stairs, holding the bottom of the mattress I had bought for sleeping at Brian's, while I carried the top. We did the same with box springs, my mom bringing up the metal frame. We stopped on each of the landings, breathing hard, my mom making jokes about the lack of an elevator and how in shape I was destined to get.

"Great spot, Vicki," my dad said as I walked them through the small kitchen on the right and past the bathroom on the left. The hall opened into a wide living room and the far wall hosted a set of six vertical Victorian-style windows. Looking out, there was the stucco wall of another building, but if I tilted my head up, my view was largely unimpeded, revealing the open sky. From the far-right window, the apartment commanded a sliver of a view of the Golden Gate Bridge and a smatter of green from the Marina.

"You sure you'll be okay here alone?" my mom asked as my dad and I set down the last of my belongings, a cedar hope chest my grandma had given me and that they had brought down for me. The large walk-in closet off the living room was stuffed with book boxes and clothes. The kitchen and bathrooms each had a single box to unpack. The only room with furniture was my bedroom, so we went in there to sit.

"You know Dave doesn't like how I'm running the company," I said, flopping down on the uncovered mattress.

They exchanged a glance. They sat close together, my dad curling around my mother, and it reminded me of how they used to jitterbug for us kids in our kitchen, my dad tucking her into him with his arm around her, the rhythm of "Rock Around the Clock" playing on the record player. It was always a relief for me to see them connecting this way, where I wasn't somehow in the middle, childishly concocting some distraction designed to alleviate the tension. They both leaned forward at the waist to look down at me.

"What?" I said, shutting my eyes to avoid the scrutiny.

"We're just worried about you," Mom said. "We know you and Dave are having some troubles." I wondered how she knew that.

"Not really worried," Dad said, "because we know you can do whatever you set your mind to, but—" Dad evoked his old motto. "You know, if first you don't succeed, try, try again. Maybe try to talk to him again."

"I've tried," I said a little too shortly. "Maybe you should be worried about him. I'm going to be great. I've got big plans for Foghorn."

Neither of them said anything and I tilted my head back to look at the window where I had already hung a curtain to block the view of the apartment across from me. I felt lonely and anxious, it was true, but I didn't think any of it showed.

I added in a smaller voice, "I don't know what to do. He doesn't even like me anymore, I don't think." I felt weepy all of a sudden and I stopped talking.

My mom got up to get me a tissue.

My dad reached over to squeeze my hand and then said, "You know we love you, kiddo." He leaned over and planted the same wet kiss on my forehead that he had always given me since I was a child. I started to cry.

My mom handed me the tissue and they both waited until I was done. "Let's go get some dinner."

"Okay." I sat up, resolved. This was no time to resort to *Victim MorGrim*. I gave myself the former victim's pep talk: Time to toughen up.

* * *

At the next meeting with the Book Festival board, I presented an idea to expand our name and mission beyond the festival and become the San Francisco Bay Area Book Council so we could introduce year-round programming which would even out our funding. It was also the meeting where I was to become president. After the meeting, the executive director and I scheduled a trip to New York to meet with *Publishers Weekly* and the American Bookseller Association to pitch them a story about the Book Festival, the Book Council, and the burgeoning San Francisco Bay Area publishing scene. A few weeks later, *Publishers Weekly* captured the renaissance in a multiple-page article and Foghorn was one of the featured presses. I had a copy on my desk ready to show Dave the next time he challenged me on the benefits of my involvement with the Festival, but of course, by then he was no longer challenging me about anything.

* * *

Tight end Rodney Shaw stood six-feet-six-inches tall and that—and being the only Black man in the Marina—turned heads. He met me for dinner, and I enlisted him in my promotion for our new edition of the Raiders book for the Fall. I pictured an autograph party that would sell books and generate funds for a scholarship in the name of another alumni player's son, who had inexplicably died during his high-school football practice a few months ago.

Rodney had a close-cropped beard that balanced his receding hairline, now at the halfway mark on his enormous head. He was handsome with penetrating eyes, and mid-dinner, he grabbed my leg under the table. Our flirtation went back a few years to the start of the publication of the Raiders book, but it had never veered into direct contact.

After dinner we walked along Chestnut, noticing the new trendy shops that had opened with their cream-colored throw pillows on their rattan sofas. Rodney took my hand when we crossed the street and when we made it to the other side, did not let go. I looked up at him and laughed.

"Rodney, what are you doing?"

He grinned. "Being friendly. I've waited a while."

"Oh, yes, I'm sure you've been sitting around waiting."

Casey and I had stopped seeing each other two months ago and I hadn't had a romantic thought since. I let Rodney pay for a motel room off Lombard, not wanting to take him to my place. I was keeping it for myself. We didn't turn on the lights.

"You are very attractive. Attractive, but goofy, too. It's cute," he said, pulling off his shirt.

I wasn't feeling goofy just then.

Afterward, he dressed and leaned down and kissed me, his lips tender against mine. "You know that once people connect like we have, they are connected forever. It's like strings across the universe. Even if we never saw each other again, we'll always be connected because of this night."

I pictured the imaginary strings, entangled across the universe from all the meaningless sexual encounters. I smiled to think what a mess that would be and my contributions to that mess to date. I dressed and walked home, the cool air coming off the bay rinsing me off, tingling my skin. I suppose that was one of Rodney's better lines. I wanted to tell Dave about it so we could mock the strings across-the-universe concept together. We could add it to the Morgan lexicon as the new definition for the one-night stand. Instead of "no strings attached," it would be "strings permanently attached."

I chuckled as I traveled along the sidewalk, rehearsing the story I might tell Dave. If I could get him to laugh, that would help. The City rattled and purred around me with cars, buses, and people in the throes of another urban night, yet by the time I turned onto my street, I was the only one. I turned the key to the door of my building and began the trek up three flights of stairs.

It was good having one person between me and Casey, just as Casey had been one person between me and Sully. I did not know how many more would be necessary, but it seemed like a kind of progress.

* * *

As we signed a slew of new titles, I heard Dave's voice in the back of my head, cautioning me to slow down, to not get so far ahead of our cash, but he didn't say any of those things to me, the old fight finally gone. Dave and I were in a place we'd never been before. We didn't know how to talk to each other, and so the best we could do was avoid one other, calling on years of our parents' tried-and-true marriage strategy. It didn't help that he and Allison were avoiding each other, too. All our group conversations were strained.

Dave spent more of his time at the apartment he'd taken up the street, where he could read unheeded. He now came into the Boiler Room at nine a.m. and left at five p.m., often disappearing before I could say goodbye.

I called Brian at his new apartment in downtown Portland from my desk one night. He was settling in he said. I asked, "What's up with Dave?"

"He's on a reading program, he says. Reading all of Nietzsche."

"Again?"

"He's reading them this time in German."

"He's teaching himself German?"

"That's what I understand."

I looked for ways to engage Dave, but each time I tried, extending an invitation to my new place for dinner, for instance, he shut me down. He hadn't been there yet and it didn't look like he was ever coming over.

"Gotta get some reading in tonight, Vic," said Dave, now permanently the hermit version of himself. That hermit wasn't hostile to me, which was preferable, but then he had almost no sense of humor, which left me feeling truly alone. I got a brief burst of happiness the morning I cornered him in the parking lot to deliver the "strings attached" story about Rodney Shaw.

Dave commented with mild judgment and a hint of his former humor, "Way to stretch yourself, Sis," before drifting into the office.

* * *

With Dave encamped on the other side of the City reading, I now had my evening hours. And my own apartment. So that fall, I tried dating. I remembered attending some fair in my teens where a palm reader had told me I'd marry a man named Mitchell after I told her it was a name I loved. I decided that was as good as any as an organizing principle and would help pare the field down, so I decided to date men named Mitchell exclusively.

Mitch Russo, a successful publisher of computer books, sported the look already made popular by Steve Jobs. His company was also distributed by PGW, but the majority of his business was done outside the book trade. After dinner, he walked into my new apartment and noted with shock the complete lack of furniture.

Two minutes later, I showed him out. I pictured his three-story home banked into the side of Mount Tamalpais in Marin and realized that publishing outdoor recreation guidebooks as part of the book industry meant a humbler route of which my apartment was a reflection. To that humiliation, I owed the purchase of my couch, bookshelves, kitchen table, and dresser the following weekend, checking *yes* on "Immediate delivery" despite the substantial fee.

Mitch Samuel, the smarter-than-thou entrepreneur whom I met at the Chamber of Commerce, wanted to meet for drinks but postponed three successive times—he was that important, I was to understand—before I stopped taking his calls.

Then there was Mitch Ably, whom I initially appreciated because he was a meditator, but who otherwise possessed no real attractive physical or personal qualities other than his name and the insurance that came with knowing he was a friend of Allison's. But after one date and one overnight where awkwardness reigned in the form of guttural growls in a high bed already overburdened with Ikea pillows, I realized I was done.

He broke it off suddenly before I could, a fact that irritated me, with another woman slyly appearing on the scene. I considered banning dating from my activities, even if their names were Mitchell. Who had the energy for it?

SAN FRANCISCO, 1992

Published: 14 titles
Partners: 3
Employees: 10
Annual sales: $1,200,000

When a girlfriend who I'd met long before Foghorn called about getting together, I invited her to attend the AT&T Golf Tournament in Monterey with me. I had hundreds of the new edition of the golf guides for California shipping to their media tent for giveaway to golf writers from around the world. The tournament team had sent passes for me and a guest. This girlfriend was the only one who had survived the Sully era, and only because our divorces had happened at the same time. We'd gotten together to commiserate.

She ran the public-relations department for a high-tech company on the peninsula, and her high wages were reflected in her sharp business attire. She lived in Pacific Heights while I lived on the other side of the Lombard divide, the Marina. Close to the top of the heap, but not quite. My outfits ran frumpy because I didn't much care how I looked, but even I knew there were times when frumpy was strictly frowned upon, and this golf tournament would be one of them. I got a new outfit.

Rodney Shaw would be one of the celebrities playing there as well. I thought I might try to catch up with him.

In Pebble Beach, we watched the tournament during the day, then flowed through a string of parties that evening. Rodney never materialized, but the next morning, I awoke next to someone I didn't know but whom I had obviously found attractive enough the night before. I had no idea where I was, the room generic enough to be a hotel, but possibly a personal residence. He looked at me, blue eyes blinking and friendly, and I bolted out of bed and dressed quickly, calling for my girlfriend, who emerged in the doorway similarly disheveled. My head reeled and I felt the kind of nausea born of drink and disgust. I gestured and we beat it to our car, quiet for the first twenty minutes until we found the freeway, and as our speed crept up, we mutually agreed to never discuss the incident again.

A week later, I received a postcard at work that had Burt Lancaster on the beach on his back in a torrid kiss with Deborah Kerr from the movie *From Here to Eternity*. When I flipped it, it read: *May you heal from him and find real love*, in small handwriting I didn't recognize, with no signature. It wasn't Casey, nor any of the Mitchells. I had obviously let my *Victim MoreGrim* self leak to this stranger, reciting the tale of Sully Cavanaugh and my suffering at his hands, still working the old wounds.

I was embarrassed, thankful I had been the one to pick up the mail at the office that day. I tucked it away and decided never to go out with anyone ever again. I steeled myself. I could be perfectly happy as a publisher without a personal life.

* * *

Deep into the spring season, I finally got Dave to accept my invitation for a beer and dinner after work. We drove around the Embarcadero in silence, looking for a parking place. At the Fog City Diner, we took side-by-side seats at the counter so we didn't have to wait. The diner was jammed with people, most wearing suits or business attire and buzzing with conversation, which eased the quiet between us.

"What are you reading now?" I asked him, encouraging a philosophical discussion as a foolproof strategy for getting him to talk.

"Two things. *Thus Spake Zarathustra* and *The Will to Power,* which comes from Nietzsche's notebooks before he went crazy," Dave replied. He paused as the bartender brought us our drinks and took our food order.

"Why did he go crazy, anyway?" I sipped my beer. I promised myself to only drink one.

Dave took a big gulp of his beer. "He had terrible health problems his whole life, and then he may have been manic depressive, too, or had syphilis. No one can say exactly. He wrote all his books before he was forty-four, if you can imagine that."

"Brian told me you're trying to read them in German."

"The thing is, Vic, Nietzsche knew Greek, Latin, Hebrew, and French because he wanted to be able to read texts in the original language, and I want to be able to do that, too. Otherwise, you can't be sure what he really said. I can already see where the translators have gotten it wrong in places."

"It probably would have pissed him off how the Nazis took his work and used it for their own purposes."

"You have no idea how angry that would have made him. He all but denied his German ancestry in the end because this idea that the German way was the only way really annoyed the hell out of him. And antisemitism, too—he fought against that."

"How did it get so misinterpreted? People translating wrong or what?"

Dave looked at me, surprised at my lack of what he might consider basic knowledge. "His sister was a religious fanatic, and married a guy who hated Jewish people. She had control of his papers at the end."

"Ah, it can always be traced back to the evil sister," I said, half kidding, half not.

That made him laugh and I joined in.

"Well, I've been thinking. Before I go crazy, too—" He stopped and took a swig of his beer, and then turned on the stool to face me. "It's time I left Foghorn."

"What the hell?"

"I'm saying, it's time."

"It's time? Is that what you've been trying to do? Leave?" I asked, pushing my hand to his chest as if to physically stop him.

"Trying. Trying. Trying. The whole thing is trying. Look, nobody really takes me seriously because I am, at my core, an unprofessional, impractical, philosophical romantic. And you know this. I always give myself away. I can belly-laugh like I am the town fool and the next moment sober up for a good long series of Nietzsche quotes."

He stopped and took a drink. "I'm not challenging myself anymore. The problem is I never want to step into the same river twice." He paused. "Can a river ever be the same twice?"

"Not good." I frowned at him fiercely. "If you left, what would we do without you?"

Dave laughed. "Same thing you're doing now. I'm a speck in the cog of a large machine into which you keep adding parts. I'm out of it already. I'm obsolete. You just haven't been paying enough attention to notice, Madame President."

A wave of nausea gripped me. "This is not funny. I don't think it's a good idea."

"Good thing you have a million good ideas. I'm replaceable. You also have a million new employees, all thrilled out of their minds to be publishing. It works. My time has come."

"No, Dave, no, please." I refused to believe it.

"I'll give you plenty of time. When I turn thirty, and then I'm going. I'll wait until the Spring list is out," Dave said. And then, though I hadn't asked, he added, "I may go back to San Diego, or travel."

I tried to think of how to persuade him to stay.

"I'll take another," Dave said to the bartender. "You?"

I shook my head in a double-duty no. "Look, how will you live?"

"I can always get a job. I've done everything. I can do anything."

I pictured him a moment out in the wide-open world without Foghorn, without me. A flash of guilt stabbed my chest. I had let way too much time go by without talking to him. How long had it been? How long had it been since we mutually discussed where we were going with Foghorn? Now it was just Allison and me, confirming and making plans.

I thought how much I wanted another beer right now. My throat constricted. "I want you to be happy. I do."

"Don't talk to me about being happy. What kind of argument is that? That's the worst kind of argument for anything. I want to live the life I want to live."

I had an idea. "This is what we'll do. We'll figure out your ownership of the company and send you monthly payments so you don't have to work, so you can just read wherever you are."

Dave paused a moment, debating whether he should allow this.

"Maybe." He looked up from his beer. "Nothing too crazy, though, enough to live on only. Enough for a philosopher to live on, that is."

"I don't know if I can do it without you, Dave. I mean, it's always been you and me. I'll now be the girl in the yellow bathing suit asking everyone, did you *See More Glass*?"

He chuckled at the Salinger reference. "You're doing perfectly fine without me."

I opened my mouth to defend myself, but he cut me off. "And I don't mean anything bad by that. It's just not for me anymore."

Dave looked at me closely. "Strange as it may seem, just because I'm leaving, I'm not doing this in opposition to you. I want you to get this. I'm doing this for *me*. Nietzsche said, 'Become what you are.' You've already done that. You're clearly a publisher. I need to become what I am, and I can't do that at Foghorn."

I couldn't think what to say; I leaned my forehead on his shoulder a moment and then when I sat back up, tears streamed down my face.

"Vic, please, it's hard enough."

But I knew I wouldn't stop trying to make him stay.

* * *

Allison strode into my office and sat down. "Have you been listening to what's going on?"

I shook my head. It was after seven p.m. on a Thursday night, the last day of April, and we were both working late; me, working out the promotion for a bungee-jumping event to launch our new thrill sports title in June; and Allison, trying to get a book to the printer. Everyone else was gone and the place was quiet. I preferred this time of day because of that. I knew she did, too. We were like twins in that regard, hermits at heart who strangely had organized our lives around public interaction.

"The City is locked down because of the reaction to the Rodney King verdict. People are rioting. We're supposed to stay put," she said. We picked up the purr of a helicopter in the distance. We looked at each other.

"For how long?" I asked.

"No idea. They said on the radio that fires are burning on Market Street and there's looting. They called a state of emergency and there's a curfew in place."

"We'd both have to cross Market Street to get home." I walked to the glass front door. I stood a moment, looking out. The light had drained out of the City, the usual fog covering the skyscape, no sign of the street-level disturbance taking place a mile away.

Allison came and looked too. "Yep. We're stuck here."

"It's like the City feels and absorbs everything."

"Righteous anger can't be contained." Allison flicked off the lights in the lobby. We stood for a moment in the dark. I thought of Dave, maybe unaware of this in his monthly rental up the street.

"Want to move your computer down to my office so we can be together?" I asked.

She brought down a printout of a book that was going to the printer this week. "I think I'll do a hard-copy edit." She set the book on the table and took a seat. I handed her one of the yellow crocheted blankets my grandmother made that I kept in a basket behind my desk.

"Here's a lovely blue one," I said, testing her Salinger. Her Morganness.

She laughed. "*It's a yellow.*"

We put our blankets across our laps and settled in to work.

After a while she looked up. "Is Dave leaving because of me?"

"No, I think it's me, actually. I frustrate the hell out of him, as if that wasn't obvious to everyone." I hadn't had this conversation with anyone yet, not even Brian, so far away it seemed in Portland, and my voice grew thick.

"You want different things," she said.

"No, we want the same things, but we just go about it differently." I tried to think of what Dave might want. Beyond Foghorn, what was there? Love, maybe, but we both had failed at that. And all those *permanent strings* with strangers. But through all that love and not love, we had managed to survive by banding together. Now what would happen?

Another helicopter chopped through the air.

"Crazy out there," Allison remarked.

"I've always loved this City."

"Me, too. Even though I live in one of the worse neighborhoods." She laughed.

"Maybe we'd better stay here all night. It's not like we haven't done it before."

"That's your and Dave's old schedule. I usually try to quit by two a.m."

"He is the hardest-working man in the publishing business," I said.

"He'd be that way with anything he took on. Now it's reading." She smiled. "Remember those 53 Steps, outlining every step of the publishing process?"

"Maybe when he leaves, I'll get a rest." I tucked the blanket around my knees.

She snorted. "You're kidding, right? You're the hardest-working woman in the publishing business. Knowing you, you'll just double your efforts."

"Do you think there is anything we can do to make him stay?" I asked. "Maybe we could put him in charge of new business development."

"He wants to go, so no. He's the most stubborn person I ever met."

I thought about how Dave considered happiness to be a poor measurement of a good life, but it remained my primary measurement. "Are you happy, Allison?"

"I'm kind of a hot mess, if you must know, but don't tell anybody," she said.

"You mean in love?"

"Love, life, you name it." She shook her head and a rueful smile appeared.

This surprised me. Everyone—me included, apparently—equated beauty with a perfect life, and I realized that wasn't a fair assessment. It denied the humanity everyone else was allotted.

I said "Me, too. And I'm definitely not happy. I'm really not happy he's leaving. I just can't get over it."

"You don't think it was inevitable?"

I looked at her, surprised again. "You do?"

"Frankly, yes."

At midnight, we decided to make a move to go home. I followed her car with my own down DeHaro. We cut over to Division and onto Van Ness to cross the city. The streets were bare and when we crossed Market, I looked to my right. I could make out bonfires downtown and I felt the unease of an unfamiliar and dangerous undercurrent in a city I thought I knew.

* * *

Everything about the American Booksellers Association trade show in Anaheim felt stressed and off that year. The only location we could come up with for the Independent Travel Association annual ABA event was the Knight's Room of the Medieval Times in Buena Park, which lacked the magical ambience of a New York City cruise around the Statue of Liberty. Yet, our participating publishers had grown to thirty-eight. I was happy that Anna was at the helm, and I could share the load of coordination.

I brought in a few staffers to work the Foghorn booth. Every ABA had its share of parties in the evening and hangovers at the booth in the morning, and I wasn't alone in experiencing that. The ABA trade shows were intense runs of daytime work and nighttime fun. The night before, several of the travel publishers had gone bar hopping, and I barely remembered the return to my room at the hotel. And now, Publishers Group West was making its mark on the trade show by hosting coveted parties in the late evening, featuring major bands. As a publisher, we were always granted tickets.

For the PGW party, I just wanted to make an appearance, then go rest. But two beers later, standing at the bar, I noticed a *Publishers Weekly* reporter and approached with an introduction. As soon as I opened my mouth, I realized I had had too much to drink. The embarrassment I felt when she cut me off was keen. Later, on the sidewalk as I walked back to my hotel, I saw her again, and made to apologize, but she walked away as soon as she saw me. Here was a solid indication that maybe drinking and business did not mix. When I got back to the room, I sat in a hot bath, thinking. There could be no more drinking, I decided. No men. No alcohol. No mistakes. No embarrassment.

* * *

Our thrill sports guide charted the best places to bungee jump, surf, parasail, hang glide, skate, and more. In June, I sent invites to Bay Area media and local booksellers to join us for a bungee jump at a site we had set up with a company in Vallejo.

Dave came along reluctantly, hating to leave the office when he had so much to do now that he only had a few months left at Foghorn. But I had begged, telling him this would be the last thing we'd be able to do together before he left. His job was to monitor the handing out of books based on the clipboard of names I had printed for him. It was early and the morning was gray. At the site, cars whooshed by on the adjacent freeway, drivers peering over as they flew past, wondering what was going on.

The crane with the platform rested near the ground and the operator gave me a hand up. I looked down at the dozen journalists and booksellers who had gathered. A great turnout. I held up the book and described what was in it, introduced our author, and explained how he would be going first to demonstrate.

Up the crane went, me clutching the side. I had been terrified of heights my whole life, thinking much like Freud's fear of trains, that mine came when my father held me as a baby of three months over the railing of Seattle Space Needle for fun and my mother's terror flew up and into me, permanently lodging there. I clutched the railing and tried to focus on the freeway directly across from us. Someone was talking to me, but I hadn't heard a word. With a small bump, the platform came to a stop, and I uttered a gasp. The operator opened the gate. Our author was already strapped into the gear, but the operator looked over each of the fastenings again. One of the straps hung out longer off his back.

"Did you check that one?" I said from my corner, holding fast and nodding my head at the strap.

"Yep, all good," the operator said cheerfully. Our author moved to the gate opening and stood there, ready.

He hollered down to the people on the ground, "Ready?"

The platform kicked back with his takeoff.

"Argggghhhhhh." I screamed involuntarily. I shut my eyes. I heard him shout as he hit the bottom of the bounce and shoot back up.

"Yeeee-haaaawww!"

When the platform descended to the ground to take on the next jumper, I stepped off carefully. Dave came up to me and took my arm as I wobbled a bit.

"You okay, Vic?" he asked and I nodded.

"Must sit," I said. He pulled up one of the operator chairs and I plunked myself down. "Can you go up with each of them?" I asked Dave. "Just talk up the book and the company. Be friendly."

He looked at me strangely. "Me? Friendly?"

"Maybe not," I said. "Oh, hell, forget it." We watched as each of the booksellers climbed onto the platform and jumped.

"What?" I looked at him.

"You don't think anyone can do anything without you. Or without your advice."

"What? Not true." I scanned my recent activities, searching for an example I could give him.

"No, think about it; you are the queen of the command form. If you're not in charge, you won't participate."

"Neither will you," I shot back.

"Not true. I'm participating and have been for the last year, and I'm definitely not in charge."

"Do you want to be in charge?" I questioned him. "Really, do you?"

Dave settled deeper into his folding chair. "Vic, this may come as a surprise to you, but I've never been interested in publishing."

"I don't believe it." I said. "You *are* interested in publishing, or you were in the beginning." We watched another jumper pitch herself off the platform. He didn't reply.

"Jesus, let's never discuss this damn business again, then," I said, irritated.

He laughed. "Okay, Slim Bob. No need to get testy."

The last rider finished, and the operator called over, asking if either of us would like to go up.

Dave shook his head. I shook mine, amazed the operator hadn't put the clues together. Meanwhile, most of the journalists had left to write their stories and get them in the paper.

In the office the next day with our coffee cups full, we spread the paper in front of us, featuring a huge photo of a reporter springing through the air, the freeway behind him. Dave conceded the promotion had been a good one. The paper had even included a photo of the book cover. At lunch, Dave came back with burritos to celebrate, and we ate them in the Boiler Room of my office, apart from the rest of the crew. For a moment, we were a team again, Dave and me.

Most of the time, though, he preferred his reading. Less frustrating, he said. As a testament to prove I had heard him the year before, I had moved this summer's Junior Publishers Program out of the office to a school site in the nearby Mission District, and hired a teacher to manage the daily program. But it still took a tremendous amount of my time, and I spent hours each day during the last week of the program so we could get the book project finished.

Dave said nothing when I saw him back at the office, refusing to discuss it at all, but not because it angered him, but because he no longer cared. I saw that now. For Dave not to have an opinion was like death to me; it meant he really was leaving.

Allison and her team had an intense spring with all the new books, but finally the last title, the Washington and Oregon camping guide, was printed and in the stores. The Fall list would begin in August. Before it did, Dave would be gone.

So when the Junior Publishers Program was over that July, I concocted an outing that would be part celebration, part goodbye, and part team-building, the last part of my secret agenda to get the crew ready for fall.

* * *

For a group of outdoor-recreation guidebook-publishing employees, we were a sorry and reluctant sight. In front of the rafts at the Salmon River where the eleven of us stood, the lack of athleticism was apparent. I, their fearless leader, stood, my skin translucent below my shorts, leaning on an oar, waiting for instruction. The only Foghorn outdoor experts on hand were Allison and our author Phil, the only author we were allowing along, partly because of his good nature but mostly because of his expertise in white water rafting. Allison was apparently a skilled river rafter. Her mysteries ran deep, as Dave and I had often joked. She had the least body shame too; she wore a bikini top and shorts. Allison made sure we each were secure in our life vests, pulling mine tighter than I liked.

Phil stood at the water's edge and loaded us in. His face was serious as he tried to make raft placements that were balanced with their occupants' athleticism, an obviously difficult task. My raft was the least talented in this regard, and perhaps out of deference for me as his publisher, he put me in charge of the navigation. He reviewed the basic navigation strokes and while he did, it occurred to me that when we interviewed anyone for a staff position, we never asked if they were campers, golfers, hikers, rafters; that was beside the point. We wanted people who could edit or format or research or market and that was a different breed than the people for whom we were publishing our guidebooks.

John Aberdeen had kept us in check for the first years, since the books were largely his, but the list had grown well past him. I was happy Allison was at the editorial helm. Who knew what obvious mistakes we might make otherwise?

Dave stood at the side of a raft by himself. He hadn't spoken to me yet this morning. I knew he'd rather be working or reading—anything but this. He was in Phil's raft.

"We could drown the whole company today and that would be the end of Foghorn Press," I told Phil and Allison so he could hear me. "Whose idea was this, anyway?"

"Yours, I believe. Team building. Isn't that what this is about?" Dave's hands were on his hips as he peered down river. His round glasses sat on his pale face, reflecting the light. I tried to determine if the mocking had any humor in it.

Allison laughed and put her hand on my shoulder. "Maybe you should have said no to sitting on the Chamber of Commerce board—too many team-building ideas." Allison was always the great peacemaker. She was still fulfilling Brian's role of bringing us together.

There was a little flare of the old Dave for a second. "I've got your team-building right here, fellas."

Allison and I both laughed, too hard. Dave turned away and joined Phil at the river's edge.

"This river is damn cold. I thought she meant we were going down a metaphorical river," Dave said to Phil as he stepped into the raft. This early in the morning, there was still shade along the sandy beach.

The three rafts fanned out with Phil in the lead, Allison next, and me, bringing up the rear. By midday, the heat was oppressive. Phil spotted a shady harbor and pulled in and his folks scrambled out. Allison followed with her crew, and then we bumped in behind them, my legs sticking to the plastic side of the raft.

"Sunscreen?" I offered to the crew lying on the soft sides of their raft. The new editorial assistant was clearly miserable. He took the cream and rubbed it on his thick arms, which were already glowing a bright red.

Allison and I conferred. I had slathered sunscreen all over, yet I could feel the stiffness of my skin from being in the sun. My hat covered my face, but the reflected light from the river had gotten me, nonetheless. My lips burned. "Maybe another hour?"

"It's an hour and half, probably."

Fifteen feet away, Dave whistled the *Deliverance* banjo theme from the shade of a tree. He was lying flat on the rocks of the beach with a towel over his eyes.

Phil sat next to him and chuckled. "Don't worry, just over that ridge of trees is suburbia."

"Good, I'll stop guarding my colon." Dave sat up. "What's the rating on this river?"

"Just a two." Phil laughed.

"Doable. Totally doable. We will survive it," Dave said.

"There's a rocky patch coming up at the end that'll challenge everyone a bit, anyway." Phil added, glancing around at the immobilized crew huddled on the river beach.

Two hours later, we arrived. Phil negotiated the rocky patch for his raft. I could see Dave furiously paddling with the others at Phil's command. Once clear, they turned sideways, floating backwards with the eddy and, before getting out, they watched as our raft headed into it.

Boulders littered the river, jutting up through the surface. Spirals of white water spun off them, turning the whole river into a broiling bath of foam. The decibel level had crept up considerably as we approached.

"Uh-oh," the editorial assistant in my raft shouted. He glanced back at me at the rear of the raft, where I was supposed to be navigating. I had three people in my raft besides me, their lives in my hands. Just to our right and ahead, Allison sat at the helm with her two passengers on either side, everyone markedly calm.

"Jesus, Mary, and Joseph," I said, a coping term I had learned from Casey. Out of the corner of my eye, I saw a campground on the right bank of the river, populated with red, blue, and yellow tents. A perfect shot for the cover of the California camping guide, I thought.

I gave directions to veer right, but we charged forward into a flat rock stationed just under the water. For a moment we were perched there, stuck.

Then the pressure of the water behind us sent the top of the raft over our heads, dumping all of us into the water. I bobbed up, the blast of cool water soothing my burnt skin, but I was facing upriver. I twisted around just in time to see the big rock in front of me. My knee caught it and the pressure rather than pain told me I was hurt. I bobbed farther down the river, where the others were being retrieved by Phil and Dave. Our raft was flipped on the side of the beach where the rest of them waited. I floated over to them, my life vest doing the work.

The sand came up under me and I stood up. Blood ran from my knee and the moment I came out of the water, it ached. I dropped back down, squatting in the chilled current.

"Hurt?" said Phil, walking over.

I nodded, and he did a quick examination.

"Stitches."

"Ah, really? Never had stitches."

"You'll love it. I'll take you over to the hospital. Let me get you something to stop the bleeding, though."

Dave ran over. "Vic, you hurt? Do you want me to take you to the hospital?"

"Phil can. You go make sure everyone has a good time at dinner. One of us should be there. We'll come when it's sewn up."

The hospital gave me three stitches and Phil kept me entertained with his rafting stories. I didn't watch the needle going in and out. Ten years my senior, he'd taken on rivers all around the world. That was his calling, he said, and though he appreciated the chance to write about each of California's rivers for Foghorn in a guidebook, he didn't have much interest in doing it again.

"That's a hospital stitching record," said Dave when we finally got to the restaurant. He smiled at me and waved us to the open seats they had saved.

I slid into the chair at the end. Everyone was having a fabulous time. Drink and food were more of our shared currency, anyway. Stories about the trip were flying around. Dave sat center table and gave a dramatic account of the final rapids that led to my injury while I stuffed myself with pizza.

"Foghorn survives!" Everyone clinked their glasses together. The waitress brought the bill to Dave, and he scooped it up.

"Dave, what are you doing?" I asked. I did a quick calculation, thinking about how he'd get his last regular check when he left and thereafter would only have his reduced philosopher check, namely half.

"What I want," he said, standing, slipping the bill into his pocket, and making his way to the host stand in front.

I stood and got everyone's attention. "Listen, everyone, Dave cannot afford to pay for everyone so it would be great if we all could pitch in."

I collected and stacked up the money and put it at his place.

"What's this?" he said when he returned. Everyone had left and we were alone at the table.

"Dave, you can't afford to pay for everyone."

He stood up, reddening. "This isn't any of your business. It's mine. I want to pay for everyone."

"Well, it makes no sense."

"It makes sense to me. It's what I want to do. Why can't you let me?"

"Take the money. It's already here and I don't know who put in what now."

"You don't even see it, do you?" He walked away, leaving the money there.

"Dave?" I called after him, but he was already out the door.

To get home, I hopped on the back of Phil's motorcycle, the vibration and noise keeping me from thinking too much about what had happened, my knee still numb. Back in the city, he dropped me off at my car, which I had parked in front of the Boiler Room.

"Is it bad business to date your publisher?"

"Probably, especially this publisher."

"Well, think about it," he said and he leaned in to kiss my cheek before shutting the door to my car.

Phil was a good guy, and good-looking, too, but I wasn't going to mix business with personal anymore. My knee began to throb and as I drove home, I kept seeing Dave's face. I replayed the restaurant scene, thinking about what I could have done differently, but that quickly expanded into a list of everything else I had failed at, especially in regard to him. The recurring theme was that I thought my ideas were the best. I was the big sister, ultimately, and that title meant I was right, and I knew what was right for everyone else. Maybe okay at work, but maybe not with people I loved. Somewhere on Van Ness, midway to my place in the Marina, I shut the inquiry down, unable to reconcile my supposed victim status with my assertiveness.

I lay in bed that night, unable to sleep, needing a diversion. I summoned Metaphor Woman, feeling her rallying optimism igniting a thousand plans. The Little Red Engine burned inside me: *I think I can, I think I can*. Of course, I could, when it came to most things. I disdained any plan that was small or without glory. I had never been humble nor patient, something very few men could handle. Casey couldn't.

Maybe Dave could, but I had left even him behind with all my glorious schemes. I realized he had hung on as long as he could.

* * *

With two weeks to go, Dave and I had a new mission to get everything set up. Our last Morganization. It was how we worked best together anyway, with a deadline and with heavy furniture to move. To house the editorial and production team, I added the second floor to our lease. We purchased four fifty-dollar used desks at the furniture depot down the road and loaded them ourselves up the stairs on a weekend. We moved the Book Festival out of the conference room off the main lobby and to the back portion of the second floor. We found a used conference table that fit, and installed it with matching chairs. The Boiler Room, where I had my office, was now the marketing wing. We assigned cubicles, one for sales and another for publicity. And the production room in the back of the building became the business office and storage.

Dave brought in more computers to accommodate each of the new employees and upgraded the machines we had. We were Mac people by constitution, but a few PCs crept into the mix. Dave called in a consultant to coordinate our computers, set up the printers, and link the entire office. The consultant's laughter carried through the building as she and Dave worked and at lunch, they disappeared down the street to our local sandwich place. He was already acting differently, enjoying himself in a way I hadn't seen for a long time, obviously relieved to be leaving.

Allison came into my office. I grabbed the stacks of files I had left on the chair and set them on the floor, and she sat down.

"I met someone," she said.

Allison went through men like a hand through water, but she never declared it. Even as of today, we had never really discussed the fact that she and my brother had been an item. So this declaration had my attention.

"Who? What? Where?"

"I actually met him in the bookstore."

"Not the self-help section, I hope."

"No, the computer section. And he's a Mac guy, too."

I smiled at her. "These things happen." I thought of how I didn't even want it to happen to me anymore.

"How do you think we're going to do without Dave?" she asked. "I'm a little worried. Lately he's been putting in so many hours and does so much, we're not even going to know what we're missing until something goes wrong."

"He's doing the best he can to set us up so it all goes smoothly." Dave didn't want to be called back in—I could tell. He wanted to exit permanently. I beat back the ache that had been creeping up on me all summer. "Did you review the finances yet?"

"Yeah, Dave's right. We're a bit pressed for cash right now. I'm not sure what the solution is." Allison put her hands under her chin, framing her face. Her nails were bit down so a painful-looking red ring ran along the top of each cuticle. Noticing me looking, she quickly curled her fingers under. We were more alike than I'd realized. This was the same woman who had kept us going for the past few years with "absolutely," but it had been stressful for her, too.

"Maybe we should go to a bank. Are we big enough for a business loan?"

"Dave would never want that, Vicki. His mantra is 'no more debt.' "

"Dave is leaving. My mantra is growth, and that means we're going to need a credit line." I leaned forward, thinking about what I would do with a hundred thousand dollars.

"It's a risk." She channeled Dave for a moment, her eyebrows questioning.

"PGW's banker would be the best shot. They understand the book industry and the cash-flow cycles. I'll make the call."

"I suppose we could hire a real chief financial officer after Dave leaves."

I sat up a little straighter, suddenly excited. "Yes, let's get someone who has done all this before, and who can prepare the documents we need to get a good line of credit."

* * *

When I arrived at work that final morning, Dave had Brian's car backed up to the office entryway with the trunk open. The front door of the office was ajar. I went in and called his name. No one else would be arriving for another two hours.

He appeared around the corner with his computer. "Taking this. I downloaded everything of Foghorn's onto the new machine."

"You bought it. You should take it." I followed him out to the car as he loaded it in the trunk.

He turned to me. "You can call me if there's anything you can't find. I tried to lay out everything in a straightforward way, so whoever comes in can find everything." We were both staying as professional as possible.

"Thanks, Dave. What's your plan?" I knew, of course, but it was the only thing I could think to say without getting emotional.

"Leaving today. I'll fly to Paris from Portland, then I'm going to Budapest. Probably come back to Portland. I've always wanted to try Portland."

"And then you'll live with Brian when you come back?"

He nodded. "We'll see. He said he'd keep my stuff when I start traveling."

"Will you keep me posted?" I felt my chest constrict and I knew I might cry.

Dave turned to the trunk and fitted a blanket around the computer, dropped the hood, and latched it with the key. He turned back to me.

"Vic, I don't want to have a long goodbye. I can't take it. I'm ready to drive, man."

I couldn't speak and so I nodded.

He leaned forward to give me a hug. I held onto him too long, and he pulled away. "We can write to each other. We'll be old fashioned letter-writers, you and I."

I nodded again, my throat choked. "Like Virginia and Vita."

"Like Theo and Vincent." He smiled at me and climbed into the driver's seat.

He started the engine. I leaned toward the window and tapped it, and when he rolled it down, I said, "Yo, Butler, bring me some adventures."

His car turned out the driveway and I watched as he headed downtown, where he'd hit the bridge north.

Inside, I sat at my desk and shuffled through my papers. The Boiler Room felt cold and desolate. I got up and put in the Dylan tape so I could hear "Tangled Up in Blue." I hadn't heard it in a year. Dave had left it on top of the stereo, where he'd known I'd find it. I walked through the offices, back to Dave's space. All his books were gone. The new computer sat with mouse and keyboard, ready. His office had access to the sliding glass doors leading to the back porch, which was walled in on three sides, the street sidewalk above us.

I remembered the feral cats we had living there last year, and how a class of preschoolers had once toured our building at the request of a teacher trying to expand their horizons about books and publishing. But when they saw the cats, that ended the tour right there, and I always laughed to think they would have some primal association for the rest of their lives between books and cats, the thought of one triggering the other. That was how it was with me and Dave. The association I had with publishing ultimately had less to do with books, and everything to do with Dave and me.

What would happen now that he was gone?

The ache in my chest radiated and I needed to work. I walked back to the boiler and reorganized my desktop. I wrote him a letter and when it was done, I wiped my eyes and did one of the few things that always made me feel better. I took out a new yellow pad and wrote down my list of to-dos for the day.

* * *

If I was telling myself the truth, the discomfort that came with revisiting my hometown washed over me the moment I drove over the county line and made my way up Highway 101. The memories of all that had happened here struck me without order or relevance: the moments of being too drunk at a party, the awkward dates, the overwhelming and pervasive sense of floundering far into junior college, when I finally met Sully and generated more trauma for myself. The memories seemed to stack up, waiting for me, the play button hit as soon as I drove into town; all this, despite all my achievements in the City with Foghorn. Here in Sonoma County, I was boiled down to an eighteen-year-old girl still trying to figure it all out.

That was why I had scheduled a meditation retreat for myself immediately after this high-school reunion was over. To regain myself. In the meantime, the question of why I had agreed to go to this event kept cycling.

At the reunion, the thirty-three-year-old former cheerleaders gyrated in a circle in the middle of the room, drinks in hand, to the pulsing tones of Elton John's *Goodbye Yellow Brick Road*, and I immediately regretted coming. The dogs of society were howling, I thought. Most of the women of my class wore little black dresses whose hems crested at the top of the thigh, as if high school had left a permanent watermark that had been uncovered again for the night. Makeup hung a little too desperately on faces with blue eyeshadow and bright lipstick, hair still framing heads like '70s icon Farrah Fawcett taught us.

I had not gotten the memo, just like I hadn't in high school. I wore fitted black pants with wide bell legs that swung about my calves when I walked, my black cowboy boots emerging and retreating with each step. A kimono top of bright blue with bursts of green and gold flowers with knotted buttons and short sleeves covered my top half. There was another advantage of Casey not being in my life for the past year and a half, and it was that without all that late-night dining, I was thinner. I had pulled my hair into a knot at the back of my neck, but loose strands escaped around my face.

Into the middle of the evening, when the drinking had reached its height, people embracing sloppily though only two hours before they had just met again as strangers, I perched on the end of a table behind a crowd, nursing a bottled water. I had kept my resolve for a month now to not drink. At the reunion, looking around at what happens when you did drink, it was easy to keep on track.

A classmate with round glasses and a bald pate walked toward me. He wore too groovy a shirt for the '90s and carried his own bottled water. I did not recognize him and glanced down at where his badge should be. He had taken it off and when I looked up again, meeting his eyes directly across from mine—for he wasn't tall—he smiled widely at me, uneven teeth cheerfully exposed, nodding his head as if he was pleased I had made it. He said nothing and I said nothing in turn, my mind racing, wondering, who the hell was this?

"Mitch," he offered.

"Mitch," I said slowly. We had two Mitches among our five hundred graduates in the class of 1977. One was a nerdy guy who was in all my advanced-placement classes, in the back row, never talking, slouched low in his seat, reading to himself. The other was one of the most popular guys in our school, a thick-bodied football player who ran with the cool crowd and had a slab of auburn hair that matched equally auburn eyes.

The man before me had no hair, but I recognized the warmth of those eyes.

"Mitch DeArmon?" I tried, disbelieving.

"Yep," and he laughed like the Buddha might, jolly but inexplicably caring at the same time.

"Vicki Morgan, right?" he said.

"Yes, that's me." I smiled widely too, but quickly tamped it down to a small smile that hid my excitement and my teeth, perfect after years of junior-high-school orthodontia. I saw he was still burly, with wide shoulders trapped under his button-down shirt and further fortified by a gray vest. His chest hair burbled up from the top buttons. I remembered then the high-school knowledge that Mitch, at age seventeen, had been able to buy beer, primarily because he was able to grow a full beard.

I knew him as I knew most of my classmates, not simply as Mitch, but as Mitch DeArmon, per the hundreds of role calls that all students endured. First and last. Yet there was something else that my thirty-three-year-old self knew immediately. I *knew* him. Blame it on the pheromones.

Another classmate approached Mitch with glee, extending his hand and shouting, "Mitch fuckin' DeArmon. Damn, man, what have you been up to? This is the first time I've seen you at one of these reunions. What the hell, man?"

Mitch glanced at me apologetically as I stepped back, the guy's enthusiasm generating its own space. I started to turn to walk away, but Mitch touched my arm lightly, asking me wordlessly to stay. When the classmate finally left, Mitch asked if I wanted to go out to the café tables, where we could talk without being interrupted.

We talked about the strangeness of the reunion and being here, like this world still mattered somehow when it did not matter to either of us. His friend had persuaded him to come despite his misgivings, and I had surrendered, too, to the calls from acquaintances, people I used to know, whose mission had been to drum up attendance.

We talked about our lives. I shared about the business and how much I'd put into Foghorn and the changes that were coming now that my brother had left the company. I would have to reinvent myself and that was one of the reasons I was driving south of Yosemite for a silent meditation. For him, it was the desire to work with people rather than at the butcher shop where he'd been since he turned eighteen, and I could see it so easily, his counselor self.

Occasional shrieks and the battering of glasses against each other floated out to us, but we were in a dreamlike dance of first disclosure— so much so that two hours later, when everyone started drifting out, we were shocked into real time by their goodbyes over the iron gate that separated the outdoor café from the parking lot. We were set back in the corner, the potted plants creating a natural shield that kept people from stopping to talk to us.

When a large group had passed, Mitch leaned forward across the table, his elbows bent and his head low, his chin above his crossed hands. "You know, you and I have a shared past."

I leaned forward too, mimicking his secretive posture. "We do?"

He smiled, regarding me a moment. "You don't remember?"

When he smiled, deep clefts sprung up in either cheek, accenting the warmth and openness of his face. It was a very nice face, I thought. Broad and browned by the sun. And his eyes—I felt steadied by them.

"Remember? Remember what?"

He paused and looked down at the table as if embarrassed, but then he looked up and said carefully, "The party on Middle Rincon Road?"

I hesitated, suddenly anxious.

"You were pretty drunk, I think," he added.

Dimly now, I remembered a back room of a house and falling to the floor with someone in a mutual make-out session. I remembered pulling my shirt over my shoulders and over my head and depositing it next to us before experiencing a slow gain in consciousness about where this might go if I let it. I remembered how I swam back from letting that happen by sitting up, my hand on my front pants zipper. I pulled on my shirt, staggered up, and out of the bedroom and some-how, no idea how, left the party. I remembered the next Monday at school, avoiding Mitch DeArmon's eyes in the crowded hallway and pretending nothing had ever happened. I had pushed it so far away, I hadn't remembered it all until this very moment.

I shoved my chair back and stood. "I gotta go." I lunged for my purse, feeling a flush over my face. I hated coming back home for this reason—these sneaky memories, that sense of being revealed in a way I never intended and couldn't take back.

"Wait, wait!" he said as I fished for my keys in my purse. "I just wanted that out in the open, didn't want to pretend that it hadn't happened."

"I have to get back. I'm leaving in the morning," I stammered. When I got in my car, I gunned the engine and backed out, ready to get out of town as quickly as I could. The old ghosts were starting to assemble. I was happy to be going to the meditation, where no one could reach me for ten days. As I pulled out, I saw Mitch return to the table. It wasn't a glass slipper, but earlier in our talk at the table, I had given him my business card with my home number handwritten on the back. Now it was sitting on the glass tabletop.

* * *

When I got back from the meditation, I had two calls on my answering machine from Mitch, one logging the day before and the other, the day of my return. The meditation had eased my qualms. I called him back and we talked again for three hours. He came to San Francisco the following Saturday and we walked Golden Gate Park, talking for ten hours. By the following weekend, we were officially together, both realizing this was different than anything we had experienced before.

But it was August and with it came football season. That meant it was time to activate my selling strategies for the sports books each weekend. For the last few years, I had set up book signings with members of the local NFL Alumni Association, football greats such as Leo Nomellini, Bruce Bosley, Marv Hubbard, Jack Tatum, Jim Otto, and Raymond Chester. They met me in shopping centers throughout the Bay Area to sign our sports books for fans. They sold easily to sports fans who valued the signature as much as the book, guaranteeing thousand-dollar weekends if I hustled and worked both days.

I explained to Mitch that I was the only one at Foghorn who knew how to sell and, with that, our weekends together quickly reverted to lengthy phone calls.

At a signing with Leo Nomellini in the South Bay, I met Vince Rhode, fifty-something and a former alumnus of the Baltimore Colts. He spoke to Leo for a minute and moved over to address me, towering over me at six-foot-five. His blond good looks were tempered by too much sun, but he never let go of his smile. His polo fit tightly.

"How many professional sports books you got?"

"I've got a series of football histories, with baseball and basketball on the horizon," I said.

"Did you get licensing?"

"Don't need to because we're in the book business."

"Do you work with local media and teams?"

"Somewhat," I answered. I collected twenty dollars from a customer and Leo took a book from the pile to sign. A small boy stood next to his dad and waited. When the signature was complete, Leo shook the father's hand again, then the son's, whose face expressed the awe of the small in the presence of the huge.

Vince pressed his card into my hand. "You need a marketing director who knows this market, and I do. Can I come talk to you?"

The next day in my office, Vince spread his huge frame over the chair. Dave had always been unconvinced about the sports books, but my theory was that better marketing was the key to their success.

"What can you do for us?"

Vince laid out a plan of attack that encompassed working with the teams to help promote the books.

"You have those contacts?"

"Yes. I also have contacts in the NFL Alumni Association. I'm an alum myself."

"How much?"

Vince looked at me carefully. He wrote a number down and pushed it over for me to see. "All I need is this and I'm good to go."

The number was reasonable, far less than I'd expected, in fact. Which made it doable. I looked down at his résumé. A series of marketing-director jobs, none longer than two years.

He leaned forward, his elbows on his knees. "I'm not going to play games with you. I need this gig. I've got two kids in high school at home and a mortgage to maintain, and I need the work. I'll get this job done. I also know golf, if that helps. I could do premium sales for the golf guides, too."

I sensed his desperation. Here was a good old boy with a different story. He was honest, at least. I suspected Dave might like him. So might Mitch. "You'd work from the office?"

"I would."

"And weekends, selling the sports books?" I thought about the time I could spend with Mitch finally.

"Yes, weekends, evenings, whatever it takes." He smiled at me, watching me weigh that.

"You'd report to me. Do you have any trouble with that?" I was twenty-two years younger than he was.

"None."

I started him the next day.

PART III

A REAL PUBLISHING COMPANY

SAN FRANCISCO, 1993

Published: 18 titles
Partners: 6
Employees: 18
Annual sales: $1,300,00

A month after he left, I dug out the first letter Dave had sent me. He'd returned from his travels and moved in with Brian. I kept the letter in my top right desk drawer where I could reference it after everyone else had gone home for the day.

A letter for Metaphor Woman,

Vicki, my sister, here's what I want you to understand. Do not ever fear you'll lose me. We are connected forever on the most fundamental level. No truth can wipe it out, no spouse can rip you away, no quandary insoluble, no fate overriding. I trust you completely and I don't mean that in a constricting way, only that we are even deeper than trust.

And then there was requisite Nietzsche, offering a definition of our relationship.

We, You and I, are in battle, but I find it pleasant. Don't you want in me your greatest enemy so as to be greatest friend? I think the best we can do for each other is to offer ourselves up as a mirror for the other. But to be a mirror one must stay shiny, hard, strong, receptive, versatile, yet human. You are the sun of a solar system. Only between two solar systems is true friendship possible. The sun's energy is almost infinite. Don't feel guilty about your excess; you could easily supply NY with all the electricity it needs. And now is the time to do it.

Love, Dave

I folded the letter and put it back in the drawer. Dave would forever make me better than I was, make me reach higher than I thought I could. Dave had his life to live, and I had mine to live, too. We were obligated to be everything we could be. A Morgan notion. As I looked into the future, there was the absolute realization that now, I was ready.

The stage was mine.

* * *

Dave had been gone several weeks. Allison and I met in Foghorn's lobby. She limped, having hurt her foot on a recent hike. It was wrapped in gauze. I would have to drive.

We were already late and had to get downtown to California Street to sign the deal with PGW. We had a scant ten minutes to get there. Anyone who has lived in the City for more than a day knew such a feat was impossible. It took us ten minutes just to get to Market Street, and that was flying through the back streets.

"You never want to be late with lawyers," Allison said as I crossed onto California.

"PGW's lawyers, luckily, but still," I said, swerving in front of a Muni bus to make the light.

"Parking is impossible, too."

"Watch for parking spots and I'll watch, too. Is there a garage near there?"

"There it is." Allison gestured toward a looming building. We both scanned for garages and found none.

"What time is it now?"

"It's fifteen after."

"Jesus. Stressful. Can't even flip a U-turn." I turned to go around the block again. We both were quiet, concentrating on finding a spot.

"Goddammit. This is ridiculous!"

"What are you doing?" Allison held tight to the door bar as I swerved.

I pulled up next to our destination again and pushed the button on my door to roll down Allison's window. A young man about our age in a three-piece suit walked next to us on the sidewalk.

"Excuse me." I raised my voice. "Pardon me!"

He looked over and stopped.

"We need help." I saw him glance at Allison. Thank God for beauty and the susceptibility of men. "Could we ask you to park this car for us?" I jumped out and Allison followed, hobbling onto the sidewalk. The car was still running. Allison put twenty dollars in his hand and named the garage we had passed a block over.

"I'll need your business card," she said. "Leave the keys with the attendant, okay?"

He flipped a card out of his pocket and stood a moment on the sidewalk as we made our way to the steps of the building.

"Okay," I heard him say and he walked around to the driver's seat.

"Thank you," Allison called. We walked through the big glass doors and I ran to the elevator to hold it for her.

The lawyers were waiting on the fifth floor and Ferris was already there, ready to sign. I signed as the majority partner and then Allison signed as a minority partner. It took fifteen minutes. PGW now owned a quarter of Foghorn and I owned less than half, but we had a quarter of a million dollars to build, money we didn't have to pay back.

I practically skipped while Allison limped cheerfully to the garage, and, when the attendant presented us with my car, keys inside, we high fived about that win, too.

* * *

We hired another marketing director for our outdoor and recreation titles. Vince added another staff member to help him work the sports shows. Allison added more editorial staff and a production manager. I added an acquisitions editor. We needed a receptionist. In a matter of months, our payroll hit sixteen, up from ten in 1992 when Dave had been here six months ago—an increase of more than a third.

But we still needed a finance person, a chief finance officer to be more exact, somebody who could wrestle with the numbers and offer them up to the new bank with confidence, and in a format that would be persuasive for the maximum credit line.

Our top candidate came back to interview. We brought him into the conference room. Allison pulled the curtain across the screen door and we took a seat across from him.

He was on the thin side, his face sporting a scraggly black beard. His square black glasses were of the variety worn in the 1950s. He wore an open-collared shirt, no tie, under a jacket that accompanied jeans. I allowed Allison to interview him, watching him carefully as he answered her questions in a soft voice, while I glanced periodically down at his résumé. After each answer he smiled, tilting his head, and we smiled back.

It was impressive, his résumé. A major insurance company, a dot. com start-up, a manufacturer. And he had all the right answers. Had he worked with banks? What size of credit lines did he manage? What reports had he put together? What software was he proficient with? What challenge might he foresee working in a new industry?

Allison nodded at each response and checked off the questions on her yellow pad. And lastly, how did he feel about working for women? She looked up.

"I've always worked for women," he said, smiling slightly, as if he were counting off each of those women now in his head. He didn't have any direct experience with publishing, but then, not many people on the West Coast did. We wouldn't hold that against him as we didn't hold it against ourselves, I told Allison later.

In the negotiations later over the phone, he held out. To compensate for the fact that the salary we could offer was significantly under the going rate for CFOs, a fact he pointed out—we offered him a bonus of a one-percent share in the company that would kick in a year after working, then sold him on our growth plan, of which he would be a part. We gave the same deal to a highly recommended public-relations director and completed our professional team.

* * *

Our new acquisitions editor, Sibyl Abercrombie, had red hair—not the color of mine, however, but a bright flaming red that had sprung from a bottle and further accented the sharp lines of her pale face. Her whole being suggested the fragility of some other world and she conducted herself with deep earnestness. Using the model I developed, she was to sign books across the country to expand our various series. She reported to me.

Above her desk, which we had situated at the top of the stairs in a mild separation from the rest of the editorial department, she erected a canopy that hung in a graceful swath tacked invisibly through the folds to the ceiling. Behind her on the windowsill, overlooking the parking lot, an array of candles with scents of musk and myrrh. The candles were lit, their scents wafting down the open staircase into the lobby.

As I topped the stairs, she was on the phone with a would-be author and I glanced to my right at Allison, who was at her desk working. Her new team members each sat at their desks, eyes focused on their screens.

No one looked up, their keyboards clicking as they edited. The rest of the room was spare, nothing on the walls, just desks in a room with Allison's crowded deadline calendar looming above them.

I sat in the Victorian armchair Sibyl had brought from home and across from her desk. The deep velvet high-back of the chair created a further separation from the rest of the desks deeper in the room.

She hung up the phone and looked at me expectantly. "That was a new author in Florida, who I'm working with to do a dog lovers' guide there."

"Great." I nodded. I had given her the list of acquisitions I wanted and she was going after them systematically.

Her cat-eye glasses rode low on her nose, and its chain draped around the back of her neck. I thought once again how everyone new to publishing thought they wanted to be an editor, and this was the uniform they wore. I had a stack of résumés on my desk from would-be editors that I had to turn over to Allison for the new editorial assistant position she was hiring for.

"What about the camping guide for New England? Are those guys signed yet?"

"I let them go. They weren't right." She folded her hands and set them atop the stack of file folders in pastel colors. She leaned forward and quietly said, "I've been wanting to tell you this, but I have other ways of determining whether the author is going to be the right one for the book."

"Such as?"

"I'm clairvoyant."

The clicking behind me stopped.

"I can do a kind of psychological scan over the phone when I'm interviewing them about potentially doing the book, and those two did not make it. They would never have made the deadline, and they are not a good match for each other or us. We would be in trouble from the beginning if we signed them."

I hesitated. "This clairvoyance, what do you see, exactly?" I leaned forward, my elbows on the desk now.

"I read people and can see if they are carrying any energy that might make it impossible for them to do the books." She paused as if to assure the room, raising her voice slightly. "I try not to do it at work, except when I'm calling authors, of course."

She picked up the files and straightened them by tapping them on her desk, and then set them down again with her slender fingers.

"I see." I stood and glanced over at Allison, who raised her eyebrows.

"Dave's not sorry to have left, by the way." She hadn't met Dave. She was hired after he had left. "But it seems you'll meet again someday on the Avenue."

"You're quoting Dylan?"

"I have no idea where that came from." She smiled sweetly and as I left, she picked up the phone to call another author.

In just a few months, her unusual methods bore fruit. She had signed all the authors who encapsulated "the right energy" and our expanded list was ready to announce.

* * *

Nearly every week now, I was enlisted to speak at conferences and trade meetings about marketing and promotion. I regularly appeared in print, radio, and television, either for one of our books or as an expert on publishing. *Entrepreneur Magazine* included me in their 40 Under 40 article of up-and-coming entrepreneurs. The University of California Berkeley Extension Program had an overview of book publishing, a one-day course for which I was invited to speak. Soon I was teaching the class at the annex in San Francisco to a class of a hundred with George Young from Ten Speed Press, who, equally frumpy as me in his baggy pants and jacket with patched elbows, provided an overview of the book publishing world and the fashion sense within it.

With the expansion of the Book Festival to the Book Council, our year-round programs were in effect, and the staff there had grown to four. In addition to the Junior Publishers Program, we now had a Read-Aloud Day with the City of San Francisco and small grants for teachers. I had completed the City's Leadership Program. Mayor Willie Brown's office invited me to join a task force. I couldn't stop, the affiliations piling up like mad in a corner in a room already packed with good ideas for Foghorn I couldn't wait to unveil.

I developed the Books Building Community program. We adopted nonprofit partners for each of our titles and, by including a page about them in our books, their logo and mission riding our back covers, each of our titles received promotion in the nonprofit's outreach. We gave them two percent of our profits. For the dog-lovers' companion books, we matched with the SPCA; the hiking books, with the American Hiking Society; and for our park titles, we found the National Park Conservation Association (NPCA).

Soon I became a board member for NPCA and an advocate for the annual March for Parks events coordinated each March/April and the sanctioned event producer for San Francisco's events. Producing and promoting events was becoming my religion.

I drove to Reno for the *Outdoor Retailer* show and presented a workshop to outdoor retailers that included them becoming recreational resources for their customers by carrying outdoor titles in their stores. We partnered with them in a promotion to help build The American Discovery Trail. *Outdoor Retailer* ran an article featuring both me and the press. Our outdoor retail sales were increasing exponentially, and we engaged a sales rep group to represent us while I sold directly to REI, Big Five, and other chains.

In all this, I was possessed by a kind of quantum madness that held neither time nor my energy as finite. I fit Mitch snugly into the weekends when he drove down from Sonoma County, then redoubled my work during the week to make up for those "lost" work hours.

There were incongruities. Starting my second year on the San Francisco Chamber of Commerce Board of Directors, I was headed to the third floor for a board meeting. I stood crammed into the corner of the elevator, driven back by an onslaught of suited executives. The CFO of the brokerage that occupied the top ten floors introduced himself and, discovering I was a publisher, mentioned his dream book—as if I, in my sensible shoes and ratty jacket, could be the broker of dreams for men in three-piece suits with six-figure incomes.

I handed him my card, but then my imposter's syndrome manifested itself as I felt my half-slip slide from my hips—I possessed only one slip and the elastic was long gone. I leaned against the elevator wall to stop its slide. When the door opened, I stood up straight and, murmuring a little *thank God* to myself that the elevator was still jam-packed, I felt the slip drop with a soft swish to the ground.

I smartly stepped out of it, ignoring it like a misbehaving pet I had disowned, and then I wedged my way out of that small space without looking back.

There was no *time* to update the wardrobe, I told myself. But then, I didn't have the inclination, either. In those heady days, I said *no* to nothing, the word *yes* far preferable as it promised to elevate Foghorn's visibility, and my own, with every commitment I undertook.

I doubled down in all my glorious frumpiness.

* * *

I met Mitch at the door of my apartment. I shut the door behind him and slid into his hug and we held ourselves there, resting in the weight of each other. He was a big man, thick chested, his arms still defined by his sports career in high school and junior college, and the years of weight training. Often, he explained to me as we sat down for dinner that evening at our favorite Mexican restaurant in the Marina, that was all people saw.

"They're not seeing you at all, if that's what they see." I said. I met his eyes.

His laugh rumbled out, deep and soothing. "People are easily intimidated or scared. I have to work to make them feel at ease."

"I have that problem a bit myself—with how people see me, I mean," I ventured.

"I can see that. People are probably intimidated by your accomplishments. I have to admit I am."

I snorted. "You're not!"

"I am. I had to talk to one of my friends to help me out. I told him I'm dating a woman who is a publisher and makes way more money than I do."

"I don't make that much money."

"More is more. I'm a butcher, remember? Plus, even if it's a dollar more, as a man you have this idea you should make more. I'm letting go of it. And the publisher thing is a big deal, plus all the other stuff you're involved in," Mitch said.

"The four-page résumé, you mean?" I thought how my love of work had challenged Casey. "I'm glad it's not stopping you from liking me."

"I really like you, Vic." His auburn eyes trained on mine, and I glanced down, then back up. "It may be getting closer to love," he admitted, "which is why I'm going to push myself through all these thoughts about myself not measuring up."

My chest suffused with warmth and I leaned across the table to kiss him. "You measure up."

"I'm still thinking of becoming a drug and alcohol counselor, but of course, that's even worse pay. Will you still like, ehhh"—he squeezed my hand—"*love* me if I'm making next to nothing getting started?"

"It seems like something you were born to do, a way you could really help a lot of people." I thought how I'd come to rely on his help in processing the grief I felt about losing Dave. Despite having Allison and Mitch in my life, I still had a spot only Dave could fill. I missed having my brother around, someone who got my humor instantly and built on it, an alchemy that we alone shared. And now his letters, though regular, were less personal, instead infused with philosophical discussions reflecting his reading rather than our shared life.

I shook my head loose of those thoughts. "Can I tell you about my project now?"

Mitch laughed. "Yes, go right ahead." Mitch offered pretty good council in business too. He was willing to hear about it, at least.

I explained how I was implementing Books Building Community with each book and just that day had talked to the SPCA about our dog-lover's series. I smiled at him.

"Win-win," I added.

"It's like what Ben & Jerry's does with ice cream?"

"Yes, exactly—that's where I got the idea."

"Seems like you can do anything you set out to do, so do it. Now you get to help some people too."

"That's what I'm thinking," I said.

"We'll dedicate ourselves to saving the world." He smiled and this time, he let me pick up the check.

* * *

That April, I tested my new events-as-marketing concept. At six a.m. the day of the first event, the radio producer waved me in. I sat on a high stool while the host delivered a commercial message, and the producer bent a large round mic from a metal arm to my mouth and exited. Bob Bentley was the most uproariously cheerful morning radio host I had ever met. His Saturday outdoor show commanded great respect in our offices, as we could see a direct correlation between an appearance by our authors and book sales. Aberdeen had been a frequent guest whenever a new book of his was released. This was the first time I had been a guest, however. My mom listened from the green room, ready to haul over to the event site with me the moment the interview was over.

Before it began, Bob flicked a switch and addressed me. "It's raining. Is it still on?"

I assured him it was. A green light switched on, and Bob gave me the thumbs up, indicating we were live.

"Good morning this fine April seventeeth. We have showers today but we're thinking that won't stop some of you outdoor lovers. We have Vicki Morgan, publisher at Foghorn Press, here right now to talk about the March for Parks event happening today on Angel Island. Vicki, I understand that this is a fundraiser to help save the park?"

"Yes, it is. Our state parks are under siege, with budget cuts threatening closure. Foghorn Press is producing this event to help save Angel Island. Folks who join us today will enjoy a ferry ride to the park, a hike, a picnic lunch, live music, and receive a copy of John Aberdeen's new hiking book, and he will also lead one of the hikes." I had the patter down.

"So the event is still on, even though it's raining?"

"Yes, it is. In fact," I paused, "I just discovered that it's raining all over the Bay Area, but with one exception. It's not raining on Angel Island."

Bob looked amused. "It's not raining on Angel Island. Metaphorically, you mean?"

"Metaphorically and literally," I replied, knowing Dave would appreciate the metaphor part.

Bob's eyebrows shot up and, catching the humor, he said, "Well, I'm not letting the rain stop me. I'm going myself today, folks, so I'll see you out there." Bob recapped the event for the audience and signed off.

"Not raining on Angel Island, eh?" He smiled over at me.

"I guess we'll find out when we get there." I hopped off the stool. "Thanks for the interview. We'll see you on the ferry!"

* * *

More than two hundred and fifty attendees, adorned with rain ponchos and jackets, showed up. They crammed into the interior part of the ferry as we churned toward the island through the rollicking white caps of Bay water. We had no walk-ups that morning, and seventy of the ticket holders had decided to opt out. I felt queasy from the rocking of the boat, but kept that to myself, looking out to the island in the front, trying to will a break in the rain.

I felt a twinge of guilt again, looking at my mother. Yesterday had been her birthday and I'd had her compiling all the names for the registration table; the frenetic preparations for the event had totally eclipsed any celebration, especially with my father helping Mitch, Allison, and the other volunteers who had set up on the island the day before and camped on the island for the night.

We docked at the pier on the east side and everyone disembarked. I could see Mitch and my dad standing shoulder to shoulder on the pier, baseball caps covering their heads. They had a lot of similarities. Both were gregarious and open to people, something I pretended to be more than I actually was. Both would do nearly anything for me, as my mom had pointed out the night before. My parents liked Mitch, but who didn't like Mitch? His integrity and honesty were obvious to everyone. Not, as I wrote to Dave, a Last Man.

The rest of the volunteers who had camped there piled up behind the two men on the pier and onto the island itself. My dad waved both arms in greeting, like the ferry passengers had arrived at Shangri-La. I loved that about him, his sunny ebullience. I could always trust that my father would exceed even my enthusiasm. He rallied the others and soon everyone was waving at the attendees on the boat, welcoming us to land.

The Angel Island docents in Victorian-era costumes carried themed umbrellas to protect their outfits. I spotted John Aberdeen's cowboy hat in the crowd. The docents would lead most of the hikes, with John leading one group. I walked down the gangway, escorting radio-show host Bob Bentley to greet John. I saw our author Harrison Wolf there too, shorts and undershirt irrespective of the weather, ready to lead a hike. All authors were on deck for this event.

Allison assigned the rest of the arrivals to their docents and they wandered off on two separate trails. The rain had not ceased and, in fact, seemed like it was gathering momentum. I circled up Foghorn's volunteers and staff, who shivered in their blue ponchos. What to do about the band, the presentations? Was there any place with cover where we could stage them? The volunteers had already worked out a site and led me to the barracks up the hill, to an assortment of ruins that had a roof with three walls still standing. In one corner, a concrete floor, still intact, housed the band that was in the process of setting up their sound system.

Mitch and my dad started erecting three ten-foot awnings in an attempt to shelter as many of the returning hikers as we could. The park service brought in a generator for electricity, and it purred steadily in the corner.

Allison stood next to me, surveying the situation. "You won't believe what happened last night."

I motioned her to follow me as I walked around the shelter testing for leaks. "Tell me."

The books had already been dropped off, two hundred and fifty copies of the hiking guide for the giveaway, now covered by a clear plastic tarp. It had been a good idea to have the volunteers here overnight and figure all this out. Everything had changed due to the rain.

"Harrison tried to climb in my tent. Like it was an accident."

"*What?*"

"Yeah, essentially, I work my ass off cooking dinner for our thirty volunteers in the rain last night for two and a half hours on this old stove, so I'm totally exhausted, and he walks up to my tent where I've collapsed and after everyone's gone to bed. I hear the door zipper and I sit up and said, 'Who is it?' "

"He says, 'Oh, Allison, is that you?' like he stumbled upon me by accident."

"You're kidding me. Did he leave then?" I motioned to a few volunteers where they could put up another one of the tarps.

"He said if I was cold, I could join him in his tent."

"Allison, we have to do something about this."

Allison wrung out her hair and retied it in a ponytail. "What can we do?"

We both turned to look up the pathway.

"Oh, my God, are those some of the hikers, back already?" I motioned up the trail and we both looked to see about a dozen people walking fast for the shelter, no docent in sight.

"They're coming," I hollered. I turned to Allison, hearing Dave's assessment of Harrison again in my ear: *lecherous.* "Listen, we have to deal with that guy."

"I know. It's getting weird." She gave me a quick hug and ran off to help the incoming hikers.

Our new public-relations person charged up in a golf cart and ran into the shelter, her head lowered under her poncho. She was in charge of VIPs and lunches. She'd come to the island from the Sausalito side in the small private boat we'd rented for the event.

"Lunches?" I inquired.

At her direction, volunteers started loading them in from the back of the cart. She told me each box had had to be rewrapped in plastic against the rain, which was why she was running late. She had to get back to go pick up our star guest, who was waiting at the boat.

Drenched, the incoming hikers claimed their lunches and books, and found a spot to huddle in the cement bunker. I asked the reggae band to play and soon the music made it impossible to talk. In an hour, we had a hundred or more hunched over their lunches, with more people streaming in.

Not much later, the golf cart zoomed up to the bunker and out hopped environmentalist and actor Mike Farrell, who had played B.J. Hunnicutt on my favorite show, *M*A*S*H*. He ran onto the side of the stage in his bright-green rain poncho and a cheer went up among the crowd. I introduced myself and we conferred briefly while the band finished its song, then I addressed everyone with a welcome and thanked them for being there. I introduced a park advocate, who described the park's special attributes. He thanked the docents and Foghorn, ending with, "I hope you'll come see us again when it's not raining."

"What rain?" I said as I stepped back up to the mic, but no one laughed. "Is Bob Bentley from KGO back from the hike yet?" I inquired into the mic. Everyone looked around, but no Bob. I looked over toward the golf cart, but our public-relations director shook her head vigorously. I handed Mike Farrell the mic and he spoke passionately about our parks for fifteen minutes, the crowd's energy rising in response. After the cheering had subsided, the band resumed.

The rain was slicing sideways now, and the awnings leaned with the pounding wind, the area beneath them encroached by water. People pushed closer together under the cement bunker, but a growing group stood outside the shelter, pelted by the rain, unable to fit inside.

While Mike spoke to some of the hikers, our public-relations person approached me. "Bob Bentley wants to get off the island now. He's over at the pier trying to get on the boat to Sausalito. I told him no, that the boat had to stay there to take Mike Farrell, but he's throwing a huge fit."

"He's just standing on the pier?"

"He's climbed in the boat and refused to get out," she said, shaking her head. "And the boat only holds three people: the driver, me, and Mike Farrell. I don't know what to do." She was a professional pub-lic-relations person, and if she didn't know what to do, I sure didn't.

She shook her head. "It's bad to have Bob Bentley so mad at us. He screams at me every time I see him."

"He seemed so nice this morning. Why's he mad at us?" I said. "If it's the rain—we can't help that." I wondered if our future radio cover-age was in jeopardy.

"He says you misrepresented the weather and the length of time he'd have to be out here. He doesn't think he should have to wait with everyone else, either. He wants off now, he says. He lost it when he found out Mike Farrell was brought in on the private boat, but he wasn't. He's threatening a lawsuit."

"Oh, for fuck's sake." Good ol' boys still popped up everywhere.

"I think I have to have to give him my spot and let Mike Farrell fend for himself once he lands. Otherwise, we'll have a big scene," she whispe-red to me. Mike came toward us, and we both put on a smile. I thanked him and she led him out, both adjusting their ponchos before dashing to the golf cart. I heard her explaining to him that he would be joined by Bob Bentley, and I was sorry that the last thing Mike Farrell would hear about us would be Bob's complaints. But it couldn't be helped.

I turned back to the crowd, but it had dissipated considerably. Where had they gone? I walked outside and looked toward the pier where the ferry had docked what seemed a lifetime ago. Over half of the attendees were waiting there for the ferry to take them back to San Francisco, but unfortunately it wasn't set to arrive for another hour and half. My dad was down there, running up and down the line. A few times, I saw him point back to the bunker where the music still played, but no one budged. The rain drove down mercilessly, and waves slapped against the pier. Angel Island had turned into the *Titanic* and everyone was scrambling to get off.

Later that day, around five pm, the event over, we stood on the dock in Sausalito across from Angel Island and the City, watching the sun finally push through the clouds, the wind now reduced to a light breeze. We'd said goodbye to the last of the participants, cleaned up the bunker, and used the golf cart to haul everything over to the ranger's station, then took the late ferry back to Sausalito. Once there, we loaded our cars and said goodbye to the volunteers who, despite being soaked, seemed happy with their service, hugging us all goodbye as if we'd just come out of a natural disaster in which we'd all been the rescuing heroes.

I walked Allison to her car and she said, "Did I ever tell you that I'm not that fond of humans?"

"Wildlife is definitely not the scary part of the outdoors, I guess."

"Now you're paying attention." She grimaced and whipped her car around and out of the lot, waving her hand out the window. I couldn't blame her, thinking about the incident with Harrison Wolf.

I crossed the parking lot, catching up with my mom and dad, who were leaning against the car, talking to Mitch. They all turned and took me in, like I had interrupted a private exchange of which I might have been the subject. I suggested dinner in Sausalito, partway home for my folks. They agreed with alacrity.

There was a nautical theme to the restaurant, the wheel of a ferryboat sat above us, along with a wooden carving of captain's head, covered with a yellow slicker, protection against the raging sea and the rain. *Irony, so tasty*, I thought.

"Well, everyone had a good time," my dad said after we'd ordered.

I laughed. "That might be stretching it, Dad. I would say everyone survived it, and that's probably the best we could hope for under the circumstances." Mitch took my hand under the table, and I smiled at him.

I pushed my empty plate back after eating. I was waiting for the waiter to bring my mom a slice of cake for her delayed birthday celebration.

My parents sat close together, and I thought maybe the event had unified them, as it had the rest of the volunteers. "How was the camping?"

"Well, since no one brought their rain fly, it was pretty wet," Mitch said. "I mean, we got some sleep, but not much."

"Not much at all," my dad echoed cheerfully. "But we were up early anyway, trying to figure out where to move everything. Good thing we had Mitch here with some muscle."

Mitch laughed. "Yes, I'm good at moving heavy things, like books." He squeezed my hand again.

"We didn't sleep much either. Pre-event stress, right, Mom?" I looked over at her. "And we had to be at the radio station so early." She didn't look worse for wear, but I knew I did.

"Dad, what were people saying when they were on the pier and having to wait all that time?"

"Well, a few were trying to tell me that it wasn't supposed to be raining on Angel Island today. They heard *that* on the radio this morning, if you can believe it." He shook his head. "Some of them said they'd never listen to that radio guy's show again, the outdoor guy, Bob Bentley."

Mom and I looked at each other and, in our exhaustion, started to laugh.

* * *

The dog guidebook to the Bay Area had been one of my more brilliant editorial finds. The author's proposal about the best spots to take dogs won us over immediately. I signed the fabulous illustrator Phil Frank to do the whimsical illustrations, elevating the guidebook to one that screamed fun. Now Sibyl Abercrombie was signing authors across the country for the series and it would soon become our second largest series in terms of sales after the camping and hiking guides.

One morning, the dog guidebook author called me about a theft of her work by another publisher. Luckily, she had set a trap to catch any such encroachment. On an unnamed small bridge on a dog-friendly hike that she featured in the guidebook, she had created a name of her own and put it in the guide. When that same name popped up in a knock-off guide that had just been published out of Southern California with a publisher no one had ever heard of, our author had proof of plagiarism, along with other phrase-by-phrase matches she had discovered throughout. I was incensed, my editorial integrity affronted.

I engaged a lawyer and we went after them. We won. They were ordered to destroy the twenty-five thousand copies they had printed and provide legal proof of the destruction.

Then, only a month later, *we* were in the doghouse. I got a call from another Bay Area publisher claiming that a new author we had signed had pirated one of their climbing books. It was one of our points of integrity that all our guidebooks were thoroughly researched and written by authors who were outdoors people, who had walked every trail, camped in each camp, people who had been there. I was mortified. This author had all the right credentials, except the integrity one. And he was partnering with Harrison Wolf to write the book which encompassed the whole state.

Now I had to call in the new author and fire him. I had to work out restitution with the other publisher. Plus, we had to find a new writer to replace Harrison's partner, and quick. The new edition was due to the printer in just a few months, luckily making the current offending edition obsolete.

"I can write it." Allison leaned forward in her chair, where we sat around the huge conference table. Her hair was tied back and her sweatshirt was stained with sage-green paint from some home project. "You'll have to get someone to replace me here at Foghorn. But until then, I could do both, and our editorial team can pitch in."

"You'd have to work with Harrison Wolf," I said, turning over the idea.

"Which I already do," she said.

"Closer still, like daily contact. As his co-writer, you're on the same level with him and that makes it different. You know how crazy he is around you. It might not be the best for you, or for him, for that matter."

"I can handle Harrison." She smiled quickly. "You know, Vicki, this is what I've been wanting to do. Write my own guidebooks."

"Your own guidebooks?"

"Yes, I've been thinking of a cycling series for the Bay Area, for instance."

I nodded, considering. "That's a good idea."

"Plus, with me, you know I'll do the work. I'll do each climb in the book and you know the work will be my own." She grinned. "Think of all the time it will save. I can get that new edition out in months, so the current one can be replaced. I've already done some climbs with Harrison, so I know how he does it."

I studied her carefully. "You have?"

"I love to climb. He loves to climb. It's a good time to talk to him about the books when we're climbing." She glanced out the window, then back at me.

When I didn't say anything, she asked, "So you agree that I should step in and take over the guide?"

"Yes, do it, baby." I stood up. Allison was capable of anything. This rock climbing skill was one of those extreme ones though. When had she learned to do that? "You can get everything organized in editorial so the team can function without you until we get someone else. It could take us a while." I paused at the door. "Do you want to tell Harrison, then?"

I realized I hadn't had many conversations with Harrison since Allison had taken over editorial—or since the night on Angel Island. But she said she had handled it. For that I was grateful, but I was also a bit nervous. You had to monitor Harrison Wolf to see which direction he was headed, especially now that he had multiple books with us. Once Allison became an author, that would be a job I'd have to reclaim.

* * *

The American Booksellers Association in muggy Miami came and went. I took a crew of four, who manned the booth while I had meetings. At the show, I confirmed content licensing deals for our outdoor titles with Microsoft and also Encylopedia Brittanica, who was exploring the new technology of CD-ROMs, both deals providing cash to the bottom line.

A successful show. I was on automatic pilot for most of it, my head continually returning to California and what I would need to do now that Allison was leaving.

SAN FRANCISCO, 1994

Published: 22 titles
Partners: 5
Employees: 18
Annual sales: $1,600,000

Vince had recently brokered a trade with the local sports station KNBR, trading our sports books for airtime so our commercials now ran on the sports station regularly, prompting Ferris Wiley to remark, "I'm hearing about Foghorn Press everywhere, every time I turn on the radio."

We worked with the Giants, renting VIP suites and inviting booksellers to the game. We worked with the 49ers and staged signings with the NFL Alumni Association before the games in the Candlestick parking lot. I jumped in and coordinated Book Council publishers' donations to a nonprofit resulting in a halftime photo on center court at a Warriors' basketball game. With Vince at work, it seemed we had finally discovered the sports-history marketing formula. Vince, our very own good ol' boy, represented us to the Bay Area Sports Hall of Fame, the professional teams, and sports media.

Because of increased visibility, we'd stepped up the publication of the sports histories, contracting sports writers across the country to write them. We planned to tap into the marketing potential of each team and use writers from those regions to help us do it. I thought about who might handle the editorial organization of that project best and realized it was probably Sully, my ex now of several years. I hadn't seen Sully since our divorce was final, our business always trans-acted by phone and as briefly as possible. But I knew he had remarried, because I'd had to sign off on an annulment so they could marry in the Catholic Church.

Vince and I met Sully in my office. When Sully walked in, he had his one-year-old son tucked under his arm like a football. I didn't know he had a child. It surprised me—and surprised me more when he handed the boy over to me to hold at the start of the meeting, the scent of baby powder traveling with the child. I bounced him on my knee gently, noting his chubby legs and arms, and his green eyes so much like his father's. I thought how history might have gone differently if Sully had gotten sober when we were together. But alcohol hadn't been the only thing that had made him a bad pick for me, I reminded myself. I handed the child back.

I explained how we wanted Sully to manage the freelancers we were bringing in for the new collector's editions. When the meeting was over, I thought that perhaps family had changed Sully—he had been so affable. Vince shook his hand and left. I handed Sully the con-tract I'd drawn up.

"I expect a bigger advance than what you've got here. I'm doing all the work," he said, looking at the contract.

"You already agreed to it over the phone," I said, astonished, then more astonished at myself for believing him to begin with. He was always affable in front of other people I remembered, but when we were alone, the true Sully came out. I felt a wave of appreciation for Mitch.

I sought my publisher tone. "That's a higher number than we've budgeted for and makes the books much riskier. The advance already compensates you for that work."

"It's a deal killer," he said, issuing me the grin that included the dimple. The baby made a gurgling sound.

I hesitated, tamping down my rage, so easily accessed all these years later. "A bigger advance is a deal killer on our end."

We both sat. Then he set the contract on my desk and then ges-tured impatiently for me to hand him the pen. When I did, he snatched it and signed the contract, leaving it there as he tucked the baby under his arm and left.

It felt momentous. A small internal victory that I would have shared with Dave if he were here. *Codependent, Never More* I'd tell him in my next letter.

* * *

Ambition, however, is a different beast.

"The annual book trade show this year is in Los Angeles, in our home state," I ventured in a meeting with Allison and our CFO. We were sequestered in the conference room for my next big idea. It was Allison's last week in the office before she became a full-time guide-book author. "I want to create a California experience for all the bookstores and media who are coming. We'll have a camping tent, a climbing wall, a golf green, book signings with football players, there on the convention room floor. All the activities matching our title list."

They both nodded, following along.

"To do this, I want to take ten booths, a whole corner."

"We usually take only one," Allison said to the CFO, who nodded. He had one ABA under his belt, the Miami show of last year, and, now in his second year at Foghorn, he was better able to track the financial costs of each of our promotional endeavors, as he had something to compare it to.

"How much does a booth usually cost again?" he asked.

"For where we want to be, on the main floor, about five hundred dollars for a ten-by-ten," I said.

"So you want to increase that by nine booths."

"That's right, I need a thousand square feet," I said. "There'll be a huge banner from the ceiling that will read *California Experience*. I'll send out invites to all the booksellers and media and invite them to come by. It's going to make a big statement."

The CFO looked stricken. He glanced at Allison. "I'm putting together the new spreadsheet for the bank so we can get our credit line up to pay for the spring list. How much money are you going to need?"

"I can do it all with ten thousand dollars, I think. I'm going to need to bring a few people with me. Vince, for sure. Maybe one of the interns."

We met the next day to review the money we'd need to implement the *California Experience*. Our CFO produced some spreadsheets from his folder and fanned them out on the conference table. "I'm having some trouble making it work for May and June, because so many printer bills are coming due those months."

I nodded, looking down at the month-by-month cash flow statement he had created. Both May and June dipped into three-digit negatives.

"Is the credit line in here?" I asked.

"This one has the current credit line figured in. This line here." He pushed another sheet at me and pointed and I looked at it. Still negative.

I looked up at him. "What can we do?"

He smiled warily. "I guess you could just do a regular trade show and not the *California Experience*. Even without it, we're going to be negative and we're going to have some challenging months."

"I'm pretty sure that's not happening." Allison looked over at me. "In fact, I bet Vicki's already reserved the space."

"We *are* doing it. We just need to find the money," I said. "Can we up the credit line, or maybe defer some of the printer payments?"

He gathered all the sheets and left, his shoulders hunched. "I'll try to rework it."

"I can just hear what Dave would say," Allison said. "But I'm not going to stop you, and our CFO certainly isn't going to, either. Everything you want, he does. You want the numbers to look a certain way, he'll do it. It's not strictly honest. But that's how we got that last credit line."

At the mention of Dave, I winced. I'd been fighting his voice in my ear ever since I'd had this idea. "I pitched the bank last week on including Foghorn in their ad campaign featuring their clients. If we're picked, they will have a bigger stake in our success."

"It's too bad the trade shows don't generate immediate income." Allison drummed her fingers on the table. "We probably can't keep relying on the bank's good faith or our CFO's pyrotechnics for the long term."

Allison wasn't like Dave; she would never confront me directly, though she would state her objections. But afterward, when the sales as she predicted didn't add up to all we spent and I was unable to point to any big gains from the extravaganza I had staged, Allison was a full-time guidebook author and I was answering only to myself.

SAN FRANCISCO, 1995

Published: 22 titles
Partners: 6
Employees: 20
Annual sales: $2,100,000

How big a canvas could I have? I was looking for a site for our third March for Parks event with the National Parks Conservation Association. Coming off the last two years' events, my imagination envisioned an event of epic proportions. It worked on me throughout November, and I finally called the Golden Gate National Recreation Area to set up a meeting to talk. With their buy-in, I'd do it. They said yes quickly, based on the relationship we had forged the year before.

With the Presidio of San Francisco becoming a national park, coupled with the twenty-fifth anniversary of Earth Day, it would be big. I'd reassemble the volunteer event crew from the previous year and then I'd back off all my other extracurricular responsibilities. Kathryn, at the Book Council, had begun to have a similar expression to the one Dave developed when I started working for the Book Festival. My attention had turned from the Book Council to March for Parks and it frustrated her, as I was still the president. I reminded her that her frustration would be short-lived, as it was my last year.

I needed someone to cover me at Foghorn Press. An associate publisher. I immediately thought of Carla Tribetti of Sun Books, who had become a good friend after our stay in the apartment in New York during the trade show a few years before. She had the experience to elevate Foghorn. I drafted a letter with my proposal, including a battle cry to come and reinvent publishing with me. I offered her a stake in the company to sweeten the deal. A month later, she was installed in my former office in the Boiler Room.

I moved my office to the last available space, a room on the third floor in our 4,400-square-foot building. My view of downtown San Francisco from Potrero Hill was panoramic and epic, an ideal hub for launching the biggest event of my life.

* * *

At the same time, Mitch and I were ramping up in our relationship. At the start of the year, we had moved in together to a loft South of Market. A contact of Mitch's from the Bay Area men's group he belonged to had offered the place to us while he went on an artist's retreat to Baja. The generosity of the low rent made it impossible to say no. So, though Mitch had declared himself not a City person, he moved to San Francisco.

The enormous paned windows overlooked the on-ramp to the Bay Bridge, where thousands of cars passed every hour. The loft was three blocks from the Townsend Building, where Dave and I had first worked together at Foghorn, and just a block from the Embarcadero waterfront. The loft was industrially hip and open, with inlaid floors and a fourteen-foot ceiling, a complete upgrade from the Marina district apartment where I had spent the last four years. Furnished with a white overstuffed couch, loveseat, and chair; a steel-topped table with wicker chairs; and enormous modern art pieces—one covering an entire wall with heavy black textured paint and a small figure diving through the blackness—our sophistication level shot up the moment we moved in.

Mitch and I knew we were going to get married, that was understood. But Mitch would not propose and ignored my proposals of marriage, which I had begun uttering now in the third year of our relationship with a little too much ferocity and eye contact. After a while, I stopped talking about it and took direct action. After sex, I assumed a headstand, directing spermatozoa down the vaginal highway to my waiting ovaries. At thirty-six, I had begun to have a daily dialogue with my hormones, admonishing them to settle down so I could concentrate on work.

But the seesaw was starting to tilt in the favor of the hormones. I secretly began taking prenatal vitamins and stocked up on pregnancy books. It was my new favorite topic. Mitch fended me off, suggesting that rather than have children and then make the necessary life changes, it would be better to make the changes, then have the children.

He was waiting for that, he said, and when I didn't understand, pressing him again, he offered, "You can't simply add another bullet point to the end of your résumé that reads 'Mother.'"

That made me angry enough to stop discussing it.

Then, in April 1995, the busiest month of my life, the twenty-fifth anniversary of Earth Day swinging like a giant and deadly wrecking ball toward me, he did want to talk about it. Mitch had followed his dream and taken a job as a drug-and-alcohol counselor at St. Anthony's Farm in Sonoma County; his was the late-night shift. He got off at two a.m. and, now that we were living together in the loft, he drove the hour home through Sonoma and Marin counties, across the Golden Gate Bridge and across the City on his motorcycle, usually crawling into bed nearly frozen at three a.m. Usually I heard him come in through the heavy front door, but this time I had not. I had finally fallen asleep after tossing and turning, the event coming up Saturday churning through my brain. I was worried we hadn't generated enough publicity, and all day I'd been on the phone talking to media about it. Mitch slid into bed and wrapped himself around me, the chill across his skin burning against the heat of my sleeping limbs.

"Vic," he whispered, jostling me awake.

I ignored him, breathing rhythmically as if still asleep.

"Vicki," he said, sitting up on his elbow and shaking my shoulder gently.

I opened my eyes slowly and turned toward him.

"I've been thinking and I think we should go ahead and get married." I didn't say anything for a beat, and he added, "Like next week."

"Next week. What?" I sat up. "What?"

He smiled. "I was just thinking it's time."

"It's been time for the last year," I countered, "in my humble opinion, of course."

He laughed. "Okay, shoot me. Now I agree. Would you rather be right or be happy?"

"Look, I'm not going to come off this crazy event and then run out and get married. You made me wait all this time, so now we have to have a plan. And that plan has to have a three-month lead time."

"Okay, we'll do it in June."

"Okay, June."

"No wedding."

"Agreed. We already did that with other people. We're too old. We should just run off and get married."

"New Mexico? Or maybe Arizona. Make it a vacation?"

I pondered the choices. He was taking me off my game. I had an event *this Saturday*.

"How about we talk about it after the event?"

He laughed. "With you, it's always after the event, after the event."

"After the event," I said loudly, flopping back onto the pillow.

"Getting married is the big event, bigger than the twenty-fifth anniversary of Earth Day. Or, at least, maybe someday you'll think so," he said, settling back into the covers.

"Oh, my God, after the event, Mitch." I flipped over and drew the pillow over my head, but I still heard him laughing.

* * *

The event team I assembled had met with the Golden Gate National Recreation Area staff at Fort Mason to review the plans for the Twenty-Fifth Earth Day Celebration weekly for the last several months. We now numbered sixteen team members and had directors for each aspect of the day, from the concert to the hikes to the cleanup projects to the festival to the food vendors to the kids' activities to publicity. I had disappeared from Foghorn life completely and taken Foghorn's public-relations director with me, though she was still expected to do work for Foghorn.

I borrowed money from Foghorn to fund the event, but assured Carla that it would be repaid after it was over. Earth Day 25 was designed to not only publicize the Presidio's attributes as a new national park, but also to provide $50,000 in seed money to the Golden Gate National Recreation Area to jump-start some of the projects that would transform the concept into a reality. I was confident the event would generate that from the concert ticket sales and the exhibitor booths we'd sign up.

When I ran through the borrowed cash in February, two months before the event, I borrowed more.

The night before the event, I stood on the Fort Scott Field above Crissy Field in the Presidio. It was six thirty p.m. and I'd just completed a television interview from the site. The crew's van was winding out of the park past the concert area where we'd erected a stage and fencing. My dad and mom were there, of course, helping mark the spots on the grass where each of the vendors would go.

Mitch was down below, setting up the tenting for the registration booths. I'd be up all night, I knew that. Even as ready as we were, I'd be in the pre-event state of worry, running through everything again and again. To me, every event at this point felt like I was about to descend a giant slide, and that once the descent began, there was no stopping it. In this event, more than any of the others, it seemed as if everything was at stake.

I realized I was hyperventilating. The dangers of an unchecked imagination spread in every direction. My dad walked up to me, his shirt sweaty from work, and upon seeing him, I burst into tears.

"It'll be fine, baby doll," he assured me, enfolding me in a giant hug. But I couldn't stop. "You'll be fine, it'll be fine."

I tried to soothe myself by telling myself that at this time tomorrow, it would all be over. When I finally looked up—my eyes felt puffy and raw—the deserted site was dark and there was nothing left but to come back in the morning.

* * *

The next day, the weather was event-perfect. I dashed between the three stages we had set up. At the free Global Food Fest and Earth Fest, children gathered to put together a thirty-foot-wide picture puzzle of the Earth. The smell of Aidells chicken apple sausages wafted over the seventy-five booths, showcasing food vendors as well as businesses with environment priorities such as Aveda, Ben & Jerry's, and Tom's of Maine. Radio and television stations, plus environmental groups from The Earth Day International to World Environmental Network to the Yosemite Fund; and government entities such as the U.S. Forest Service to the U.S. Environmental Protection Agency were on hand.

We had environment-related exhibits as well. Folks could visit the Rainforest Expo, which recreated the atmosphere of the tropics and included more than one hundred live exotic plants and animals. They could peruse the Endangered Species Art Gallery. They could walk through the United Nations' Fifty Flag Walkway—created by children from recycled pillowcases—or join in the United Nations' celebration of their commitment to environmental sustainability. They could take home the twelve-page event program we'd created, stamped with the official Earth Day commemorative pictorial cancellation issued by the U.S. Postal Service.

Gazing out from the concert stage to the thousands of faces, I welcomed everyone and then gave the mic to environmental sage and author David Brower to address the reason we were all there. Five name bands played the main stage. These were interspersed with speeches and calls to action for Earth Day from representatives from the Golden Gate National Recreation Area, The National Parks Conservation Association, AmeriCorps, the City of San Francisco, and Earth Day International.

Allison was in charge of the March for Parks hikes and restoration projects, with hundreds of participants. Occasionally, her voice sparked on the walkie-talkie with an update that everything was going well. John Aberdeen led hikes. Harrison Wolf managed a climbing wall. There were no improprieties from him.

I had put Mitch at the concert gate as the ticket collector / bouncer. When I checked in with him, he pointed out some people ducking under the far fence which had been built around the five-acre concert site. We watched as more came in on the other side of the field.

"What can we do about it?" I was alarmed. Ticket admissions to the concert had been my main hope for revenue, but the grassy space was so large, there was no way to regulate it. I called the Park Service to see if they could help monitor it with their team, but they lacked the man power. Every person was already assigned to some part of the event.

"We can't do anything about it," Mitch said finally.

And then it was over.

* * *

More than fifteen thousand people attended, but of course I had budgeted for double that. The success of the day that the rest of the team reveled in wasn't a conversation I could enjoy, knowing the numbers. I alone bore the huge financial loss. Embarrassing me, too, was the minuscule amount of money raised for the park. I told myself that the restoration projects and the publicity had benefited the Presidio and that was something. But it wasn't what I had promised.

When I had borrowed money from Foghorn and others, I had never considered a scenario in which I wouldn't make enough to pay that back. Now it was all my personal liability, a crushing $120,000 worth of debt. I wondered how I was able to convince so many to allow me to take this kind of financial risk. Dave, if he had been here, would have been at me relentlessly to defend my decisions.

When I tried to discuss the event with Mitch, he refused to talk about it beyond making his point that the stress and exhaustion hadn't been just mine. He was uncharacteristically stern.

"Using yourself up in pursuit of your big ideas is your choice. Using up everyone around you in the process is a whole different thing." He was referring to himself, my parents, Allison, everyone who helped me because they loved me and wanted to support me. I had learned that my father, a diabetic, suffered insulin shock that day. The cost of the event to my relationships and the people I loved ate at me. That cost was one that, until now, I had never calculated into anything I had ever done.

I stayed home for a few days, trying to think myself out of the situation. No solutions came. In the months following the event, as I struggled with how I might pay what I owed, an interior dialogue began cycling through my brain, questioning my ability to regulate and have limits for myself. Sorting through my years at Foghorn, I could find no proof that I had ever exercised this ability or listened to anyone who had tried to stop me. My optimism needed balancing with common sense, but was common sense even in my arsenal of character traits? I thought about my parents' car spinning out on the Grapevine and the trailer hanging over the cliff.

Suddenly, I couldn't trust myself.

*   *   *

If I hadn't just come off the fiasco of Earth Day, walking into the Grand Ballroom of the Hyatt in downtown San Francisco as one of the honorees for the annual Women's Entrepreneur of the Year breakfast that May would have been the culmination of so many dreams. Foghorn had a table for eight and sitting there, in addition to me, was our CFO, our public-relations director, Sibyl Abercrombie, and Vince, along with some of our editorial and production team, young and obviously uncomfortable out of the office.

Vince had gathered the event programs featuring my photo and bio for the Hall of Fame entry table he'd created in the Foghorn lobby. They were stacked next to him. He had been on a mission for months to promote me and the company.

He addressed everyone at the table. "It all adds up. What'd I tell you? Vicki's been featured in *Entrepreneur Magazine*. Costco just had that big feature story in their magazine and *Outdoor Retailer* wrote up Vicki and Foghorn, too. It doesn't stop. It just goes through the roof and we're all making it happen."

Vince was feeling what I should have been feeling, but couldn't. Despite his membership in the good ol' boys club, I liked Vince. And while he was always angling for his own advantage, he managed to do a lot for Foghorn's benefit, too. In him, I recognized myself, always working the angle, but believing in something greater too.

As the event hosts ascended the stage to the podium, I checked my jacket pocket again, feeling for the script for my speech. The night before, I had rehearsed my speech to Mitch, who generously did not mention the irony of being honored for community service, especially community service that had so completely kicked my ass. Usually when speaking, I used talking points and spoke extemporaneously, but for today's speech, I had memorized what I planned to present, the script there merely for security in case I drew a blank.

I still believed it was good business to give back to your community. It was a formula that worked, except with extremists like me, who gave past their own capacity to give. Or maybe, as Dave might have said, created from their ego rather than reality. I left those caveats out, though.

I had never spoken to an audience of a thousand-plus before, and I had been up most of the night before worrying about it, so when the vice president from Bank of America started to introduce me, I tightened. I took a deep breath, then dissociated from my body, a trick I had used in the past. I wasn't Vicki in this instance—I was an actor sent to play her part. Then, when she called my name, I sent that actor to the stage.

When the talk was done, I heard the applause and then a rush of flash photos followed me to the middle of the stage, where they handed me the glass trophy. I could see my name had been etched upon it and after a series of handshakes with a number of assembled Bank of America VIPs, I was done.

"Great job," Vince whispered loudly across the table when I took my seat. I scanned the Foghorn faces gathered there. I wished Mitch was there, Allison too, and my parents, and even Dave, but just as quickly I was glad they weren't. I turned to watch the *Entrepreneur of the Year* award winner take the stage. I thought I read in the program her sales were $10 million annually, and looking at her at age forty-five or so, I could see that she'd been at it a lot longer than I had. A feeling of empathy for her washed over me. I wondered if it had cost her all it had cost me to run a business, to earn the right to be recognized like this. But then, she probably had been willing to pay that price.

And now, strangely it seemed, after all my efforts to grow my empire, I was beginning to understand that maybe I was no longer willing.

* * *

Because Mitch and I planned to run off and get married in June, and I was still in shock from the massive debt I owed on the Earth Day event, I sent Carla, our new associate publisher, to the book trade show in Chicago, the first I hadn't gone to since starting the company. I had a concept for a stark, modernist booth, with just a podium-high table in the middle of a ten-by-ten carpet with a large sign featuring our name hanging from the ceiling above the table. Dramatically simple and impactful. Exactly the opposite of what I'd tried to do previously at the ABA in Los Angeles with the *California Experience* booth and where the expenditure was never recouped in sales as I had hoped.

Carla called me from the hotel the night following the setup day; apparently the image didn't translate.

"Everyone kept coming by and asking if our booth got lost in the shipment," she said.

"Did you hang the banner above the table?" I asked, perplexed.

"Yes, but it just looks like we don't have a booth at all."

I reviewed it again in my mind's eye, but before I could say anything more, she said, "I just ended up renting a booth from the convention center."

"You did?"

"It was all I could think to do. The show starts tomorrow."

I surrendered. I still hadn't told Mitch exactly how much money I had lost, and we were getting married in two weeks. The number had burrowed into my head and no amount of spinning it as a promotional or public-relations cost could diminish it. My optimism had backfired now twice in a row, first with the *California Experience* and now with the twenty-fifth anniversary of Earth Day.

The first had been a company expense that everyone had tried to dissuade me from assuming. The second, in an effort to show my confidence in the plan, was a debt I took on personally. Then there were all those books I'd signed for Foghorn based on their promotion potential—the Olympics book, the World Adventure guide, a Hawaii fitness book—that lost money. I couldn't second-guess Carla, when at this point I no longer trusted my choices.

* * *

"No gifts." I said, inviting some of the Foghorn and Book Festival staff to the celebration party at my parents' home following Mitch and my return from our elopement in Arizona. "No gifts," I said over the phone to the few girlfriends I still knew from high school. I was pretty sure I was one of those terrible brides who had never sent thank-yous for the gifts for my first wedding and I didn't want a repeat.

"You guys got married in a balloon!" said Allison, presenting us with a card to which a balloon was attached. We were sitting on my parents' backyard patio; the veranda was warm but a breeze and the cool drinks made it nice. My dad and mom had outdone themselves in the yard, getting ready. My dad had put in a cactus garden and, with my mom's help, a new set of rose beds separating the garden from the lawn. Everything felt lush, green, and open.

Mitch and I had to tell the elopement story a few times.

"We were looking for a minister when we were downtown in Sedona, and then we found out he was also a balloon pilot. We got married five thousand feet up."

My dad shook his head in disbelief and said to Mitch, "I can't believe you got her to get married in a balloon. She does not like heights."

"She's got the top floor up those metal stairs in the office; you can see right through to the first story when you go up." Allison laughed. "She takes those pretty slow, I notice."

"She won't go up on the roof at the loft," Mitch said. "If I do get her up there, she stands ten feet from the edge. Says she feels like she might accidentally tumble off."

Everyone laughed.

"Jeez, fellas," I said. "Maybe we could talk about someone else's complexes?"

"Now that you're married, you can talk about Mitch's issues," Allison prompted.

"Right now, he's perfect. I'll let you know in ten years."

"Imagine how many issues you might have if you were married forty years," my father interjected, joking and peering over at my mother.

She was sitting next to him in one of the porch rockers, and her lips pressed into a tight smile. "Right. Anyone want anything from the house?" She rose and took my empty glass. Mitch took a big swig of his soda and handed her his as well, thanking her. She squeezed his shoulder.

I grabbed the discarded plates from the picnic table and followed her to the sliding glass door and inside.

"Everything okay?" I asked, taking the glasses from her and placing them in the sink. "You seem a little tense."

"No, no, everything's fine," she said with a sigh. "I'm happy you're here." She looked out the garden window at everyone gathered in the backyard. "I wish Dave and Brian could be here too."

"Well, it was pretty impromptu and it's just a barbecue, really."

She stood over the sink and turned to me. Her face grew serious and I noticed the lines under her eyes.

"I'm happy for you and I'm happy for Brian. You both made good matches for yourselves." My brother Brian was getting married to another professor at the university where he worked.

"Who knew, Mom? Who knew you could marry for love?" I rinsed a dish stacked next to the sink and handed it to her at the dishwasher. "I don't know why Sully and I even got married. Maybe it was just the next thing to do on the list."

I peeked out the window to see Mitch, my husband, laughing loudly with the others. No low volume for that guy. No cynicism. How was it that he wasn't a good ol' boy?

"Your dad and I probably weren't the best example." She frowned briefly and then started sliding in the plates and glasses as I handed them to her.

"You love each other," I said, but she didn't answer, her lips tightening.

I tried again. "You loved each other once, right?"

"Better get back to the party," she said, and she shut the door to the dishwasher, twisted the knob to turn it on, grabbed my hand, and pulled me back outside.

* * *

When we drove home, it was after nine p.m. and, as exhausted as I was and happy about the party, I couldn't shake that undercurrent of sadness I'd picked up from my mom. I kept stealing glances at Mitch, poking at him with questions I wasn't verbalizing.

Finally, as we were turning up Lombard in the City, he glanced over at me. "What is it?"

"Do you think we could ever get divorced? I mean, we both are divorced so we know it's a possibility."

He turned right along the waterfront, the City brightly lit on our right and the shadows of the water vibrating darkly on our left. "Let's make a pact to never say the D word, or ever think that's an option."

"That's all it takes, huh?"

"That's all it takes."

* * *

After we parked the car, we rode the elevator up to our loft. On our front door, an official sheet of paper was taped at eye level and as we got closer, we saw it was addressed to Bill, our landlord, Mitch's friend who was now living in Baja.

FORECLOSURE NOTICE. Legal Notification. You are in default...

Mitch spent the next three days trying to get Bill on the phone. When he did, Bill confirmed he'd been in foreclosure for months. He confessed the rent money we sent him supported him in Baja. He felt terrible about it. Did we want the furniture? We could take it. He was sorry. He'd send someone to collect the paintings.

Sensing an opportunity as we climbed into bed that night, I said. "Let's move to a place where we can raise kids."

Mitch laughed and poked me in the side. "Now you're getting the order right."

* * *

After the honeymoon and barbecue, I returned to the office to find my usual workload being handled by Carla, as I had hoped when I hired her. I liked sitting up in my office at the top of the building where I was free to make my schemes. But none was occurring to me following my huge event loss, so the job I assigned myself was to look for new markets. This was a risk-free endeavor, it seemed to me, and would benefit Foghorn by providing more revenue. I kept an eye on acquisitions of new titles and our strategies there too, meeting with Carla and our new editor-in-chief, a woman Carla had hired, to discuss where we were headed with the outdoor recreation and dog series and the sports histories.

I resisted any new ideas I might have had to expand beyond the regions we had already targeted. I had no new events planned.

At our business meeting, Carla pushed a bill in front of me across the conference table. Our CFO had brought a tall stack of papers with him. It was a thirty-five-dollar bill for some office supplies.

"Pay it," I said.

"We can't," Carla leveled with me. "We can't pay it and pay all the others, too. That last Costco return hit us really hard."

"Everything's starting to come due," our CFO said, blinking furiously. "And we've already pushed off the printers as far as they'll go. After ninety days, they won't print anything for us on the new list. We'll need to get different printers or cancel books."

"No canceling books," I said, "What about the credit line?"

"Maxed."

"Payroll?"

"We've got that put aside for the next two cycles, but look here—this month might give us some trouble." He pointed at the red ink coming our way.

"What we really need are more sales," I said. "Can I have the numbers on all the top accounts?"

Carla pushed a spreadsheet over to me. Everyone seemed to be performing fine, I could see, but often a well-placed call from me would drive another order. "I probably can get another five thousand to ten thousand dollars from these accounts," I said. "I'll make the calls this afternoon."

"Let's meet daily until we figure this out," Carla said. "We have that meeting with the bank next week and they are going to give us trouble about this." The bank had chosen Foghorn to feature in their marketing campaign and now Foghorn was splashed on billboards and ads throughout the Bay Area. That might motivate them to provide more leeway, I thought.

"I've contacted that local sports publishing company about buying the publishing rights to the sports books, and there's interest," I said. Last year's upsurge in production costs could be directly correlated to the cost of printing the sports histories as part of that expansion, and sales hadn't been enough to offset it. Carla had pulled me aside to discuss whether the costs overrode the benefits, and had encouraged me to ask around and see if there might be a buyer.

Vince still advocated for the sports series, probably wondering if he would have a job without those books. Ever since I had consulted him on a possible sale, he now accosted me regularly in the halls to quiz me on what was happening with the sports books.

"Keep selling them until I tell you to stop. Regardless. Even if we sell the rights, we still have inventory to sell," I told him.

At the door, Carla shook her head, channeling Dave. "Those books have always been a thorn in Foghorn's side."

Our CFO looked up at me, hopeful. "How much could we get for the series, do you think?"

"Enough to get us through a few months, but it might take me a month or more to do the deal, and that's if I don't get any grief from Sully." I frowned. "Look, I know Foghorn is still holding onto some of those Earth Day expenses and I'm trying to pay that back."

I thought about the four personal credit cards I had applied for to cover most of the debt. It was a stretch to think I could get another, but I was trying.

I stood up suddenly and they both looked up at me.

"I've got to get to work." I backed out of the conference room, then grabbed some coffee from the kitchenette in the lobby and beelined it up the stairs, unafraid of the gaps below that opened to the first story. I was going to turn this around if it killed me. After all, work was what I did best.

* * *

In late July, Allison had set aside three days to do eleven hikes in Yosemite as part of the new edition of the California hiking guide. She invited me to go with her. I realized in the thirteen years I had run Foghorn that I'd never actually gone hiking or camping. The only vacation I'd had was my recent elopement trip with Mitch. Allison now worked from the trails or her car, and occasionally from home. We hadn't seen one another in weeks, and that had been part of my reason for saying yes. And I was stuck waiting for the sports publisher to get back to me about the sale. The timing was made better by a thought I'd had that Foghorn might actually do better without my interference, anyway.

She picked me up at the office and as we headed out the Bay Bridge, I caught her up on all the Foghorn news: My shopping the sports books to a buyer, our wrestling matches with the bank, my stepping in to drive sales, and my plans for financial redemption by finding more markets. Hours later, we were still chattering about Foghorn, as befits two business partners who were now more like sisters.

She drove, the car descending through the granite terrain, on a windy road that would take us to the valley floor. Allison pulled the car over, a cliff tumbling below us, and we got out. I stood, my back to the car, heart racing, while she walked to the edge, pointing out the spires and lakes below, naming each of them.

"We're headed over there for the first day. We'll do three hikes there tomorrow. Then we'll go further south." I followed her hand along the big expanse. "We'll end up there for the night, so we can do another trail in the morning. You'll love that one; we'll hike along a waterfall. Did I tell you about my new idea for a book? A guide to waterfalls!" She grinned.

Two days later, we had stripped down and were lounging in the waterfall near the trail and under the low pines. I stretched my legs out, feeling icy water undo the soreness in both calves.

"So, not to ruin this beautiful experience, but how's it going with Harrison Wolf?" I asked.

"Well, it's getting weirder. He actually drove by my place the other day, back and forth, really slowly, and that freaked me out."

"Was your new boyfriend there?"

She nodded. "I think that's what's triggered all this. I may have to file a restraining order."

"Oh, no. How will you work with him?"

She sighed. "That's the problem, isn't it?"

I hadn't told her about the message that Harrison Wolf had left on my machine just two weeks ago, an act of desperation on his part.

I told her now. I could still hear her voice on the recording he sent me prefaced by his emphatic, 'I know she loves me, just listen.' Then obviously spliced together, the words from her mouth now condensed into one sentence, 'I love you, Harrison.' I had listened twice to confirm that splice and then saved it on my answering machine—as evidence, perhaps. I leaned back in the water, submerging myself below the neck. "He's not well."

"Oh, my fucking God. Erase it, please. I never want to hear it." She shook her head and stood.

I thought about how she had never cussed until Dave and I schooled her in the Morgan lingo, which demanded such adjectives.

"He has a studio." She was silent. "It's such a great house, huge, but he lives there by himself. Think of all the money he's made from his Foghorn books."

"More than you and I will ever make," I said. "How strange is that, given all the risks we have taken as publishers?" I hesitated. "You know, we could make that kind of money if we sell it."

She looked at me. "Sell the company? Are you thinking about that?"

"It's spinning around in my brain. Especially as the money gets tighter."

"Might be harder to sell if they knew one of our top authors is, well, not right."

"It took us a few years to figure it out. Maybe I don't bring it up."

"Uh-oh." She nodded at the rock where we'd set our clothes and the backpack with our lunch. Allison had unzipped the pack and a brown bear lumbered toward it, and then stopped to sniff. We both watched silently as he plunged his head in the pack and emerged with the sack.

Allison had warned me against carrying any actual food in our pockets because, as she pointed out, "Bears are only looking for one thing, and it's best if you don't have it." When he'd gone, taking the food with him, Allison said, "At least he left our clothes."

On our final day, I was keeping up with her on the trail, lagging only ten feet behind as she cut through the path down to a miniature lake. Mounds of rock crested throughout the smooth surface of the water, islands we could wade out to for a rest.

"I don't know if we ever really got over Dave leaving Foghorn," she said as we lay on our backs on one such island.

"It's been three years," I said slowly. The warmth on my face and body was hypnotizing and I felt the hurry-up energy so natural to me dissolving.

"It's not the same, though, is it? It isn't like it was when it was just us three, trying to build a publishing company from scratch."

I opened my eyes and shut them again, the brightness of the day blinding. "It's never been the same. You're right."

"Remember how he kept trying to get you and I to commit to writing everything down on those sheets and following a plan? The 53 Steps. He's so brilliant, I think it's hard for him," Allison said.

"We didn't make it any easier, I'm sure." Maybe it would be more honest to say, *I* hadn't made it any easier. But his relationship with Allison had been one more reason to leave.

"Remember how he had me read aloud all of *Tropic of Cancer* when we were seeing each other, so he could record it and listen it to it later?"

It was good to hear her acknowledge that she and Dave had been together.

"Maybe if I had listened to him, we wouldn't be in the financial stress we are now. It's possible," I said.

"But we wouldn't have grown either. We'd still be doing seven books a year."

"But profitably." I laughed.

"It drove him crazy that you couldn't make publishing into a science. Like you couldn't lay everything out, and by doing that, by preparing, you'd know how it was going to go."

"You can't do that with life, either. Much as we'd like to sometimes."

I sat up and picked up a small stone and tossed it in the water, watching the ripples as they reached the shoreline thirty feet away. Talk of Dave still gave me that achy feeling that something was amiss.

"He's living in Germany, working on a catalog to sell American books to the Germans."

"Is he still with that German woman he met?" she asked.

"Yes, it seems serious. He might be settling down like the rest of us."

I didn't want to shock her, but I had been waiting to tell her. "I think they are having a baby."

Allison's eyes widened.

"I just got a letter from him about it, right before this trip." I added, nudging her with my elbow, joking, "When he's in, he's all in."

She snorted and I chuckled. Then we were quiet a moment, picturing Dave married with a baby. I heard the jump of a fish in the water and peered down my nose to see the ripples widening across the surface.

"You know that woman, Jody Jacobs, who died last spring? She ran the PR agency?"

"I've heard of her. I think you used her once for something, right?"

"Yes, she publicized the Booked for Adventure party one year." I lay back down, my palms resting on the hot surface of the rounded slab of granite. "I wonder sometimes if she got herself into a corner. What happened if she just wanted out of her business, didn't want to do it anymore, but she couldn't think of any way to get out? I mean, everyone respected her, she was getting tons of business, and then she gets cancer and dies in a matter of months."

"Are you trying to say she took herself out by getting sick?" Allison said.

"It's possible, yes. And if that were true, it's because she ultimately lacked the courage to be anything other than what everyone thought she was."

Allison was silent.

I hesitated. Jesus, there was so much to tell her and, working as we did, neither of us made room for that anymore. It had helped when we were in the same building.

"There's my dad, too." I hadn't spoken about this to anyone, even Mitch. I had been carrying it around with me for weeks—ever since my mom called me at work, her voice so hushed that I could barely hear her through the receiver. And she had asked me not to mention it to my dad. But then, I hadn't talked to him either since the Presidio event and our wedding barbecue, and then it was just about the event and our balloon wedding

I started again. "My dad had a kind of nervous breakdown or something like it at his school. He had to actually go home and not come back. It was the last month of school, but he couldn't wait for it to end, so he retired. He's taught for thirty years, considered one of the top teachers in the whole school district. No retirement party or anything. Just one day, gone."

"What?" Allison shook her head. "Why? Why do you think?"

"My mom told me he said it was the kids; the kids all changed and got mean. And that's probably part of it, but what if it was the same thing? What if he just wanted to be someone else and couldn't because everyone wanted him to be the same person he had always been?"

Allison reached over and gently tapped my arm. "You let me change. And you let Dave change."

"You guys both had the courage to change." I drew my arms over my forehead, blocking my face. "A lot of us don't."

* * *

I'd heard other publishing companies were selling. Distribution was getting more difficult. If they didn't sell, they were aligning themselves with larger publishers who could solve any distribution difficulties. It made me nervous. Maybe I needed to act now. At the very least, I needed professional advice. I needed to know how to sell a publishing company. Now that PGW owned part of Foghorn, Ferris Wiley sat on the Foghorn board of directors and came to our monthly meetings. At the end of the last one, I asked for his recommendation, and he gave me the name of Calvin Walker.

Calvin Walker hailed from the peninsula, home of the dot.com phenomenon. He was an investment portfolio and a business consultant. I signed him on for a large daily fee for consulting with us once a month and, if everything went according to plan, a stake in the company. He joined the board of directors, too.

He assigned me the job of writing a business plan we could shop around to potential sellers. And two weeks after he'd made the assignment, I had it, a fifty-page document that outlined Foghorn's core businesses, our list of titles, our potential for growth, a comparative analysis of like businesses, and a section on our competition. Our CFO got the numbers together for me. Then we worked on the presentation, converting our information from the business plan to slides with graphs and charts that documented our claims. And I started to approach leads, regularly reporting back to the people who needed to know at Foghorn.

Vince stopped me in the front foyer on my way into another meeting. "Anything you need to tell me?" he said, nodding his head toward the conference room.

"I'd tell you if there was," I said, though I realized as I was saying it that I wouldn't. We couldn't let any of the employees know.

"Who's the new guy?" he asked, referring to Calvin. His suit and tie weren't the usual Foghorn attire. "Not trying to take my job, is he?"

"No, Vince. He's a business consultant, helping us to expand the line and grow."

"That's good." Vince stood a bit longer, looking in. "My youngest is graduating from high school this year. I don't need any surprises."

I went into the conference room and slid the door shut. Carla stood and drew the curtains over the glass.

I stood at the head of the table. "Here's who I've approached so far." I read off the list.

A murmur of approval went around the room occupied by Ferris, Calvin, Carla, and our CFO and our public-relations director, all with a stake in the company. "I'm open to other leads you might have, too, but I think this is a good start. The East Coast publisher got back to me within a day of receiving my letter, so I sent them the business plan. If they are interested, they'll send someone out to look at our books."

"Due diligence," said Calvin. "Did they ask you why you wanted to sell?"

I repeated the line we'd all agreed upon. "We need outside capital to grow."

"Sometimes they ask the owner directly to see if there's another reason," he said.

I pictured myself telling the interested publisher that my mothering hormones were demanding their due. I probably could have because I knew her personally, but I never would. I hadn't told the Foghorn team that, certainly. I hadn't let it slip to my mother and I might have stopped mentioning it even to Mitch. What was that all about? Feminist shame? Now the need was barely audible, even to me.

A month later, the East Coast publisher sent someone out to go through the books with me and our CFO. They were interested, but might need to wait six months until they had the capital.

I called Calvin. "Should I keep going with more leads? I don't want to count on them and then have it all fall apart with no one else waiting in the wings."

"I recommend it," he said. "By the way, Ferris Wiley called to check in on how it was all going. I didn't tell him about the East Coast publisher because I wanted to talk to you first, since that's the only one of the three he might view as competition."

"Meaning?" I said, curious now why that might matter.

"He told me that distribution is really such a low-margin business that they are thinking of branching out into publishing themselves."

"Starting one, you mean, or acquiring some?" I asked.

"Not sure, but he was interested in the payout for PGW on Foghorn once we sold it. It explains why he's been supportive of the sale, anyway. That's been bothering me, since you are one of the bigger publishers they distribute. You know, Foghorn is in the top ten publishers they represent, in terms of sales volume."

I thought about that for a minute. That was something. Ten years ago, we had started as one of a couple hundred publishers, undistinguished from the rest.

"If we sold it for the price we're asking, PGW would get a third." I paused. "I could tell the publisher that PGW is interested in purchasing the company. That might push them to make a decision earlier."

Calvin laughed. "You're a scrappy entrepreneur, Vicki. You'd say anything to make the sale."

"Not anything," I said shortly, thinking how just a few years ago I might have considered that a compliment. And though it could very possibly still be true, it wasn't how I wanted to see myself anymore.

* * *

Because of the Earth Day event loss, I had a tax refund coming. It was the only positive from that event, I told Mitch, who now liked to marvel about how he had married me anyway, despite the debt, as if his craziness potentially outweighed even mine.

I could have paid off some of the amount we owed with the tax refund, and that was initially what I intended on doing. However, sitting in my office in San Francisco, I had another thought. That amount could also be a down payment on a house. With my new credit cards, monthly payments on the debt were happening and it might be better to have a debt and a home with write-offs than just the debt. It might even be viewed as a sound financial decision. But of course, for me, it was an emotional one. I needed a home. I needed a new life. A normal one with weekends off, maybe a self-care regimen, doctor and dental appointments, friends.

The house was a three-thousand-square-foot Victorian on a half-acre corner lot that was set back from Bodega Avenue in Petaluma, a town located on the southern edge of Sonoma County. It was situated on a busy road that eventually turned into the highway leading to the coast, but we were moving from a loft perched on the Bay Bridge on-ramp, so it seemed like an upgrade. When we walked in through the back door into the kitchen, the antique stove, the retro '70s chandelier, the pale-yellow paint with its wainscoting and dated wallpaper, and the worn linoleum floors overwhelmed me. I burst into tears, causing the real-estate agent to step quietly back while Mitch approached, touching my arm.

"What? What is it, Vic?" Mitch bent down to try to see me. I had my hands covering my face.

"I don't know. It's like a family lived here."

"A few generations of family," the agent said discreetly from across the kitchen. "This belongs to the Appleton family, and the couple is retiring now to a smaller home."

We wandered through the rooms, marveling at the odd features, a closet there, the small bathroom under the stairs with no windows, and upstairs, the huge room lined with mirrors that had once been a ballet studio. The living room had two sets of bay windows, one in the front of the house overlooking the small porch and the road, and one set on the side, overlooking the redwoods in the yard.

I wanted it desperately. And apparently, the Appletons wanted us to have it, agreeing to finance us on a second loan despite our debt. Mitch's parents lent us money so we could increase the down payment.

The big open Victorian house in this rural town was ours.

As I commuted, an incongruity grew. I turned it over in my mind on my drive to work as I stalled in the sluggish lanes of 101, crept across the expanse of the Golden Gate, and chugged through the stop-and-start of Van Ness, the main corridor crossing the City. I felt myself separating from Foghorn. Not like I had done with the events and promotions for the March for Parks or the Book Festival. Those enterprises fed my entrepreneurial spirit, and I could justify them as part of the promotion of Foghorn. With the purchase of the house and the move, I actually felt a stirring that might have been closer to resentment.

I contemplated my options each day as I drove. As I entered the City from the Golden Gate Bridge, descending onto Lombard which ran along the Marina District, the location of my old apartment, I thought how life might look if I sold Foghorn.

I'd have money; everyone involved in Foghorn would. We'd be out of the financial problems we had now. At the next light, I turned right on Van Ness, and pictured the company sold and my time opening as my own. I saw Mitch and I vacationing, a dog with her nose thrust out the window, the wild breeze of a highway tumbling down all our throats. I saw myself canning, picking herbs, scooping up laughing children, tending house. With the tap of the brakes at Division nearing the office, I saw myself writing my own books in the small office off the kitchen I had claimed for my own.

PART IV

THE BIG THING

SONOMA COUNTY, 1996

Published: 20 titles
Partners: 6
Employees: 20
Annual sales: $1,900,000

I awoke with a start. Foggy, I sat up as much as I could, an uneasiness radiating from my abdomen. I inhaled. The ragged edge of my breath caught at my throat, and I felt something foreign, and my hands crept to my mouth to discover a breathing tube. At that second, that became my sole concern. Not that I had come in for an exploratory outpatient surgery to take a sample of the mass they had detected in my abdomen following a sonagram. Not that I was in the hospital when I should have been home.

I didn't know I had been hospitalized now for four days because the surgeon had accidentally cut my femoral artery. My femoral artery. I didn't care about any of it and that last part would only be relayed later, along with the information that I nearly died on the table with the blood loss. I just wanted that breathing tube out. I swallowed, launching a sharp pain in my dry throat. The constant ache was unbearable.

My mom sat at my bedside. I couldn't talk so I pointed to the tube. She shook her head sadly and whispered, "Tomorrow."

I turned to see Mitch on the other side of the bed, and he met my gaze, his expression inscrutable, and shook his head. "Tomorrow."

Tomorrow was impossible. I swallowed in agony again. The doctor came in and they both turned to her. I gestured to her, mimicking the tube coming out. She said, "Tomorrow."

As they started talking, I processed that. Didn't they see? Tomorrow was impossible. I moaned in frustration. They stopped talking, glancing at me, then began again. Then I heard a word come floating up out of the conversation they were all having without me, but obviously about me. That word was *cancer.*

Cancer is the kind of word that can close all the doors you have always left open. Life up to this point for me had been a series of open doors, rooms left unvisited but existing all the same by the promise each one held. By the time I got home from the hospital, the sound of doors shutting solidly, decisively, followed me on my slow wobbly trek to the bathroom. In the tall mirror, I eyed my lumpy stomach, where it was stapled together from the first botched surgery, invasive bruises purpling my skin.

My next surgery to remove the tumor was pending. While I waited for that, I sensed cancer propagating in the minds of others. Its mention was like the first smoke detected in a house that would surely burn to the ground. I did not reach out to try to dispel that notion, as I might have believed it myself. A month later, I was back in the hospital for that eight-hour surgery. The surgeon stood over my bed in the recovery room as I fought my way back to consciousness, reporting cheerfully that this surgery had been successful. It had cleared me of the ovarian cancer, though it had required the sacrifice of my ovaries, cervix, fallopian tubes, and uterus.

Back at home recovering, I sat in the long quiet. The sorrow was abiding. The freedom was ecstatic. The irony was impossible to reconcile. I was emptied, weak.

* * *

Dave missed the hospital stay, but got my request to see him through my mother as I drifted in and out of consciousness in the hospital bed where the IV fed me after the second surgery. A week after I came home, he came to our house from Germany, where he now lived. I sensed him standing in the doorway of the family room. I lay on the couch, the same one I had purchased when I moved into the Marina apartment so long ago, my feet facing the French doors that led to the patio and the brilliant light of morning.

I did not know what day it was. The turn of events had wiped my calendar clean, shaking out the days from their structure of times and appointments and deadlines. Every day since I had returned home from the hospital had been a surprise, a reinstituting of the basics, like breathing, walking, and sitting.

"Hey, Vic," he said quietly, stepping into the room.

"Oh, Dave." I turned to see him, but turned back to the wall, my face convulsed with an emotion I didn't want him to see.

He sat in the armchair and waited.

"Did just you arrive?" I managed to say.

"Yes, Muriel stayed in Germany. She's not feeling so well now that she's pregnant."

At the mention of *pregnancy*, I put my hands to my face, covering it for a moment, breathing hard into my hands.

"How are you feeling?" he asked gently.

I kept my hands where they were. "It's rough, but better. I'm doing better. Ovaries are overrated," I added, a hysterical chuckle tumbling out of my throat.

"Yep, they are the bastard organ of the body. They make you bleed all over your sheets and cost thousands of dollars annually in household cleanup. I'm glad I don't have them," Dave offered lightly in Morgan parlance.

"Me, too. Because there's the hormone factor."

"More murders can be tied to the hormonal influence of ovaries than any other organ." Dave nodded, trying to make me laugh or at least smile.

I said, "I strongly disagree with women's activists who believe women who have periods are fit to run the country. On certain days, we will push the button and go nuclear."

"You managed not to push the button at Foghorn all these years."

I studied him to see if he was being ironic. "Buttons have been pushed, believe me."

We sat a moment, looking out into the yard. The trees overhung the deck and the willowy branches tossed their heads rhythmically with the breeze.

"I want you to come back to Foghorn and take over. I can't do it anymore. You have to do it. I was trying to sell it. You can still do that. Everything is ready."

When he didn't reply, I said, "Dave, are you hearing me?"

"I'm hearing you, man. I'm thinking."

"You have to come back here and make it happen."

"They probably won't like what I'd do."

"That doesn't matter now."

"You'd have to give me control to make all the decisions," he said.

"I give it. You have the control to make all the decisions."

Dave sighed, bowing his head a moment. "You're sure? Because if I move back, I'll want to run the company my way until it sells."

"There're all sorts of problems now with cash flow and the finances. It all needs to be scaled back. Only you can do it."

"Okay, I'll talk to Muriel tonight and see what we can do."

I nodded and smiled at him, relieved that I could let go, finally. And with this solution, Dave would return to the States. "You'll bring Muriel and the baby here, too."

"Yes."

"You can live here with us, upstairs. We can set the office up there, too."

"Mitch won't mind Foghorn taking over the house?"

"It's already taken over our lives for years, so I don't see how it's any different."

"Vic, I'll go down to the office in San Francisco when I leave here and see what's up and what's needed."

"Thank you, Dave."

He leaned down to hug me, and he let me hold on.

SONOMA COUNTY, 1997

Published: 14 titles
Partners: 6
Employees (Volunteers): 5
Annual sales: $1,700,000

D ave made the preliminary arrangements to move the company up to Sonoma County, and then he went back to Germany. They waited for the baby to be born, and then all three came to live at our house in Petaluma in the new year.

Dave had miraculously uprooted the business as it was in San Francisco, letting the employees go and loading up the inventory and some of the used office furniture. Old books were now stored in our basement and the newly published were in the carport behind the house. The ballet studio in our Victorian was transformed to an office, and all of a sudden, I was upstairs, sitting at a desk, making sales calls to our outdoor accounts. In that wide-open room where little ballerinas had done their pliés, we had managed to get three desks, a room divider, and a number of dinged file cabinets and bookshelves, remnants of a greater time.

On the same floor as the office, Muriel and Dave and baby Mia were settled in the one bedroom with their own adjacent bathroom. But Muriel spent her days below. She was a ferocious cleaner and I could hear the vacuum cleaner running in the family room beneath my feet. She'd already done the dishes, scrubbed the kitchen floor, and wiped down the cabinets. My idea of housecleaning had always been a simple effort to address what was most visible. Cleaning *underneath* or *behind* had never even occurred to me. Since Muriel's arrival, she had had plenty to do because of it. I felt a certain shame, but my motivation for life itself was so stunted that I poured the two hours' worth of energy I had into the business before simply sitting at my desk and moving papers around.

So we began again. But in the mornings before I climbed the stairs to the office, I went to Muriel, who had already determined the next cleaning project, and stood with the broom or a rag in hand and Mia in the bent of the other arm. I lifted the child into my arms, wrapped the plush white blanket over her feet, and walked out onto the backyard path that wound through our half-acre property. Her six-month self blinked at the lemon tree I pointed out, the yellow orbs brilliant as a children's pop-up book against the faded boards of the shed. I adjusted her so she sat on my hip, and she reached out to bat at the swollen fruit nearest us. I snapped it off and gave it to her and she put it to her mouth, her eyes widening with the deep scent. We bent over the fish pond, watching the bolts of orange flit across the bottom, the crown of her head filling my nostrils with baby shampoo.

The pressure of her weight against my chest warmed me in a way I had never felt anywhere else. A kind of madness descended over me for a moment, like it did each morning before I had to go back into the house and resume work. I allowed myself to imagine she was my child.

* * *

It was the end of the month and our sales were off, so I had been on the phone all morning asking for orders from our biggest accounts. I heard myself pitching the new edition of the camping guide and upselling another hundred books. My specialty was always asking for more, bumping up the sale one notch higher. I called over to Dave, "Another order from REI. Getting close to the goal."

"Keep going, Slim Bob. You're hot." Dave looked up from his computer.

I looked at the chart I had constructed for myself. The sales goal was at the top, and every time I made a call, I took the marker and made another line closer to it. I leaned forward on the desk on my elbows, my fingers crossed, and I pushed my thumbs into my forehead. I was tired. Deeply tired. I shut my eyes.

Dave's chair scraped along the linoleum.

"I'm going to go check on Muriel and Mia a minute," he reported from the top of the stairs. He stood there a moment. "You okay?"

I jerked up. "Good. A little tired, but good."

I heard his steps receding down the stairs into the kitchen. "There's my girl."

I listened a moment to hear Muriel's response, but it was only a murmur.

I picked up the phone line and held it to my chest. The buzz from the receiver roared in my ears. I set it back down in its cradle. It was all too much.

When I picked it up again, I felt the heft of it in my hand. Extending my arm, I let it hang there a moment, the buzz insistent, before lifting it to my head and slamming it against my skull twice, the hard edge of plastic launching a bump and bruise that I would revisit for days. It was something safe to feel.

* * *

Dave stood with a clipboard for our end-of-month inventory ritual. His face glowed in the garage-port light, divinely white. Above him, the funnel of light harbored a thousand insects swarming the bulb at the top of the post, while a misting rain absorbed into the sponge of darkness. The hair receded on Dave's head in two arcs at either corner of his forehead. It was wet and shiny and his glasses had specks of water on them from the short walk from the back door to the carport where we had the books temporarily stored.

The rain dripped from the tarp we had thrown over the awning. On the high side, Dave had dug a trench and now, as the rain picked up, the water started to trickle to either side of where we stood.

"This is not a long-term solution," he said. "Bad for books."

"Yep." I nodded. I listened for a moment, the slap of the rain insulating us from the cars that churned by in front of the house.

He handed me the clipboard and I took it and pulled the pen from behind my ear. "Ready." I stepped into the carport onto one of the pallets we had lined the carport with to keep the books elevated off the gravel.

It took us just a half hour as PGW had most of the inventory now, the rest delivered with everything else in the move north when Dave had made the break with San Francisco months earlier.

"Have you talked to Ferris about buying the company? They'd probably just buy it after you get everything in order."

"Not yet. I'm thinking we should get some space north of here, in the industrial part of Santa Rosa," Dave said.

"Warehouse space?"

"Warehouse and office. We don't need to be paying PGW all that money in storage each month. It wouldn't be bad to get the office out of your house either."

Dave had been making the decisions for the company for the last six months, so I nodded.

"It'd give you and Muriel and Mia more room upstairs anyway."

"That's the other thing." He paused, taking the clipboard back from me and staring at it a moment, before meeting my eyes again.

I heard Muriel push open the screen door and yell for Dave.

"Right there," he hollered back. "We're almost done."

He turned back to me. "Vic, Muriel wants her own house, and we found one near Mom and Dad."

"You're moving out?" I turned to the house and saw it was lit from top to bottom, every room shining in the rain. It was a huge structure—bigger than Mitch and I needed—a large rambling family house with rooms that sprung off each corridor. You could wander the many rooms and even get turned around in them. I thought of the office space upstairs. Now what would it be?

I glanced at him. "When?"

"We put an offer in on a house today. After we get settled, I'll start looking for space for the business."

I followed Dave into the house, the screen door snapping loudly twice behind me. Mitch was at a men's meeting somewhere. I pulled out one of the wicker chairs, my elbows resting on the kitchen table, my hands clutched together, covering my chin and mouth. Muriel was feeding the baby at the head of the table, a bottle bobbing vigorously against Muriel's hand as she sucked. Dave slid into a chair next to her and squeezed her small feet, which bounced with the rhythm of the bottle.

I congratulated Muriel on the new house and waited. She glanced at Dave and, flushing, began to describe it to me: the open space, the backyard, the wood floors, the one level, the kitchen cabinets, the work that needed to be done planting grass in the front yard, and perhaps some paint.

"I hope you get the house, Muriel. It sounds perfect."

She beamed and Dave smiled back at her.

* * *

I turned off Todd Road in Santa Rosa and drove down a country road. The left side was open to the fields, indicative of what the county had looked like before all the enterprisers had come in, replacing grazing pastures and orchards with the metal buildings now lining the right side of the road.

Dave had handled most of the move himself. Mitch and I helped load the books into the truck from our carport and basement. I actually hadn't been much help—still unable to lift anything, according to the doctors—but I directed Mitch and Dave when a piece of furniture came too close to a corner or a wall as they moved it. They had wrangled the desks down the stairs and out onto the driveway, where the furniture sat like an outdoor office on the pavement until they were loaded into the U-Haul. We had done this move a million times, Dave and I.

Dave's and Muriel's stuff had gone out a few weeks before, but there hadn't been much, and they moved everything by car. They had to buy a bed, though we offered them our guest room setup. Muriel wanted everything new, and hers. I couldn't fault her for it, but it worked on me, too. I don't know who had been waiting at the other end to help unload their stuff or the business furniture. Probably my dad.

But here it had been two weeks, and I still hadn't made it up to the office.

I turned the car into the driveway and followed a line of corrugated metal warehouse doors, counting to five before I found ours. Foghorn Press, our old original plastic sign—still a vivid blue—was attached to the glass door. Dave had found it somewhere and repurposed it. The warehouse door was rolled up, and when I got out of the car, I could see the boxes stretching back one hundred feet, each book on its own pallet with plenty of room to walk around. In the front, by the chain for the roll-up door, was a table with the packing materials for shipping. The UPS sign read *YES* and rested against the opening, visible to the truck that would come that afternoon. I stood gazing inward for a minute, before I pulled back and went in the glass door to my right. A tinkle of bells activated when it opened, announcing my presence, and Dave popped out of an office on the right to greet me.

"Hey, Vic!" Dave practically shouted. He reached forward to hug me, "Check this out! See who's here!"

As with each of these warehouse spaces, the corner had been built out to accommodate offices and there were three small rooms, the entry in which we now stood leading into two others. Dave's office was in the front. His desk dwarfed the space. Another room forked off his and I peered in and found both of my in-laws sitting at desks, one against the back wall where a window opened onto the warehouse, and the other against the wall to my right.

I stopped in the doorway. "Whoa!"

My father-in-law was in his mid-sixties and had been an accountant all his life, and even though he'd been retired for nearly five years, he still wore the approved accountant uniform: black horn-rimmed glasses and a pocketed shirt with short sleeves.

He grinned at me, "Well, hello there, Vicki."

My mother-in-law, formerly a bank manager, sat at the other desk, bent over a stack of invoices, her right hand running the adding machine in an undulating whirl that stopped when I came in.

"You're lending yourselves to the cause, I see." I bent to give each of them a hug. "I knew Dave would find good people to help him. I just didn't know it would be both of you." I thought about how my in-laws had camped outside my door the entire two weeks I had been in the hospital. Every day they had come and sat there, guarding the door, daring the cancer to advance. They were loyalists, like Mitch.

"Professionals, and they work for cheap, too." Dave laughed. "As in free."

"All in the family, too," I said.

"That's the best part. I'm going to give Vicki the tour." Dave escorted me out.

I followed him over to the shipping area, where Muriel had magically appeared. She had a tape gun and was applying it zealously to a box of books, then her lean arms quickly snagged another box, filled it with books, and sealed it. The labels were all lined up on the plywood table, ready to be affixed. She paused a moment and grinned at me, then grabbed the next stack of books.

"Muriel does the shipping now." Mia was asleep in a car seat on the concrete floor next to her, undisturbed by her mother's wielding of the tape gun and the ripping sounds that echoed through the warehouse. I thought about waking Mia and bringing her along with me on the tour, but Muriel would most definitely disapprove. I imagined the heft of Mia's little self on my hip.

"You're going to like this," Dave walked back into the warehouse. I followed him. He turned right and behind the stack of books was a desk, and there sat my mother.

"Oh, my God, what are you doing, Mom?"

"I'm editing the books. Well, proofreading, really, and also checking facts."

Dave beamed at me. "She's really good at it, too. All that experience at the stock brokerage—she's got a great eye for the details."

"You left your job?" I was both shocked and delighted.

"She wasn't too thrilled about the place she worked at anymore, so she retired. I think it was easy for her to do, right, Mom?"

Mom and I exchanged a glance that told me that she was making another one of those mother sacrifices she had built her mother career on. She had on her brave, we'll-face-this-together face.

"You didn't call Brian in from his teaching post in Washington, did you?" I turned to Dave.

"Just to help move some of the furniture and generate a hernia or two, but he had to get back." Dave paused. "I'm joking, of course."

"Of course."

"Dad helped move the stuff into the warehouse and he comes each afternoon to help me do inventory and move stuff around," Dave said, scanning the pallets. "That's why it's so organized now."

"Morganized, up and down, and all around."

"And now we come to your spot."

We walked to the back of the warehouse, where an alcove had been created between two pallets, the rear of the space against the corner of the warehouse. There sat my old desk with the previous month's goal sheet taped to the top of it and a plastic two-shelf in-box in the corner that was full of papers. The phone sat there, ready. The chill of the warehouse was catching up with me and I would have to grab my jacket and a Grandma blanket from home for my knees in order to work here.

But just as suddenly, I knew I couldn't work here. It was too much, this going backward and starting again. I peered up to the ceiling, where the fluorescent lights buzzed mercilessly. Jesus. How to tell Dave? I felt incredibly tired and leaned back against one of the pallets stacked with books as Dave talked about the new Spring list and how we needed to get all the initial orders in, especially for the new camping guide.

The baby woke up and her crying filled the warehouse for a minute, until Muriel stooped down and picked her up. I heard her murmuring to her and in the ensuing quiet, the buzzing from the lights reasserted themselves and I felt faint.

"I've had to cut back some of the books. Harrison Wolf's guides for instance." He chuckled. "Vic, you all right?" Dave stopped talking. He patted the chair, my old chair, where I might sit.

"I'll come back tomorrow and start, not feeling so good today." I retreated a few steps and then turned, walking through the warehouse to the lit opening of the roll-up door, Dave on my heels.

"Love you, Mom, love you, Father-in-law, Mother-in-law," I hollered back into the building, "Bye, Muriel. Thanks, Dave. It looks really great here. Great." I walked to my car and when I pulled out, I saw Dave standing in the doorway, watching me. I raised my hand in a backward wave and drove, waiting to cry until I hit the freeway that would take me back to my home.

* * *

It took Dave two weeks to realize I wasn't coming in to work. I deferred for the first week, citing exhaustion, but by the second week, I could only communicate by not communicating. I didn't call. I didn't go. I pulled myself from the deep covers of the bed and saw Mitch off to work, then climbed back into bed, thinking I'd read Salinger's *Nine Stories*, but sleeping instead. The steady purr of cars passing the house let me know the time of day. The sounds of elementary-aged kids screaming in the schoolyard across the street as they chased each other or as they flew across the monkey bars or soared in the swings punctuated the naps I took in the backyard in the afternoon. Suspended in my own washed-out grief, lying on the lounge chair, I watched the sun cut through the tree above me, the soft light shifting across the deck.

"Vic, are you coming?" Dave's voice shot through the phone at the end of the second week.

I paused a minute on the line. "I can't right now, Dave."

"You can't right now, or you can't ever again?"

I sighed and looked out the front door at the string of cars waiting for the light. It turned and they all pulled forward, and I dropped the curtain.

"I don't know."

"Vic, you've got to say the big thing. Say it and then I can go get someone else to do the marketing. If you don't say it, it hurts everybody."

"I don't want to say it. I don't want to feel it, either."

There was a long pause on the other end. "So you're saying it."

"I'm saying it. Okay, yes, I'm saying it." I paused, looking for some comic relief. "Hear me now and hear me later."

"Okay, I'm hearing you, man."

I felt a crying attack coming on. "I'm sorry," I managed and hung up quickly.

Dave sent a check at the end of the month with a note that read:

Vicki. Remember how you supported my philosopher days? Here's a monthly check that isn't much but should get you through. We can take it off your ownership percentage if you want to keep it coming for a while, until you figure out your next big thing.

Love, Luke Thrasher

SONOMA COUNTY, 1998

Published: 20 titles
Partners: 6
Employees (Volunteers): 5
Annual sales: $1,700,000

M itch sat on the edge of the bed, watching me. I pushed up and tried to smooth down my hair.

"What?"

He glanced up at the window above the bed and I noticed it was dark. "Just got home and you didn't answer."

"Sleeping. I was sleeping."

My pregnancy books, a library of twenty or more volumes, were scattered on the floor, dinged and scuffed, and he looked at them carefully.

"I threw them in the trash, but then I thought someone else could use them, so I dug them out again. Maybe Muriel, but she doesn't need them." I sniffed.

"What do you want to do, Vic?"

"Now, you mean, or in my life? Because, right now, I want to go on sleeping." I shut my eyes for a moment and when I opened them, he was still looking at me. Mitch was the epitome of patience.

"It's a very big house," I said, shutting my eyes again. "I'm almost forty," I added. His fingers brushed gently across my cheek.

* * *

Sometime early that spring, my energy started to return, and I had a sense that I actually might live free of the cancer. I started to pace my house. I walked around the bottom floor from the living room to our bedroom to the long hall to my office, then through the kitchen and then dining room. I went up the stairs, unoccupied since Dave and Muriel and Mia had moved, along with the business, to Santa Rosa. I walked to the front window overlooking the street where I could see the playground for the elementary school. In just a few minutes, the kids would come rushing out of their classrooms shrieking and calling to one another. Mitch had his job at St. Anthony's, but he had taken another, working at a friend's deli to make up for the income I was no longer generating, so it seemed I was perpetually alone.

Adoption is not a simple process, but I thought I could use my skills to tear through the obstacles. Learning the lay of the land was the first impediment. Fly to China and adopt a child from an orphanage? Implant your husband's sperm in another woman and wait for nine months? Get on the list for a newborn? All those required time and patience and money. I, of course, had none of those. I had to have children and I needed lots of them now.

We enrolled in the foster / adoption program through the state. There was a class, inspections, references from our friends and family to check out, and forms, lots of them. When it came time to fill out the forms, I checked the box that read three or more.

In May, we had a phone call.

And in June, they miraculously arrived. Three children—two girls and a boy, siblings ages seven, four, and two. Our children. With their presence, I felt new air finally return to my lungs. The long, melancholy breath I had held for the last year expelled and was gone, and joy, a kind I had never experienced before, not even when I married Mitch, coursed effortlessly through my limbs.

Every day was a perfect day for bananafish. For imagination. In the drowsy summer afternoons, we'd all crowd onto the lawn chair which was folded down to fit us, a boat upon the sea, each child tucked snugly against a different part of me, the baby situated in the middle of my lap while the waves crested around us. We'd see the bananafish. We'd feed the dolphins off the side, the birds that landed, and spot distant whales over by our neighbor's fence. Other times, I told them stories, evoking each of their names as I cast them as heroes in Candyland, riding the secret passage in the closet to land on a pile of marshmallows, formulating chocolate bark boats to take across soda rivers.

If I dozed off or stopped too long, one of them would cup their small fingers around my face and lean into my eyes, their forehead pressed against mine, and say "Mom!" My breath would catch when they said it. Every time they said it, whenever they said it.

I happily made them breakfast, lunch, and dinner, and gave them snacks. I helped them dress, tied their shoes, brushed their hair, made sure they brushed their teeth, changed the youngest's diaper, administered Band-Aids and comfort. I sat beside the bath while they played, three small beings in the giant Victorian tub. I washed their hair into frothy hats and gave them beards, carefully rinsing so no soap got into their eyes. We walked to the playground at the empty school and swung on the swings, then walked through the school corridors, peering into windows and imagining a coming school year. We played the piano and sang and danced in the big, open living room. I was alive, present. Mitch came home from work and found us piled on the sofa in pajamas, riveted by Disney's *The Little Mermaid* on the television, and then we'd all go off to bed. How easily I had moved into the ecstatic present-tense world inhabited by mothers; a world of stories, bedtime, baths, snacks, and play. Not once did I feel time passing.

* * *

It was nearly nine thirty p.m. when the back door swung open and Dave strode in. I stood in the kitchen and looked at him. I realized I hadn't seen him or the rest of the family for a few months, so immersed was I with the kids. Mitch was at a men's meeting, due home soon.

Dave's lips were tight and his face pale. "I need to talk to you, Vicki."

I sat. The kids were asleep upstairs in the nursery bedroom we had made of the old ballet studio. I got up and walked over to the door that opened to the stairs and shut it gently, before taking a place at the table again.

But Dave did not sit. He paced the tile floor from the stove to the wall and back while I watched him. My heart churned in my chest.

He turned and placed both hands on the table and leaned forward. "Why are you trying to sell the company?"

I didn't speak immediately. I realized someone at PGW had probably mentioned it to him, that I had called to ask about the possibility. Ferris Wiley had never been discreet, or maybe Ferris assumed I'd told Dave everything.

"Why now? We finally have it rolling again and things are going well." He stopped and looked at me. "I mean, Jesus, Vicki."

I began, "You know that I've wanted to sell it for a few years now. You know that's what I was trying to do before I got sick. And I had companies that were interested. PGW has always been interested. They own shares."

"That was before I came all the way from Germany to take over the company, which you asked me to do. That was before I moved the business back up here. Before I got the whole family involved in helping turn it around."

"It'd help everyone to sell it. We'd all have money from the sale. Mom and Dad, you and Muriel. It'd be great," I reasoned, turning my hands up and resting them on the table.

"It wouldn't be great, because we wouldn't have the company. I have been working to turn this whole thing around, and now that I'm on the verge of doing it, you want to step in and take it away."

"That's not what's going on, Dave," I said. "You said you'd look into the sale of the company when you started, but you never did. Mitch and I need the money for our family. We need to pay off debt we have from the company. We've been struggling to pay it for four years now."

Dave shook his head vigorously. "You need to sign the company over to me, Vic."

"What? Dave, I built the company."

"Look, let me tell you the truth, because no one but me seems to ever really tell you the truth about anything. It's my job to tell you the truth." He shut his eyes a moment and when he opened them, his voice was calm. "When I came back to Foghorn, it was a mess. It was in bad shape. We owed everyone money. We couldn't pay the bills. There were lawsuits from Sully over the sale of the sports books to that other publisher. We had a huge overhead that made things worse every month."

I could see that the blame was headed toward me. I scowled at him. "There was a downturn in the economy. All the distribution went to shit, Dave. That wasn't just me." I felt a surge of anger. "Look around. Small presses throughout the Bay Area are selling now because it's time to get out."

"I can't believe you are saying this. No, it was *you*. It was *your* excesses. It was your inability to tell people no or tell yourself no. You were unwilling to make hard choices. You don't get your part in this, but even Mitch's dad sees it. You went too far. You lost all that money on those events that had nothing to do with Foghorn. You had the wrong people working for the company. That CFO told you what you wanted to hear, rather than the truth. You made some ridiculous deals."

My heart charged against my chest and my mouth went dry. "I'm the one who built the company to twenty books a year, Dave. I'm the one who made that happen." I was whispering now. He wasn't listening.

He reached into his back pocket, pulled out a piece of paper and, unfolding it, laid it down on the table facing me. I leaned forward to read the top: *Relinquishing Shares*.

"You don't deserve the company, Vicki. You almost destroyed it. You need to sign over your shares to me and make me the majority shareholder so I don't have to worry about you selling it out from under me or the family. It's a family business now."

He pulled out a pen and held it out. I didn't take it and he set it down next to the page with a sharp click.

"I'm part of the family, too. I need to sell," I said. "I have that right."

"You don't. You forfeited that right when you did the things you did."

"I have the legal right." I heard Mitch pulling into the driveway.

"You don't have the moral right and you know that," Dave retorted. "You know that, Vicki."

I couldn't speak. My throat tightened. I tried to think of something to say to convince him.

"Dave, what if Mitch and I need the money? I'm in serious debt because of the company."

"What you're not getting, Vicki, is that it's *your* fault. *You* got yourself in debt and you can get yourself out, but you don't want to do it slowly and with effort. You want the quick fix. And I don't think the rest of us should have to keep paying for your choices."

I put my hands over my eyes, bent forward, and took a breath to keep myself from crying.

"Read the agreement. It's a legal document. Sign it, and I'll come pick it up tomorrow morning."

He walked to the doorway, turned and said, "Selling the company doesn't solve anything. You are always going to be the way you are. There are no magical answers, no *home runs,* as you like to call them. Just hard work. And I'm the one doing that hard work now."

He stood in the doorway, the screen pushed open. "You don't even get that you have a choice. I'm telling you, you do."

I stood. As he strode out, Mitch walked in, the screen snapping shut. I grabbed him. "Mitch, you have to talk to Dave."

He turned and went back outside. I heard their murmured voices and then, as they escalated, their raised voices through the open door spinning toward me through the night air.

"You're talking about my wife now, Dave, and she's still weak from being sick. The company nearly killed her. All those hours she worked is what nearly killed her, and you weren't here to see it. I was. She did everything she could for Foghorn, way beyond what was reasonable. I'm going to protect my wife. You just— "

Mitch's voice dropped off, then picked up again. "I guarantee that nothing good can come from this. The whole family will pay."

I heard Dave's door open and the engine start, and Mitch yelled after him, "That's the difference. I'm the only one who doesn't give a fuck about the business."

* * *

I'd been called a lot of things. *Metaphor Woman,* by a lover more enamored of my sexy sorrow than by my heady explanations. *Unprofessional,* by an employee who left us for the professional publishing circuit. *Cutthroat,* by Design School Girl as a parting shot before we could fire her. *Scrappy entrepreneur,* by an investor and adviser who honored my nerve while not exactly favoring my methods. One of 40 Under 40 by *Entrepreneur Magazine,* based on growing the company to a $2 million enterprise from a $25,000 credit-card advance. Businesswoman of the Year by the bank, although not the one that provided our over-the-top credit line that preceded our fall.

I'm sure there were other names, names I was never privy to. What my ex-husband said when I fought him for the business and won. What he said when I sold the sports books he had authored to a competitive publisher. What Bob Bentley said when stranded on Angel Island. What the Presidio said when no money was raised.

But then, none of these were family.

The morning after his visit, Dave called to see when he could pick up the document he had left for me to sign.

"I don't know, Dave." I was in the kitchen, the kids already at preschool and school, the phone cord stretching with me as I put the breakfast dishes in the dishwasher. I'd had a sleepless night trying to figure out how to make everyone happy. Mitch and I had spent hours discussing it, and we thought we might have a solution.

"We were thinking there might be a buyout you could arrange for our shares." I tried to shake the pleading tone from my voice. "That would work, because we need to get something out of the company. We aren't able to just walk away. That way, we'd both be good. I mean, you'd still have the company."

I heard Muriel in the background in her German accent say, "She needs to sign it, Dave." Dave murmured something to her, and I heard her say harshly, "No, it's not right."

Apparently, you don't have to be an American to have American dreams dashed. She didn't think much of me, Dave's wife.

"The thing is, Vicki, the company can't afford that. And it shouldn't have to." I heard the righteousness in his tone, and I knew what it meant. There was no backing him down.

"Have you discussed it with the rest of the family?" I asked. I sat down at the kitchen table, my forehead resting on my palm.

"Muriel, of course."

"Anyone else?"

"I don't want to drag you through the mud with everyone. Your in-laws agree with me that the company was poorly managed. Everyone sees that. It's more than obvious."

I was silent. I didn't want to drag anyone else into it either. He had Muriel. I had Mitch. And we both wanted what we wanted.

We both sat in the quiet.

"You're not a responsible person, Vicki. That's what running the company takes. That's what this decision takes." He took a deep breath. "That's what raising kids takes, too. Frankly, Muriel and I question whether you're even up to parenting those kids."

"What?" My heart stopped. "What?"

"Face it, if Muriel and I still lived there, she'd probably be the one having to take care of your kids."

Did he even know me at all? With this, I felt him receding from my range of concern. The rest of the family too, my membership revoked by a judgment I couldn't forestall and I suspected was even shared. Who they had deemed me to be was who I apparently was, permanently.

I hung up.

He tried calling me back. My mother tried to call me that night. But I could not answer. When Mitch got home, I told him what had happened.

"Your family isn't the sunshine family you've always thought they were, Vic. Time to realize that. We have to think of our family now."

And so we did.

* * *

When the check came in August, I called Mitch at work. The kids were playing in the back yard and their laughter trickled in from where I stood in the causeway of the open French doors, watching, the phone cord stretching across the room. The adoption had become final two months ago, a complete year after they came to live with us. My girls sat in the tree on the porch and threw down leaves like they were confetti upon my son, now three, who spun in a circle, his arms outstretched.

I waved the check like it was a flag. I remembered getting that first large check from PGW years ago, and how Dave and I had danced in the kitchen in Bernal Heights, chanting, "We're thousandaires!" Now we were hundred-thousandaires. Not rich, but infinitely better. Now, when I thought of possibilities, they wouldn't be business schemes. They'd involve taking the family on a trip to Disneyland or turning the former ballet studio upstairs into separate bedrooms for the kids. The weight of the debt I'd carried since Earth Day would be gone. We could pay back the Appletons on the second mortgage on the house, and pay back Mitch's parents, too.

Allison, with her check, would have more security now that she was writing full time. And the others—Carla, our CFO, and public-relations director—they'd gotten something, maybe not as much as I'd promised, but something. Then there was my redemption within my family, starting with my brother. As much as I felt the injustice of the injury, I longed for redemption more. It would mend the rift between Dave and me. He had been working long hours up to the point of sale, getting everything ready for PGW to take over. He had been all business with me, everything transpiring through email.

But he would see I was right about the money. As the second largest shareholder, he, too, was a "hundred-thousandaire." He could forgive me now, and I, him. He and Muriel would have time to enjoy their family. They could visit Germany and Muriel's family whenever they wanted. I would be redeemed with the whole Morgan clan. With my parents' check, my mom could relax now, leave Foghorn behind, too. Maybe she and my dad could travel like she always dreamed of doing. And I'd written Brian in as a minor shareholder at the end so he and his new wife could benefit. All the Morgans would profit from the sale.

That was what I believed anyway, at that very moment, holding that large check, imagining myself the family hero once again, and anticipating that—despite everything that had been said—good things might lie ahead.

PART V

MORGANIZATION

SONOMA COUNTY, 1999

Company: 0
Employees: 0
Partner: 1
Children: 3

After forty years of marriage, my father left my mother. He did it the day after their check from PGW arrived, the timing suggesting he felt less guilty now because he would be leaving my mom financially fortified. Anger and disbelief swept through each of us, though we each felt it on our own, not reaching out to one other.

My dad called me to discuss this ultimate Morganization, this melting down and starting anew. His plan was to leave California and move back to his hometown in Washington. He was leaving us all, I realized.

I thought of his saying, "Life can never be exactly as you'd like it to be." For him, we were the *exactly* in that sentence. In his voice I heard the ache he felt, but also the unmistakable excitement about what life might now contain. I recognized in it my own bolt for freedom from Sully years ago, then from Foghorn.

He hesitated, still not done talking. He said that once the divorce was final, he planned to marry a woman he had known since childhood who still lived in the town. I didn't know what to say, the betrayal suddenly deeper for the planning that preceded it. Then he told me he loved me and hung up.

My mother's hurt at first paralyzed her, then metamorphosed into anger that could not be suppressed. She raged while Dave and Brian and I each took turns listening, in person and over the phone. I felt the betrayal as well. I didn't find what he had done defensible, but I couldn't cast him off either. As usual, I stood between my parents, trying to negotiate a place to stand for myself in the center. And I knew my nature wasn't that far from my father's. I was dishonest, or had been, in leaving Sully those years ago. But this was my mother, not Sully. My beautiful, sacrificing mother.

Of course, it was my doing, my selling of the company, that created the opportunity for my dad to leave to begin with. And the subtle affinity I had for my dad put me further at odds with my brothers. Brian and Dave were both concerned with my mother and, Dave and I were already not speaking because of the sale of the business. Nothing was changing now. At the time of the sale, I had written a clause into the agreement for Dave that arranged his continued employment with Foghorn under PGW's new publishing imprint Avalon. I understood from my mother that that had been a bust, the publisher perhaps not receptive to my brother's proprietary knowledge and recommendations, or possibly, unappreciative of his idiosyncrasies.

After a few months, relegated to mundane tasks designed to keep him busy and out of their way, Dave took the buyout I had built into the agreement in the case of such an eventuality. I became the author of that employment disaster, one that resulted in another humiliation. With Dad gone, Mom in a depressed state, and Brian living in Washington, all Morgan family functions were now off.

SONOMA COUNTY, 2000

Partner: 1
Children: 3

O ver the year following the sale, Allison called periodically with bits of news about how Avalon was restructuring Foghorn Press. She was their author now. PGW had bought a number of its distributed travel publishers under its new imprint and began to bill itself as the premier small-press travel publisher in the country. The editorial staff redesigned the Foghorn books, removing the grid system, scaling back the enormous indices, and inputting the books into a new format with newly designed covers. I sent a sharp letter to Ferris Wiley about not liking the changes and when he fired one back that essentially told me it was none of my business, I realized I had burned that bridge.

Finally, they removed the Foghorn name as an imprint from the line of books, folding it into another press, our legacy dissolved, temporal, like everything else.

SONOMA COUNTY, 2001

Partner: 1
Children: 3

It was two years before Dave and I would speak. Dave came to the new home we had bought twenty miles out of town, a country place with five acres for our kids to roam. He drove up in our mother's car, bumping a bit too far forward into the fence when he parked. Out of the back seat tumbled his son, a small boy with a round face. A small Dave with Muriel's wide cheeks.

"Vicki," Dave called from the gate.

Our dog yapped along the length of the front fence. The child veered back, and Dave took off his cap, and from the window of my home office on the second floor, I could see Dave's head stripped of hair on top with short-cropped bands of hair on either side. I paused there, watching, until he herded the boy back toward the car.

Then I was down the stairs, out of the house, jogging toward the gate. "Dave, I'm here." The dog fell quiet.

"Oh," he said stopping. "You're looking older."

"And wiser," I offered, but he didn't acknowledge that, stooping instead to whisper something to Christoph, whom I had only seen twice since the company sale and only because Mom was watching the kids and I happened to be there with my own.

"Will he bite?" Dave was still not a fan of dogs.

"No, he just sounds fierce."

"I should have called."

"That's okay. Come in. Come in."

Our house was a comfortable one, messy with projects on the kitchen table and toys scattered in the corners. My kids were at their elementary school in town, my youngest now a kindergartener.

Dave glanced around and took a seat on the couch in the living room with the child at his side.

"Christoph, this is your Aunt Vicki. This is her house."

"Hi, Christoph," I said softly. My son's toy dump truck sat in the hallway, and I got up to roll it over to him. "Talking?"

"Not much. Mom's trying, but Muriel wants us to speak German at home. He knows more German than English."

The boy dropped to the wood floor, his hand on the truck, as he watched the dog.

I bent to rub the dog's stomach, his paws in the air as he went into his usual stupor.

Then I sat down on the chair across from Dave, my heart beating in my throat. Seeing him sitting there, I sensed none of the hatred I was sure he had for me.

"I was hoping to talk to you about something," I said carefully.

He looked at me, waiting.

"I've been thinking about writing a book about Foghorn."

"Memoir or fiction or...?"

"I don't even know. A strange blend, maybe?"

"Always walking the line."

"I've actually started working on it. And have been for this last year. But I haven't written the end."

Dave chuckled. "Are we writing it right now?" He continued, "If you're asking me for advice, I actually only know one thing about writing and that's this: If you have a gun in the first chapter, it has to go off by the last chapter."

I laughed. "Shit! Another rule broken. There's that neighbor's gun when we were at Bernal Heights, remember? And it never goes off— but, of course, all the metaphorical ones do."

"Oh, wait, here's another writing tip, strictly for golf guides and in golf terminology: All golf courses 'dog left,' " he said, playfully pointing his finger at me.

"I don't know if I'm getting the Nietzsche right either."

"People rarely get him right."

We talked about our mother and how she was doing. We talked about Brian.

"You talk to Dad?" I asked him.

"He's afraid to talk to me. Or, at least, he hasn't tried to talk to me yet." He shook his head. "You talk to him?"

"I do. He's hurting, too."

Dave snorted. "I don't buy that for a minute. He made a choice."

"If he did call, what would you say?"

He smiled at me. "Probably something similar to what I'd say to you."

I was offended. "What, we're both pieces of crap?"

"It's been two years. That's not what I think."

"And how would I know that?"

"Vicki, my life isn't about you or the company anymore. It's about my son and my daughter. And Muriel, of course."

I hung there, taking that in. There wasn't a day I wasn't thinking of Dave, I realized. Yes, there was the joy of my children, my family, but the unsettled part of what had happened with Dave still clouded things for me. Often my thoughts swirled around the guilt, what I could have done differently. Maybe I was still the codependent, ever more.

"I'd actually tell him something cliché like, the grass isn't always greener."

"No Nietzsche?" I snorted.

"Nietzsche has something about keeping your commitments."

"What commitment didn't I keep?" I demanded.

Christoph looked up from the truck. Dave looked down at him and smiled. "Why are you asking me?"

"Because after two goddamn years, I still can't figure it out. That's why I'm asking you."

He shifted forward and put his elbows on his knees. "Look, this is the way it had to go. If we held onto each other and onto the company, I probably wouldn't have this little guy. You forced me out and it turned out to be the best thing."

"Really? Because I'm not sure that's true."

"Vic, we were too close. No one else could get in."

"Too close?"

"Remember those Christmases? It was almost embarrassing how many gifts you gave me. Way more than anyone else in the family."

"I don't think it was that obvious."

"It was that obvious." He laughed.

"No."

"To everyone."

I sat, stumped.

"Not that it was a bad thing. It was just the kind of thing that kept other things from happening."

"What things?"

"Husbands, wives, kids. Those kinds of things."

I felt suddenly vulnerable, my life choices scrutinized. I imagined the conversations the rest of the family might have had about me. I had been right to remain distant. "You are so judgmental," I said, thinking back to his attack on me as a parent.

"Judgments. Facts. Those have always been a bit tricky for you to distinguish, I know." He chuckled.

"You have a little trouble there yourself," I shot back. I realized no apology would be forthcoming from him. I added without emotion, "You're kind of a bastard."

"Your favorite one," he offered lightly.

"Why did you come to see me, then?"

"You're my sister. You were the best friend I ever had. You have a part of my history. I have a part of yours. I don't want to lose that."

I started to cry, suddenly off guard. "I never wanted to lose you. I'm so sorry, Dave. I didn't mean to hurt you." Jesus, why did I have to cry?

"You forget, I knew what I was getting into. I've got philosophy to support me. Rip my heart out. Bring it on. That which doesn't kill me, makes me stronger. I'm okay. Mom said you were having trouble."

"I'm not having trouble."

"Look, start telling the truth. Write your book. Unleash *Metaphor Woman*. Let my people go." He paused to drum on the table. "I will not stand for anything but the full and honest truth, even if I look like a total asshole."

"So far, I look like the asshole," I said.

"Well, you're not. Nobody wants to read about a bunch of assholes, anyway. They want people with dimension. Why is your memory just conjuring up the asshole moments?"

"Guilt?"

"Guilt is a ridiculous emotion." He shook his head.

"It's a Morgan-sanctioned emotion," I said.

"The Morgan era was over the minute Dad called it quits and walked out on Mom. The minute Foghorn sold, he got out. Don't tell me he hadn't been thinking of leaving for years. You have to know they weren't happy. And Mom's making progress. She's moved from guilt to justified rage and you know that's good, because she's been stuck on guilt most of her life." He sighed. "You can release yourself from the binding Morgan code."

"It's overwhelming. To have worked so hard and then have it mean nothing in the end."

"Maybe not. Maybe it's liberating. Maybe you can construct your own code for life now. I don't know." Dave's eyes were hopeful.

"Well, the story I'm writing is about the Morgans—you and me, really."

The old Dave began to rally; a philosophical discussion always ensnared him. "The story should be about publishing. Not the Morgans. Publishing is the process of making public—the welling up of the unconscious to become conscious and spoken. Publishing is magic. The more scientific it gets, the worse it becomes. We discovered that. The more we tried to become a publishing company, the worse our relationship became."

"The story does keep devolving into who was right and who was wrong." I had noticed that.

"Well, just so you know, as pig-headed and stupid as I was, and as impossible as I felt you were sometimes, I am now way over it. In fact, now I find your old approach much closer to my own heart—and you were often relentlessly impossible."

He drummed his fingers on his knee and smiled. "The essence of it was this: At some point, the thing actually evolved into a real business. And it was mostly due to your influence. You have this trait, Vic, that I just don't have. You always believed in a tomorrow. No matter how ugly things became, no matter how down we felt, no matter how many returns we got—you always came back. I can walk the path pretty far, but at some point, I say *fuck it*, there is nothing further that I can learn here. And then I need to go."

"It took me a while to find my own reasons to go," I said. And here they were, my life now reconstructed in this country setting, with my kids, Mitch, and the computer summoning me to write every day. Thinking often about my next business venture and what it might be.

Dave wasn't listening. "But for you, back then, Foghorn was an extension of your being. Nothing mattered except that you had risked yourself in some way and things had to be kept in tune to that beat, the Vicki Beat." He smiled, delighted. "I don't believe Foghorn was ever in complete chaos, really. Acquisitions, design, editorial, and especially finance were only important within this Vicki Beat framework. All my systems were really useless."

Dave leaned forward to study me closely. "I've reversed my position. I was the one who wanted to make it definable, to fit into a system somehow. You didn't. You ran at it with everything you had and that was a lot, believe me. It's messier but it has more heart. And a story with heart, that's something. Just ask Salinger."

I shook my head. "I've reversed my position to your old one, though. I think I should have been more careful, more scientific, somehow."

Dave leaned back, all the tension gone, and gazed out the window as if he hadn't heard me. "I can still remember entering the DeHaro building on those foggy mornings and finding you with the music blaring, sitting behind your desk in the cave office with Grandma's afghan on your lap. Business as usual. Foghorn was as close to a real home that I ever got."

I was happy to know Dave had been thinking about Foghorn, too, what it all meant, trying to make sense of it. The time was as alive for him as it was for me. We shared that, and always would.

"Are you happy now?" I ventured.

He threw his head back and laughed. Christoph looked up at him and smiled.

"Yes, I suppose I am. Don't tell Nietzsche, okay?"

But he wasn't done with the book. "Vic, when you ran Foghorn, you were driven, bold, arrogant, smart, egocentric. Remember that? Now, as a writer, you've got to call on those traits again. You are the great *Metaphor Woman*, not *Victim MoreGrim*. No time to hold back. You'll never get anywhere holding back, Slim Bob. This is your dream, right? Make it happen."

At the sound of my old nicknames, I smiled. I didn't need permission, never had, but his encouragement, his love, still mattered. It was a hurt I couldn't seem to recover from otherwise. And that, I realized, is where I had been stuck in the story. And in my life.

"It's a comedy, after all, right? I like Nietzsche's idea that eventually everything becomes a comedy because everyone must misinterpret their motives. It is all hidden from us. Well, we have simply made it to the joke phase, Vic. Congratulations!"

He paused a beat, grinning. "It's time to do the big thing. I have only one last thing to say to you, Metaphor Woman: Get to the bank quick and make the deposit. The checks have been postdated."

I smiled back and we sat there a minute, thinking about the book and what it could be.

"Thank you, Luke Thrasher," I said. His words had released me. He stood up to leave.

"Where's the rest of your family?" I said as I rose to walk him out.

"They're visiting friends. We leave this week for Germany, so they are trying to see everyone one last time."

"How long will you stay there?"

"We may stay there forever. This country has nothing for me. I really hate it here, if you must know. I want to raise my kids away from this country."

"But Dave, you're breaking the family apart."

"Vicki, it's already broken. Everyone's concerned with their own families now. Brian is. I am." He gestured impatiently to the fireplace mantel, where I had framed school photos of my kids. "You are. You can let go of the rest."

I turned to look with him, admiring the beautiful faces of my children. I knew it to be true. Nothing could take that from me now.

He pulled his son up by his hand, murmuring something in German to him.

"So I won't see you again?" I brushed my hand over my forehead, then shaded my eyes.

"I'm sure there'll be visits. And there's email. Email me the final story." He grinned. "I'll send you an idea I have for a business there."

"In Germany?" My eyebrows shot up, that old entrepreneurial spirit stirring.

"And, of course, I'll see you again someday, on the Avenue," he added.

"'Tangled Up in Blue,'" I said.

He leaned forward to hug me, and I hugged him back. As we pushed away, our hands on each other's arms, the tops of our heads hung together a moment, wrestlers pausing.

"Don't leave anything out," he said, and, whisking Christoph into his arms, he made for the door.

EPILOGUE

The question woke me in the middle of the night. Did that last scene with my brother really happen? Or did I create it because I wanted it to happen? Adhering to the truth is the core discipline in writing memoir. Yet there's that tendency to want to clean up your past when you write about it. It may be the only opportunity life will give you to do so, and it's a terrible temptation. I believe I've done well keeping to the truth in this story. Until the end. Here my unconscious has asserted itself. This epilogue comes as a correction, truth-telling after the noble lie. If you like happy endings, this is your warning to stop reading.

Many of the things said in that last meeting with Dave came to me via his letters over the ten years he lived in Germany. And some of it, I just wish he had said. The sad truth is a relationship such as his and mine did not suddenly change, injuries forgotten. Even today, with whitening hair, I cannot muster the courage to call him to ask if it indeed did happen, because for many years now, I have let my relationship with my brother and my family lie, a sleeping giant. It was easy enough to do.

The family continued to recalibrate after my father left. My mother moved north to be near Brian and his family, leaving California and, what felt like, my family behind. Dave and his wife divorced and when he came home from Germany, heartbroken, he moved in with my mother. There they all coalesced into a universe in which my mother is the center and my brothers, her sentinel moons. Since the sale of Foghorn, I have moved from the heart of that universe to the outlying range.

As Brian pointed out in one of our rare calls, I am a risk-taker, the sort of risking that this side of the family prefers to avoid. Which I take to mean starting businesses (of which Foghorn was just the first), the adoption of three foster children, and a general lack of conservative choices that come from a life governed less by logic and more by emotion, less of practicality and more of service, less of saving and more of spending.

And there have been challenges with our kids, who now are thankfully grown and settled, but whose foster and adoption struggles were difficult to understand from afar. I've necessarily turned away from my family of origin, focusing instead on the family Mitch and I created. I've become the metaphorical Uranus in that first family's planetary system, as is my father, and, as we all know, Uranus's primary function is to be served up in jokes. As Dave used to say, you don't want dogs around Uranus.

It turns out I am more like my father. When I visit my father and his wife at their home in Washington, his health failing, diabetes taking its toll on his body, his frailty is always a surprise when I walk into the living room of their farm home and find him there in his big chair. Wobbly, he stands up to greet me—thrilled, it seems—and with a kiss to my forehead, he says, "Hello, baby doll."

For years now, my father and his wife have sustained their community. My father—a force in a small town—is the initiator and funder of small projects, the saver of families with an emergency and no savings, the laborer who restored the church and the historic theater, the spirit behind the renovated rail bridge to a trail that stretches across the state. Now in his eighties, he works to have enough equilibrium to go downtown to play cribbage with friends in the coffee shop on Main Street. Dizzy, he endeavors to weed the rose beds, lying prone on the ground.

I will always be grateful for Dave, for the Dave I loved and who loved me when we both needed it the most. Following my divorce in those lonely times, Dave saved me, and I saved him from our shipwrecked relationships—his with Julie, mine with Sully and the others—but also from the annihilation that the world inflicts on young optimists who step out alone. We were not alone. Our ascent into adulthood may have included grief and confusion—but then, because of each other, it was tempered with story and belly laughs.

"Come in, she said, I'll give ya shelter from the storm," as Dylan said.

Foghorn was that shelter.

In the early days, too, the business may have existed as an artifice to keep my brother and me together before we finally figured out how to fly on our own. It wasn't repeatable, ultimately, though we've tried to reprise that artifice over the years. During visits or phone calls or emails, Dave and I replayed our inner-circle jokes, carefully raking through the coals of Foghorn's early days for the humor that used to double us over in laughter. The days of absolutely and of Bob Dylan. But it always goes too far.

As our conversation ramps up, we arrive at a new enterprise and then we attempt to collaborate, but then the old opposition rears—Dave the way he is, and me the way I am. In these projects, my brother wants from me the type of attention and focus that I can no longer muster. I never measure up. Again and again, I fail him. The resulting judgments leave us both reinjured, and so we choose no longer to repeat the exercise and have stepped back, the intervals between attempts finally lapsing into years.

"We drove that car as far as we could," Dylan might conclude.

Metaphors still compel me, especially metaphor wedged into reality.

A few years after the company sold, my grandparents—my father's parents—were in their thirty-six-foot motorhome, a car attached to the rear hitch, travelling the Grapevine, that treacherous bald mountainous pass blasted by winds that provides a portal between the top and bottom parts of California that is our family's nemesis. They were coming down the north side, returning from their Snowbird stay in Hemet, intending to visit the Morgans still remaining in Sonoma County. It's unclear what happened next.

My grandparents missed the rest stop exit and lost their focus perhaps, when their RV was tapped by a passing truck. It bumped them loose from the guiding white lines of their lane, causing them to swerve, sweeping in larger swaths, left, then right, until finally they arrived at the cliff's edge. Unlike our story, forty years before, the RV did not stop but soared over, plunging sixty feet until it met the canyon bottom. My grandfather bled out there on the Grapevine, his leg sheared off. My grandmother lived another week, enough time to see him buried, before succumbing to her broken ribs and inability to live without her husband of sixty-plus years.

Their deaths further convulsed our already fragmented family. Beyond our father, our grandparents were our link to the great Morgan clan. Now we felt the gravity of the involuntarily amputated appendage.

* * *

Two decades later, I am at the foot of the Grapevine, on the L.A. side heading north to Sonoma County in our black Chevy pickup. Mitch is ahead in our other truck, towing our home, a forty-foot fifth-wheel RV attached to his hitch. This is one of our many commutes from the northern part of the state to the southern and back again to visit our adult children. We lean toward retirement, but we never succeed.

When I am the sole driver, I take other routes to cross the state, up and down 101, routes that cost me hours more to travel. Routes without cliffs, without history. Irrationally I fear another incident, as things superstitiously happen in threes. But this trip we travel the Grapevine, driving as a wagon train with my husband in front, my son and his girlfriend in the middle with their own truck, and me bringing up the rear. This will make it easier for me, they all assure me, this being part of a train, as if we are all connected by invisible safety ropes.

But then my body starts shaking, my hands grip the wheel as I see the pass rise ahead. I take an off-ramp and then after reaching the stop sign, I tremulously cross and ascend the on-ramp, where I pull over. I see my wagon train has also pulled over to the side of the road, looking for me behind them. I call Mitch from my cell phone, defeated.

I can't make it. I cannot drive over the Grapevine.

Hunched over the steering wheel on the on-ramp I wait, my head down. I hear cars whipping past, picking up speed, oblivious to the psychic and physical breakdown transpiring in my body. I hear a tap on the passenger window, and I look up. My son's girlfriend smiles, opens the door, and offers to drive. I let her take the wheel and move into the passenger seat and close my eyes. As we crest and finally descend onto the flat plain surrounding Interstate 5, I'm already meditating on the next time. Infusing myself with courage.

It's possible that on my next trip, I will make it.

It's that way with my brother Dave, too. These negative patterns can be surmounted. Even if it means it happens "in another lifetime," or, if need be, when we're very old and hard of hearing. When we're too tired to defend all the stuck places, and there's no danger of starting any new enterprises or having any philosophical discussions, and there's no Morganization at hand. Optimism will course through my body as it has over my entire lifetime, providing the necessary stamina to seek that elusive redemption that only I seem to need.

I'll do the Big Thing and again, it will be the perfect day for bananafish. I'll go to my brother's for a visit, setting another verse of "Tangled Up in Blue" in motion. We'll sit on a porch in our rockers, just him and me. He'll call me Slim Bob, crack open a beer—most likely a Mickey's Big Mouth—and then Metaphor Woman and Luke Thrasher will chase down one more belly laugh as we remember the time we had a publishing company in San Francisco.

THE END

Enjoy more about
Foghorn
Meet the Author
Check out author appearances
Explore special features

ABOUT THE AUTHOR

VICKI DEARMON has been in the book industry for forty years as a respected publisher, bookseller, and innovator. She started her San Francisco publishing company Foghorn Press with a small advance on her credit card when she was twenty-five, growing it to a $2 million enterprise before selling it fourteen years later. She worked as the marketing and events director at Copperfield's Books for eight years and as consultant to California's independent bookstores. She's also a writer whose short stories and essays have won awards and appeared online and in print. Vicki is one of the founders of Sibylline Press and serves as its publisher. She lives in California.

ACKNOWLEDGMENTS

This book has been floating around in my head for 25 plus years, actively being assembled for 15 of those as a novel, and finally shared with friends who volunteered to read it in its 'kitchen sink version.' Not much had been left out of that early version and like an overstuffed suitcase it sprung open easily, leaking onto the baggage turnstile--wherever it traveled--in a messy heap. To those of you who read that version, apologies go out with the thanks.

Thank you Seré Prince Halverson for kindly reading it and for your comment that you almost missed your plane because you were so engrossed. I fed myself on that comment for at least ten years. To Joanne Hartman for reading versions again and again and again, with no thought of compensation or putting me on her Dead Friend list (a list that her friends all dread and I admit I made, once, long ago) for favors as yet unreturned. Thank you for saying you laughed out loud which kept me motivated like a young comic in a darkened club who discovers the one person in the back corner actually chuckling. To my friend Christine Walker for the generosity of the book's beginning fully imagined and for enlightening me about the nature of scenes. To my former professor from UC Santa Cruz, Paul Skenazy, who really liked only the first and last scenes and therefore caused me reluctantly to return to the middle. Marlene Cullen for taking the time. For Nina Schuyler who decades ago when the first chapter emerged responded positively with, yes, there's a novel here. To my dear sister Ann Marie Brown, who demanded better syntax, less secondary characters, while supporting me to write the story that was mine to tell.

To friends like Jeanna Menze who stayed up all night to read it if only to find out what I'd been up to all those years and who I might have slept with. And the friends too who have always kept me upright, Jenny Lawrence, Michelle Murphy, and Amy Appleton, my dearest dear. To my sweet mother for being a reader always and for very specifically taking no offense. To my brother Kyle Morgan who read multiple versions and whose encouragement and laughter kept me out of grad school and kept me writing. To my beloved father whose generosity of spirit belies all that is said about him in this book and to his wife Cheryl who echoes that spirit. To my brother Mike Morgan whose steadiness over the years has always helped me balance my life, then and now. And Amy and Myst, Jim, Janene, Mike, Jana for extending my family in such a grand way. Christine and Marco for the heartbeat. Amber, Justin, and JJ. For redefining family, Vanessa and Rhett Tavernetti, Jacqueline and TJ Machado, and, of course, the grandkids who I cannot live without: Sage, Falcon, Paloma, Scarlett, and Austin.

Love to my children who are the biggest gift of my life: Brittni DeArmon Hau, Taylor DeArmon Seaton, Alex DeArmon and also, their partners, Alex Hau, Michael Seaton, and Jasmyn Hartley. Love to my husband who sees me for who I am and loves me regardless. Mitch makes it a point not to read anything I write, keeping our relationship free of old lovers and my compulsion to endlessly reinterpret the past especially when a beautiful present surrounds us.

To my brother Dave who insisted that the Foghorn story must be told, no matter how bad it made him look. I persevered, sure I looked worse. Thanks to Anna Termine who read it and saw a television series there in the kitchen sink version and cause to continue. To the agents who rejected the kitchen sink version, catching me in the biggest mistake a writer can make, thinking she's done, when in fact she is merely tired and desperate for input. Bridges burned alas. To all the writing program readers who were baffled by what kind of animal I had set before them, sensing what it would take me years to realize. It wasn't a novel, it was a memoir. And thank you Suzy Vitello for calling it out, Why don't you just call it *Foghorn*?

You all may be happy to know that at age 62, governed by some aggregated wisdom and the threat of never finishing the book at all, that I hacked through the stone, dropping 40,000 words to find the story underneath. At age 65, inspired by the Sibylline Press authors who were courageously putting their work out into the world, I finally let go of the manuscript, trusting that it was time.

To all the Fogheads who go unnamed in the book but have stayed in my heart all these years: Ann Marie Brown, Donna Galassi, Donna Leverenz, Gigi Reinheimer, Judith Pynn, Howard Rabinowitz, Samantha Troutman, Aimee Larsen, Tom Austin, Michelle Thomas, Amy, Charlie, and others too. Plus the authors, too many to name (and most, thankfully, who were never good ol' boys). For Susan Quinn who showed me a lot in the day and then circled back 35 years later as a friend. To Elizabeth Whipple for her patience with me and humor. To my comrade George Young. To all the SF Bay Area book folk, members of the Book Council, the distributors, the booksellers and small presses who lived this era with me and remember what a magical time it was. When I picture a booklover's heaven, you are all in it.

I want to thank all the trustworthy women who have joined our cause and shared their brilliance at Sibylline Press especially Sang Kim, as well as Jenny McIntosh, Hannah Rutkowski and Anna Wilhelm.

I love beyond measure the women who jumped into this publishing venture with me at Sibylline Press and are my partners in this big dream we are manifesting. Julia Park Tracey who I have known since we lived in the City and waited tables at the Red Chimney while putting ourselves through college, for the suffering girls we were to the formidable women we have become, Anna Termine who was with me back in the Foghorn days at another publisher while we became fast friends at the

ITPA parties and has said an unqualified yes to everything I ever asked of her. And Alicia Feltman who I feel I cannot live without in anything I do because she renders art and design with good nature and beyond all expectation, exceeding every idea I have and brandishing her own better ones. She makes us all better. Much appreciation to my partners at Sibylline Press as we publish the brilliant work of women authors over 50 for reminding me that our own work should be included.

I thank the booksellers at Copperfield's for teaching me the other side of the book business when I worked there, specifically Grace Bogart, Katie Smith, and Sheryl Cotleur. And all the publishers who fostered Copperfield's success. Thank you Mary Beth Thomas for the shared wisdom. Ann Seaton and Calvin Crosby and the independent booksellers of California who I worked with when we were still the NCIBA and the SCIBA. Publishers Group West for remembering me and saying yes again.

The book publishing industry and I have been together for 40 years now and it is where I belong. It has been a love affair of the most epic kind and, for the passion it invokes in me, especially, I am eternally grateful.

FOGHORN BOOK CLUB QUESTIONS

1. How was the book industry different in the 1980s than it is now? What distinguished the Bay Area book community? Why does Vicki call the 80s in San Francisco, "the heyday of small press publishing?"

2. Think about the city of San Francisco. How do you come to understand and love the City through this memoir?

3. What were the difficulties of starting and running a small business as a woman in her 20s? What obstacles did Vicki overcome?

4. How did the Morgan upbringing both hinder and facilitate Vicki's being the publisher of Foghorn. What was her style of leadership?

5. Siblings are our lifelong mirrors. What might cause you to want to work with your sibling or never work with your sibling? What bond do siblings have that limits them and also helps them grow?

6. Vicki talks about people not wanting other people to change throughout the memoir. How does she allow people to change? How does she prevent it? How is her change met with resistance by family and co-workers?

7. What is your definition of a good ol' boy? How does Dave define them? Do you know any? How do you deal with them? How does Vicki deal with the good ol' boys and what do you think of her approach? Would she have handled her interactions with good ol' boys differently if the same issues presented themselves today?

8. Talk about some of the themes and metaphors in the book. Why does the J.D. Salinger story, It's a Perfect Day for Bananafish

resonate with the Morgan siblings? Why does Bob Dylan's song Tangled Up In Blue? How have they constructed a language and humor that they alone can understand? How does it prevent them from relationships outside the family? How does Allison overcome this barrier?

9. Looking back on your life now, what are you most proud of and of what are you most ashamed? Would you include those in your memoir? Why or why not?

10. Why is it so hard to tell the truth? Who are we afraid of hurting? What are we protecting? Where and why do you think Vicki veers from the truth in this memoir? Why is the word 'nearly' in the subtitle?

Sibylline
PRESS

Sibylline Press is proud to publish the brilliant work of women authors over 50. We are a woman-owned publishing company and, like our authors, represent women of a certain age.

Mortal Zin: A Mortal Zin Mystery
BY DIANE SCHAFFER

MYSTERY
Trade Paper, 412 pages (5.315 x 8.465) | $22
ISBN: 9781960573933
Also available as an ebook and audiobook

A crusading attorney's death. Sabotage at a family winery...As threats mount and the winery teeters on the brink of ruin, Noli and Luz must navigate a treacherous landscape of greed, revenge, and long-buried secrets. Can two fearless women from different worlds unravel the truth before it's too late?

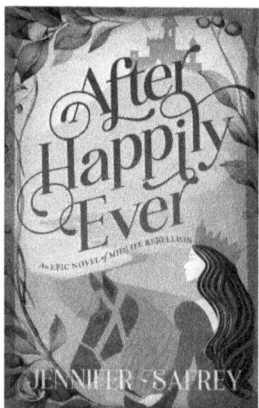

After Happily Ever: An Epic Novel of Midlife Rebellion
BY JENNIFER SAFREY

FICTION, FANTASY
Trade Paper, 388 pages (5.315 x 8.465) | $22
ISBN: 9781960573179
Also available as an ebook and audiobook

Princesses Neve, Della, and Bry are sisters-in-law, having married into the royal Charming family, and for the last thirty-plus years, they've been living a coveted happily-ever-after life in the idyllic kingdom of Foreverness. As they each turn 50 however, they begin to question the kingdom's "perfection." Can each of the women create a new happily-ever-after and will the kingdom of Foreverness survive it?

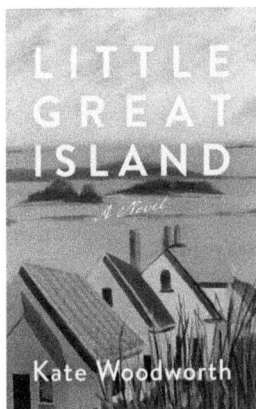

Little Great Island: A Novel
BY KATE WOODWORTH

FICTION
Trade Paper, 356 pages (5.315 x 8.465) | $21
ISBN: 9781960573902
Also available as an ebook and audiobook

When Mari McGavin flees with her son back to the tiny Maine island where she grew up—she runs into her life-long friend Harry, one of the island's summer residents, setting off a chain of events as unexpected and life altering as the shifts in climate affecting the whole ecosystem of the island...from generations of fishing families to the lobsters and the butterflies.

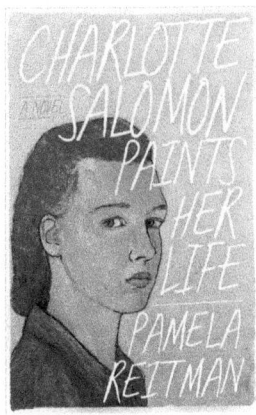

Charlotte Salomon Paints Her Life: A Novel
BY PAMELA REITMAN

HISTORICAL FICTION
Trade Paper, 392 pages (5.315 x 8.465) | $22
ISBN: 9781960573919
Also available as an ebook and audiobook

This historical fiction depicts the encroaching terror of the Third Reich and the threat of psychological disintegration of the artist Charlotte Salomon as she clings to her determination to become a serious modernist painter, to complete her monumental work "Life? Or Theater?" and get it into safekeeping in a race against time before capture by the Nazis.

For more books from **Sibylline Press**, please visit our website at sibyllinepress.com

Sibylline
PRESS

FOGHORN: THE NEARLY TRUE STORY
OF A SMALL PUBLISHING EMPIRE

"DeArmon takes readers on a thrilling, laugh-out-loud adventure as she transforms a humble dream into a powerhouse publishing house. With wit and grit, she navigates the highs and lows of building a business from the ground up—all while juggling a turbulent personal life, including a rocky marriage and a boyfriend allergic to commitment.

This behind-the-scenes look into the world of independent publishing is both inspiring and deeply human. Packed with heart, humor, and hard-earned wisdom, it's a story you won't want to put down—or see end."

—Nina Schuyler, award-winning author of *Afterword* and *In This Ravishing World*

• • •

"This is so well told and personal that every step along the way is both entertaining and heart felt. I was mesmerized and deeply engaged. A book not to be missed for many reasons not the least about what it takes to run a publishing company from ground zero."

—Sheryl Cotleur, Buyer, Copperfield's Books

• • •

"Starting with its subtitle—"the nearly true story of a small publishing empire"—*Foghorn* is an intriguing tale that reads like a novel but feels like truth in the highest sense of the word. Publishing people will especially enjoy the story of a Bay Area startup that makes good; everyone will enjoy the full nearly true story.

—John Mutter, Co-Founder and Editor-in-Chief, Shelf Awareness

• • •

"*Foghorn* is a beautifully written time capsule of a book. It captures a bygone era in publishing and a heady chapter in a young woman's life. As much a memoir about the book world as it is an elegiac tale about personal relationships—both romantic and familial—Foghorn reminds us of a time when it was still possible for a small press—and the enthusiastic soul running it—to make a meaningful mark in the world of print."

—Julie Checkoway, author of *The Three-Year Swim Club: The Untold Story of Maui's Sugar Ditch Kids and Their Quest for Olympic Glory*

"*Foghorn* is not just a tale of business success but also a story of the power of storytelling and the impact that words can have on individuals and society. Through Vicki's journey, readers are reminded of the importance of pursuing one's passions, embracing challenges, and staying true to one's vision, even in the face of adversity."

—Calvin Crosby, co-owner, The King's English Bookshop

• • •

"A publishing executive's unsparing and compelling look at the impact of a small press...this novelistic memoir focuses on the publishing business in the San Francisco Bay Area...publishing executive DeArmon delves into her tenure leading Foghorn Press and its impact on her personal and business relationships. The descriptions of the inner workings of book publishing, especially in the Bay Area, will captivate bibliophiles."

—*Kirkus Reviews*

• • •

"*Foghorn* captures a moment in time when the desk-top computer revolutionized publishing and the small press movement forever changed the staid New York centric book world. Seizing opportunity, DeArmon and her brother grow a uniquely West Coast company, Foghorn Press. DeArmon's entertaining memoir is told with honesty and humor."

—Donna Galassi, Publishing Consultant and former Associate Publisher of Foghorn Press

• • •

"Vicki DeArmon takes us on a ride through glittering, pre-Internet San Francisco as she navigates between her lust for success and yearning for family. As she makes the complex choices that shape her future, she finds her own version of feminism—one that's both unapologetic and refreshingly honest."

—Ann Marie Brown, Travel Writer